American Studies In Transition

American Studies
in Transition

Edited by Marshall W. Fishwick

Philadelphia
University of Pennsylvania Press

Acknowledgments

We are grateful for permission to reprint Richard E. Sykes' article published in the Summer 1963 issue of *American Quarterly*; and Richard Beale Davis' article delivered as a Phi Kappa Phi Lecture at the University of Tennessee in 1962, and published by the University of Tennessee Press. We thank Simon and Schuster, Inc., for permission to quote from Charles de Gaulle's *War Memoirs*; Oxford University Press, Inc., for permission to quote from Lynn White, Jr.'s *Medieval Technology and Social Change*; and Coward-McCann, Inc., for permission to quote from Alice Duer Miller's *The White Cliffs*.

The planning and execution of this volume was made possible by a grant from the Wemyss Foundation.

Introduction

MARSHALL W. FISHWICK

WHEN FRANKLIN D. ROOSEVELT TOOK OFFICE IN 1932, ONLY a handful of American Studies programs existed. Changes in all aspects of American life—and in ways of interpreting them—followed with astonishing speed. Now, little more than thirty years later, we live in a vastly different nation. American Studies is different, too. In 1955 there were ninety-three active college programs, and the number is still rising steadily. When World War II ended, teaching about American civilization scarcely existed anywhere abroad. "Discrepancy between the position of the United States in the world and its place in curricula had long been growing," Norway's Professor Sigmund Skard wrote. "After 1945 it proved intolerable. A radical change was brought on by the need for reorientation."[1]

In 1954 the European Association for American Studies was formed to coordinate the various seminars, institutes, and programs on that continent. New programs flourished in the non-western world—especially in Japan and India. Fulbright and Smith-Mundt lecturers roamed the face of the earth. American Studies was a world-wide enterprise.

Many factors, academic and non-academic, were responsible. Rapid expansion created real problems. For example, motivation seemed to outdistance methodology. The Committee on American Civilization of the American Council of Learned Societies praised the interdisciplinary approach, without specifying just what it was.[2] Richard Huber favored integrating methods and materials "through the functional interdependence of the humanities and the social sciences," but many departments refused to function that way.[3] Arthur Bestor warned us not to confuse jingoism and scholarship.[4] Meanwhile an American Studies Association was formed; its official journal, *American Quarterly*, appeared; various degrees in the new field were sought after and awarded. If there was little agreement on broad pedagogical questions, there was at least a general recognition that the overall aim was to find new patterns and meanings within the American experience. This involved, among other things, a protest against rigid categories of knowledge and the insistence on treating everything American as a mere extension of Europe. Both themes appear in essays by pioneers in the field—Tremaine McDowell, Robert Spiller, Stanley Williams, Ralph Gabriel, and Whitney Griswold, for example. In 1948 Professor McDowell formulated his First Law of American Studies: present the complex design of American life so as to reveal the fundamental diversity of human experience within which students might eventually find a fundamental unity.[5]

Such laws were easier to formulate than to demonstrate. Some scholars were suspicious of loosely-defined interdisciplinary programs. Instead of disappearing, departmental lines sometimes stiffened. It is one thing to observe, with Howard Mumford Jones, that the departmental system splits us into little groups conducting internecine wars; it is another thing to restore the peace.[6] The essays collected in this volume were not written to do battle. The contributors are not nearly so concerned with *defending* a position as with *defining* it. They have neither expected nor attempted to discover a single position or credo. Differences of approach and attitude are healthy and stimulating. Arguments between specialists (masters of the intricate microcosm) and generalists (intrigued with the vast macrocosm) continue. The latter plead for a grand synthesis; the former insist that we must know much more about what we wish to synthesize. The academic growth we seek depends not on a diminution but an increase of questions—provided they are relevant and provocative.

Those recently put to American Studies scholars by David Riesman were both:

> What can you say about your field today, in general terms? Has American Studies grown faster in state or private colleges? Have you any sense of recent major changes? Is it still a matter of missionaries and their devoted disciples?[7]

This book makes no attempt to provide "official" answers to such comprehensive questions. It is a set of random essays on certain aspects of our pluralistic culture, and as such it makes no claim of completeness. Our writers come from various regions, disciplines, and traditions. They range in age and experience from graduate students to professors emeritus. Three, being Europeans, provide outsiders' views. No essay has been edited or changed so as to conform with the style or viewpoint of any other. The whole effort is intended to be Socratic rather than dogmatic. European history has been described as man's heroic but tragic quest for a closed system. The nation we attempt to describe has created an open one. Men here have tried, in Walt Whitman's words, to "take the hinges off the door." These essays have been compiled to further that effort.

It is my hope that these essays will display the honest skepticism that marks the best recent scholarship in our field. No ready-made solution or method for our subject is in sight. "We shall have to develop one for ourselves," Professor Henry Nash Smith concludes, "and I am afraid that at present we shall have to be content with a very modest program. The best thing we can do, in my opinion, is to conceive of American Studies as a collaboration among men working from within existing academic disciplines but attempting to widen the boundaries imposed by conventional methods of inquiry."[8] This viewpoint is echoed by Walter Johnson, whose 1963 report for the U.S. Advisory Commission on International Educational and Cultural Affairs appeared under the title *American Studies Abroad*. Much remains to be done and undone in a world hypersensitive about any form of cultural imperialism.

Whatever the fate of American Studies abroad, those at home must take into account the new cultural patterns of the 1960's which, as Susan Sontag points out in *Against Interpretation*, are built on nonliterary foundations. The basic texts for today are found in the writing of Wittgenstein, Marshall McLuhan, John Cage, Claude Levi-Strauss, Siegfried Giedion, Norman O. Brown, and Gyorgy Kepes.[9] They stress new dimensions, a more open way of looking at the world. Do their ideas find a place in courses dealing with American Studies in transition? If not, why not?

Not only people, but the environment, confronts us with revolution. It took man centuries to move from the natural to the mechanical environment; then, almost instantly, to electrical. Paradoxically, with change too fast to be discernible, everything is suddenly visible: segregation, poverty, Vietnam rice paddies, the wart on Nasser's nose. So great is the acceleration that one is "out" before he fully realizes he is "in."

Modes may be verbal, aural, visual, physical—an expression, sound, look, gesture. It is the never-ending battle of Ancients *vs.* Moderns. Not the fact of transition, but the rate of transition, is uniquely ours.

To survive, a movement must be able to adapt to new environments and respond to new challenges. Many American Studies courses and research projects are guilty of the same kind of ossification and pedestrian coverage that made the movement possible in the first place. In Darwinian terms, such courses and projects invite comparison to the sad fate of the passenger pigeon.

To survive is to change and to compare. We *do* live in a global village, wired for sound. Neither bamboo nor iron curtains avail in the Age of Circuitry. The school, church, and universities are no longer inside buildings, but wherever sound and sight penetrates. If the medium is the message, what does that message say to interdepartmental studies?

The 18 essays which follow fall into three main categories. The first group centers on ways of understanding America; the second on ways of teaching whatever clues and conclusions our scholarship uncovers; and the third on the impact of American Studies and policies abroad. Hopefully the range and diversity of material will provide the impact that other fields derive from a unity which we have neither claimed nor sought.

Marshall W. Fishwick

1. Sigmund Skard, *American Studies in Europe* (Philadelphia: Univ. of Penn. Press, 1958), II, 641. For a summary of activity in our country, see Robert Walker's *American Studies in the United States* (Baton Rouge: LSU, 1958).

2. See *American Quarterly*, II (1950), 288.

3. Richard M. Huber, "A Theory of American Studies," *Social Education*, XVIII (1954), 269.

4. Arthur E. Bestor, Jr., "The Study of American Civilization: Jingoism or Scholarship?" *William and Mary Quarterly*, IX, Third Series (January, 1952).

5. Tremaine McDowell, *American Studies* (Minneapolis: Univ. of Minn., 1948), p. 51.

6. Howard Mumford Jones, *Education and World Tragedy* (Cambridge, Mass.: Harvard Univ., 1947).

7. David Riesman, letter to the author dated November 14, 1963.

8. Henry Nash Smith, "Can 'American Studies' Develop a Method?" *American Quarterly*, IX (1957), 197-208. Reprinted in Joseph J. Kwiat and Mary C. Turpie (eds.), *Studies in American Culture; Dominant Ideas and Images* (Minneapolis: Univ. of Minn., 1960).

9. Marshall W. Fishwick, "American Studies: Bird in Hand?" In *Exchange* (Department of State, Washington, D.C.), Spring, 1968.

"Nothing is more remarkable in the intellectual history of the last decades than the development of American Studies in our universities . . . It is the moment when Americans conceive of themselves to be living in a fully-developed culture, which is to be interpreted in its own positive terms, not merely by negative comparison with other cultures, which has its own history, its own laws and development, its own tone and quality, its own destiny."

—Lionel Trilling

"America's culture is above all becoming her own. The language itself, vigorous and racy, continually adding new image-making words, is proof of the vitality of American minds."

—André Maurois

"There are some nations that allow civilization to be torn from their grasp. There are others who themselves trample it underfoot."

—Alexis de Tocqueville

Contents

Marshall W. Fishwick Introduction

I

ON UNDERSTANDING
AMERICA

American Studies: Words or Things?

JOHN A. KOUWENHOVEN

JOHN A. KOUWENHOVEN is Professor of English at Barnard College. He is the author of *Made in America: The Arts in Modern Civilization* (1948 and 1962), *The Columbia Historical Portrait of New York* (1953), *The Beer Can By the Highway: Essays on What's American About America* (1961). Currently he is at work on a book about the building of the Eads Bridge across the Mississippi at St. Louis.

THE DISCOVERY AND EXPLORATION OF AMERICA HAS BEEN going on for roughly five hundred years. That is a long time on any scale except the geological. One would think that by now we would know pretty well what America is, even if we disagreed about its merits and demerits.

Perhaps we do know, but you would never guess it from reading the books its discoverers write about it, or from attending the conferences where they gather to discuss it. Conferences and symposia on American civilization are, I believe, commonly thought of—even by their most enthusiastic promoters—less as ways to settle things than as ways to unsettle them. They are set up to facilitate what is called "an exchange of ideas"—a curious phrase that suggests swapping notions as we might swap cigarette lighters, each of us pocketing and going home with the other fellow's instead of his own. Maybe some are exchanged, but very few are changed, apparently. The symposia and conferences I know about seem, at least, to have contributed very little to any agreement about what American culture is, let alone what it is worth.

15

In this essay I shall contend that part, at least, of our difficulty results from a fatal imbalance in the techniques we employ as explorers and discoverers in the field of American Studies. I shall suggest, as forcefully as I can, that we have been too ready to accept verbal evidence as if it were the equivalent of the evidence of our senses. I shall argue that we have been so preoccupied with words that we have neglected things; that we have, in fact, based our ideas of America primarily upon ingenious verbal generalizations that are sometimes laughably and sometimes tragically unrelated to actualities.

You may remember reading about Sir John Hawkins, the tough-minded and vigorous Elizabethan seaman who visited the French colony in Florida, at the mouth of the St. John's river, in the 1560's, in the course of one of his slave-trading voyages in Queen Elizabeth's good—but ironically named—ship *Jesus*. Hawkins reported, on his return to England, that there were unicorns and lions in Florida. The unicorns he knew about because some of his crew got pieces of unicorn horn from the French, who said they got them straight from the Florida Indians. So there was no doubt about the unicorns. As for the lions, Hawkins hadn't actually seen any of them, but there was no doubt about them either. Lions, as everyone knew, are the natural enemies of unicorns. It was therefore obvious, as Hawkins put it, that "whereas the one is, the other cannot be missing."

It is easy enough to see how absurdly funny Hawkins' report on Florida becomes when he accepts—as he does here—his own verbal ingenuity as the equivalent of reality. But I wonder if those of us who report nowadays on America are not as likely as Hawkins to be bewitched by our own verbal ingenuities. At all events, I shall ask you to follow me, along a somewhat circuitous route, through some speculations about the verbal traps we lay for ourselves, and about a possible way to avoid them.

II

A few years ago there was a trial in the New York Court of General Sessions that the newspapers referred to as "The Circus." It was a fantastic affair in which at one point a defense lawyer called the prosecuting attorney as a defense witness; at another the prosecuting attorney cross-examined himself; and everybody on both sides repeatedly lost his temper. Once, when the exhausted and frustrated judge was trying to follow the rapid-fire argument of one of the lawyers, he interrupted with a plaintive comment that has haunted me ever since. "The only thing you say," expostulated the judge, "that I don't understand are your words."

Perhaps the judge's remark is especially haunting because we hear so much these days about the need for greater speed in coping with words. Speed-reading is getting to be the rage. Children in school, suburban matrons, and business men are taking speed-reading courses. One wonders if they are bent on becoming participants in some sort of cosmic Court of General Sessions where, like the plaintive judge, the only thing said to them that they don't understand will be the words.

For words are deceptive enough, even if we take them slowly, as the recent studies in semantics have shown. And is it not curious that the science of semantics—the systematic study of the relation between verbal symbols and what they denote and connote, and of the way these word symbols affect human behavior—should be flourishing at the same moment in our history when we are energetically learning how to hasten over those verbal symbols? The more we are aware that words can be treacherously misleading, the more we want to race through them, lest we be misled. Perhaps we are doing so in justifiable self-defense.

For words are, in fact, deceptive and misleading—not just because they are ambiguous, as we all know they are, but because of an inherent limitation of language itself. That limitation was pointed out a hundred and thirty-four years ago by a banker in Utica, New York, who made a hobby of the study of language. His name was Alexander Bryan Johnson. In 1828 he published a small volume entitled *The Philosophy of Human Knowledge, or A Treatise on Language*, made up of lectures he had given at the local Lyceum. Eight years later he published an expanded version with the title *A Treatise on Language: or The Relation Which Words Bear to Things*, and eighteen years later, in 1854, a third and more fully developed version.

In none of its versions did the book make any impression upon learned circles at the time, since Johnson had no university connections and was unknown to the intelligentsia of Boston, New York, or Philadelphia. He sent copies to eminent men, such as Professor Benjamin Silliman at Yale and August Comte in Paris; but why would such people be interested in the ideas of a banker in Utica? As Comte said, in a curt letter of acknowledgement: "Although the question which you have broached may be one of the most fundamental which we can agitate, I cannot promise to read such an essay. For my part, I read nothing except the great poets ancient and modern ... in order to maintain the originality of my peculiar meditations." The only serious review any of the three versions received was a long and favorable discussion of the first in Timothy Flint's *Western Review*, published in the frontier city of Cincinnati in 1829. Not until 1947—more than a century later—was the book rediscovered and republished by Professor David Rynin of the University of California.

Since its rediscovery, Johnson's book has come to be acknowledged as a pioneering study in semantics and one of the most original philosophical works ever written by an American. I take both these evaluations on faith, since I am neither a student of semantics nor a philosopher. All I can say on my own authority is that Alexander Johnson's ideas have profoundly impressed me, and that the objections brought against them by Professor Rynin himself, in his introduction to the reprint, and by other semantics scholars seem to me irrelevant. I mention this only because I intend to use and develop some of Johnson's perceptions, and because I want it to be clear that I know my comments do not find support in current semantic theory.

As Johnson saw it, the radical limitation of words (their radical "defect") is that they are general terms or names, referring to things that are individual and particular. Even though we know, for example, that no two blades of grass are alike, the word *grass* suggests an identity. This suggestion of identity encourages us to disregard the different looks, feels, tastes, and smells of the uncounted blades that comprise the actuality of grass as we experience it.

Since words have this generalizing characteristic it is inevitable, Johnson argues, that if we contemplate the created universe through the medium of words, we will impute to it a generalized unity that our senses cannot discover in it. In our writing, thinking, and speaking, we habitually "disregard the individuality of nature, and substitute for it a generality which belongs to language."

One result of the delusive generality of verbal symbols is that two people can be in verbal agreement without meaning the same thing. You can say to me that television commercials are sometimes revolting, and I may reply "yes, they certainly are revolting sometimes." We are in complete verbal agreement. But the particular commercials you had in mind may not be the ones I was thinking of. Perhaps, indeed, I have never seen commercials like those you were referring to; perhaps if I had seen them, I would not have thought them revolting. I might have enjoyed them. The less our direct, first hand experience of television commercials coincides, the less chance there is that any verbal agreement—or disagreement—we arrive at in discussing them will have any significance whatever.

III

Verbal symbols, then, are inherently "defective." They are at best a sort of generalized, averaged-out substitute for a complex reality comprising an infinite number of individual particularities. We can say that a pane of glass is square, oblong, round, or a half-dozen other shapes, and that when it is shattered the pieces are fragments or slivers. But for the infinite variety of forms which those slivers in reality assume, we have no words. The multiple reality we generalize as "slivers of glass" can never be known through words. We can know that reality only through our senses, the way we experience blades of grass in lawns or commercials on TV.

This generalizing characteristic of language is, of course, its great value. It is what makes human communication possible. A language consisting of separate words for each of the particularities in the created universe would be bulky beyond reckoning. No one could ever master its vocabulary. We have good reason to be thankful for the ingenious symbol system that averages out reality into the mere ten thousand words that are necessary for ordering meals, writing love-poems, and composing essays on American civilization. And no harm would come of it if we did not fall into the habit of assuming that reality corresponds to the words we have invented to represent it.

More often than not, however, we do fall into that habit. "What is this?" our child asks us, showing us what he has in his hand. "A stone," we reply—or, if we have had Geology I, "a hunk of quartz." Long practice has habituated us to this device for eliminating all those particularities of texture, of color and form, of smell and taste that were the very things that interested the child. The averaged-out concept inherent in the word *stones* is admirably efficient for many purposes of communication, as when we are admonishing people who live in glass houses. But it does not tell your child what he has in his hand.

His senses tell him that. If he has learned anything from your words it is only that he must disregard the evidence of his senses. For the thing he has in his hand is not at all the same shape, or color, or feel as the one he asked about yesterday, which you also said was a stone (or a hunk of quartz). You have begun to teach him to interpret reality by words, instead of interpreting words by the specific realities of which they are the symbols. You have given him an effective lesson in the convenient but deceptive process by which we habitually translate the individual particulars of existence into the generalized abstractions of language. Unless he talks about stones only with people who are familiar with hunks of quartz more or less like the one he has examined, he is on his way, like the rest of us, to the Court of General Sessions.

I have magnified the difficulties he faces in order to emphasize an important point. People who have not experienced similar particularities cannot receive from one anther's words the meaning those words were intended to convey. For meaning is not a property of words, a static entity which words somehow embody. Meaning is a process that words sometimes facilitate: a process in which awareness passes from one consciousness to another. Words do not *have* meaning; they *convey* it. But they can convey it only if the receiving consciousness can complete the current of meaning by grounding it in comparable particulars of experience.

A man who has never been out of the American Southwest—who grew up in and has never left Santa Fe, New Mexico, for instance—and a man born and brought up in the Hebrides, off the western coast of Scotland, could not conceivably mean the same thing by the word *sunlight*. The less our cluster of experienced particulars corresponds to that of people by whom our words are heard or read, the less chance there is that those people will understand what we are saying.

What makes language function as satisfactorily as it generally does, despite its limitations, is that we use it chiefly to communicate with those who share the set of experienced particulars we call our common culture. One way and another we acquire some shared familiarity with a tremendous number of things. We get around, vicariously or otherwise. Even in the Hebrides there are no doubt people who have visited Santa Fe—or Las Vegas, whose sunlight will pass for Santa Fe's except among the finicky. And if our words are heard or read by those with whom we share a significant accumulation of experiences, they *can* convey our meaning well enough for all practical purposes—and even for some impractical ones as well. They can do so, that is, provided neither we nor those to whom we speak abandon our allegiance to the particulars we have experienced.

IV

So far, my argument adds up to something like this: Our words can convey meaning only to those who share with us a community of experienced particulars, and to them only if we and they scrupulously refer the generalized verbal symbols to concrete particulars we are talking about. Your translation of an experience into words can be understood only by someone who can interpret those words by referring them to a similar experience of his own. If he cannot do that, the current of meaning is short-circuited. A Santa Fe experience that might be adequately translated by the words "My wife has a smile like sunlight" cannot be the experience into which those words would be translated by an habitual Hebridean.

It seems obvious, therefore, that we must determine the limits of our community of experienced particulars. This is another way of saying that we need to discover how common our common culture is. Otherwise we will waste a great deal of energy and time in feckless attempts to communicate with people who cannot make sense of what we say.

To some extent our common culture is limited by geography. There are many places in the world where particulars like those we experience in New York, or Wichita, or Walla Walla are simply unavailable. To be sure, it would be naive to assume that geographical or political boundaries are the bounds of our common culture. A turret-lathe operator in Wichita might share a more significant community of experienced particulars with a turret-lathe operator in Bombay than with a professor of American literature who lived two blocks away. An economics student in New York or Walla Walla might share a more significant community of experienced particulars with a student of economics in Heidelberg than with a fine arts major at his own college. But the particulars that constitute American culture are by and large available in New York and Wichita and Walla Walla, whether or not the professor and machine operator, or the economics major and fine arts major, are aware of them; whereas in many areas of the world those constituent particulars are not available at all.

No doubt it is with some awareness of this problem that those of us concerned with American culture devote our efforts to programs like the international exchange of students and teachers, the encouragement of foreign tourism in this country, and the sending abroad of such cultural emissaries as Peace Corps groups, theatrical troupes, musical performers, and exhibitions of arts and crafts. Unwilling to trust to such routine agencies of international contact as commerce and the armed forces, we are deliberately making available to those in other lands certain particulars of our culture that we hope will serve to ground the current of meaning when we talk to them about ourselves. The only trouble is that we disagree among ourselves about which particulars we should make available. The State Department has its own ideas; some Senate committees have others; and private agencies like the American Legion, the Hollywood film exporters, and the Institute for International Education have others still.

The lack of general agreement about which clusters of particulars constitute the distinctively "American" experience emerged clearly from a symposium entitled *American Perspectives*, published by Harvard University Press in 1961 as one of the Library of Congress's series on twentieth century American civilization. Ten distinguished authorities contributed essays to that symposium, discussing such "clusters of particulars" as American literature, American business, American philosophy, and American popular culture. The volume was edited for the American Studies Association by Professor Robert E. Spiller (a past president of the Association) and Eric Larrabee (then managing editor of *American Heritage*). The auspices were impressive.

But despite a good deal of preliminary consultation and planning, and the best of intentions, the symposium admittedly failed of its purpose. As the editors ruefully acknowledge in their preface, "the hoped-for unity of the book did not materialize"; the contributors "found themselves in no firm agreement" either in their premises or in their conclusions.

I refer you to this book as one of the particulars I have in mind when I say that, up to now, we have not determined the limits of the community of experienced particulars we call "American culture." To put it bluntly, our verbal attempts to discover America fail because we do not know what we are talking about.

v

It is my conviction that part of our difficulty stems from an excessive preoccupation with verbal evidence. The particulars to which we refer—whether we are talking about politics or mass production, painting or social behavior—are too exclusively literary. Historians and social scientists are almost as bad as the literary critics in this respect. And so are the non-specialists.

I do not mean to suggest that novels, poems, and plays—and other writings—are not significant particulars of our culture. I think they are, and I earn my living as a teacher of courses in literature. But as I have tried to suggest, we have a weakness for mistaking words for things. We tend to forget that a novel about life in the slums of Chicago is not life in the slums of Chicago.

The novel is a cluster of verbal symbols whose arrangement conveys to us, with more or less precision, the emotions and ideas aroused in the writer by those particulars of Chicago slum life that he happened to experience. The writer's emotional responses to Chicago slum life, and his ideas about it, may be in themselves significant facts of American culture—especially if the novel communicates them to many readers, or even to a few who act in response to them. But these emotions and ideas, and the novel that conveys them, are not Chicago slum life. That is something that can be known only by direct sensory experience; and if you or I experienced it, its particulars might arouse in us emotions and ideas very unlike those we acquire from the novel.

If we can accept some such view as this of the significance of literature and other verbal documents (including "case histories" and other data of the social sciences), we will realize how necessary it is to consider other kinds of evidence in our speculations about American civilization and culture. Verbal evidence is, plainly, not enough—especially if we remember that not all civilizations have found, in literature, the most complete or significant expression of their vital energies. It may be true that the creative genius of England has been most fully expressed in literature, and that we can more or less ignore English music, painting, and architecture, without seriously distorting our image of England's achievement. But other cultures have obviously expressed themselves most significantly in other forms. One thinks, for instance, of Roman building, of Dutch painting, of German music. The fact that we are heirs to much of England's culture, including its language, does not necessarily mean—as Constance Rourke long ago pointed out—that we have, like the English, expressed ourselves most fully in literature.

In all of our studies of the past we probably rely, far more than we should, on verbal evidence, wherever it is available. As Lynn White, Jr. says in the preface to his recent book on *Medieval Technology and Social Change*:

> Voltaire to the contrary, history is a bag of tricks which the dead have played upon historians. The most remarkable of these illusions is the belief that the surviving written records provide us with a reasonably accurate facsimile of past human activity . . . In medieval Europe until the end of the eleventh century we learn of the feudal aristocracy largely from clerical sources which naturally reflect ecclesiastical attitudes: the knights do not speak for themselves . . . If historians are to attempt to write the history of mankind, and not simply the history of mankind as it was viewed by the small and specialized segments of the

race which have had the habit of scribbling, they must take a fresh view of the records.

The general pertinence of Lynn White's words to the problem of discussing American culture will, I hope, be clear. But I want to apply them in a special way.

It is important to recognize that, as White indicates, major segments of the population do not speak for themselves. Not everyone has the habit of scribbling (though it sometimes seems so). And I think it is true that in American civilization—and perhaps in what we call modern civilization elsewhere in the world—men and women whose work has most creatively expressed the energies of their times have often been non-scribblers. All of us, in so far as we rely upon our senses rather than upon verbal preconceptions, would acknowledge that American culture is expressed more adequately in the Brooklyn Bridge than in the poem Hart Crane wrote about it.

VI

I have talked a good deal about words, rather than about things. I have done so in an effort to call attention to the limitations of words as evidence of the realities that constitute our culture, hoping thereby to remove the chief obstacle to the consideration of things. If we can get rid of those verbal lions and unicorns, we may be able to see and hear and touch and smell and taste the things that are really here.

Archaeologists and anthropologists have long known how important things are as testimony. And historians in some areas have learned a good deal from non-verbal evidence. Lynn White's book rescues the non-scribbling knights and other medieval people from oblivion by examining things such as the stirrups that gave the knights unprecedented control over horses and the cranks that gave medieval mechanics new control over power. Similarly, museums of folk art, and museums like the Smithsonian Institution, acknowledge the importance of tangible objects as evidence of the culture of large numbers of people who did not have "the habit of scribbling."

It is chiefly from the archaeologists and anthropologists that we might learn techniques that we can adapt to the recognition, appreciation, and evaluation of the non-verbal elements of American culture. We must, I am convinced, learn to perceive and savor with our five senses the things non-scribbling Americans have made, in somewhat the same way that the archaeologist or anthropologist approaches the artifacts and folk arts of other times and places.

A good deal of attention has been devoted recently to the study of what are called American folk arts; but those engaged in such study can contribute little to our understanding of American civilization for the simple reason that we really do not have any folk arts, properly so called. Those we have are other people's. For the term folk arts is properly applied to artifacts made in traditional forms and patterns that originated, and survive, among groups cut off, in one way or another, from the main stream of contemporary life. The things we call folk arts are things like Navaho sand-paintings, or Pennsylvania Dutch fraktur.

Surviving remnants of traditional folk arts can still be found in isolated communities of even this highly industrialized and urbanized nation. And many are the collectors and students who cherish them. So many, in fact, that the folk arts will soon be—if they are not already—a big business. But delightful and interesting as these hand-crafted variants of traditional forms and patterns may be, they cannot tell anything much about American culture. The love of them, or the faddish popularity of them, can tell us a good deal. But the objects themselves cannot.

The nearest thing to folk arts that American culture has produced are those artifacts that I once labelled "the vernacular arts." The term has its limitations, but I meant it to serve as a generalized label for non-traditional forms and patterns of many sorts. By it I referred to objects shaped empirically by ordinary people in unselfconscious and uninhibited response to the challenges of an unprecedented cultural environment.

The principal novelties in that environment, in nineteenth century America, were, it seems to me, a technology based upon power-driven machines rather than handcraft, and a social and political system based upon the mobility-oriented institutions of democracy rather than the status-oriented institutions of aristocracy. Specifically the products of the vernacular arts were the tools, toys, buildings, books, machines, and other artifacts whose texture, shape, and so on were evolved in direct, untutored response to the materials, needs, attitudes, and preoccupations of a society being shaped by the twin forces of democracy and technology.

VII

It is my contention that direct sensory awareness of such vernacular objects provides an important kind of knowledge about American culture. Perhaps, indeed, the most necessary kind if we are searching for a community of experienced particulars that embodies the dynamic energies of an emergent American culture.

Up until very recently these important constituents of our culture were entirely overlooked by scholars and critics, and even now they are known chiefly through verbal accounts of them. It is no wonder that our verbal theories about American culture have seemed so irrelevant to people who know its everyday vernacular realities at first hand in factories and filling stations, on farms and in offices. If we are ever going to formulate useful verbal generalizations about our culture, we are going to have to look at, and handle, and contemplate the particulars of this vernacular tradition.

Ideally, of course, we should experience these particulars in the cultural context that produced them, not isolated from that context as displays in museums or World's Fairs or exhibitions. But wherever we encounter them, let us respect the things themselves and test whatever is said about them against our firsthand sensory awareness. It will not be enough to approach these vernacular things as we customarily approach the fine arts and folk arts displayed in museums. Go to any museum and you will observe how ready people are to permit words to usurp the dignity and authority of things. Some unfamiliar object on display catches our eyes, because of its form or color. We go over to examine it more closely, but before we have done more than glance at it we notice the label that the museum's curators have supplied in their ardor to educate us. The label probably provides valuable knowledge *about* the object—what it was made for; when, where, and by whom it was made; and so on—knowledge that might well sharpen our sensory awareness of the object if we returned to the contemplation of its form and color and texture. But more often than not the label replaces the thing as the center of our attention; having mastered the words we are satisfied that we have mastered the thing. So we pass on to the next display and read its label.

As Joyce Cary says, in his little book on *Art and Reality*, there is a good deal of truth in the notion that "when you give a child the name of a bird, it loses the bird. It never *sees* the bird again, but only a sparrow, a thrush, a swan." In all phases of our lives the primitive magic of words still works its spell among us, and we think that we have mastered creation by naming it. Like the child who is attracted by the form and color and feel of a particular stone or bird and asks "What is it?" we ask the label what it is that caught our eye. And like the child, we have been educated to accept the verbal reply as a substitute for the thing itself.

This is, of course, only one of many ways in which we have taught ourselves to accept translations of reality for the original. Even in non-verbal realms we increasingly encounter reality at one remove. More and more of us know the game of baseball not as a cluster of directly experienced sensations, including the mixed smells of cold beer and hot franks and peanuts and cigars, but as sights and sounds only, as selected and translated by TV cameras and microphones. Fewer and fewer of us know the taste of tobacco on the tongue, or the taste and feel of tobacco smoke, now that cigarettes have filter tips, some with the filters recessed a quarter inch away so you can't even touch your tongue to them. More and more of us experience the arts—literature, painting, sculpture, and music—filtered through some translating device. Many of us know painting and sculpture primarily through two-dimensional photographic translations that either distort the colors or average them out into tones. Most of the music we hear has been translated, with higher or lower fidelity, by microphones and electronic tubes or transistors.

These various forms of translation all differ in an important way from the sort of translation that occurs when we translate the particulars of experience into words. They all alter some aspects of the thing, but they do not generalize it or average-out its uniqueness. A photograph of a scene on some Main Street translates a three-dimensional reality that can be experienced with all five senses into a two-dimensional reality that we experience only with our eyes; but the pictorial image, like the original, is a specific and individual thing, not a generalization. Any verbal description of the scene would, on the other hand, be composed of words that are generalized symbols, each capable of standing for (or referring to) many different particulars of the same general class.

VIII

To discover America, to become aware of American culture as a community of experienced particulars about which we can effectively communicate our perceptions to one another, we must first of all be aware of the limitations of verbal translations of reality. Then we can set about the job of training our young people and ourselves to think with our senses as well as with words.

At present our educational system is almost exclusively concerned with training our capacity to think verbally. What this means is that we learn to think words such as *bridge* or *beer can*. We then think *about* those words and link them with others to form verbal concepts. These concepts are articulations and juxtapositions of words that have properties we call syntax, logic, and so on. And they can be recorded, memorized, and easily made available to others in identical copies.

The ease with which verbal concepts can be recorded and repeated is a great and powerful advantage. Word-thinking has become the basis of our educational system— except in those areas (notably the exact sciences) where vagueness and generalization are intolerable. In those areas apprenticeship, laboratory or studio work, or some other system of acquiring first-hand familiarity with specific particulars, has necessarily been retained. But so impressive are the properties of language that subjects to which its generalizing properties are appropriate—subjects like philosophy, sociology, theology, and history (including literary history and art history)—dominate the academic curriculum, to say nothing of the American Studies Association.

I do not wish to belittle such subjects, or to depreciate the wonderful powers of language. But we must not permit our admiration of word-thinking, and our respect for its achievements, to blind us to its limitations—limitations that derive from the inescapable limitation of words themselves: that is, their averaging-out tendency.

The danger is not that we will underestimate the importance of word-thinking in education, but that we will overlook the importance of what might be called sensory thinking. I do not know if there is a better word for it. But I know that just as we can think the words *bridge* and *beer can*, we can also think the appearance of a bridge, or the appearance of a beer can. That is sight-thinking. As Alexander Bryan Johnson remarked, the properties and limitations of sight-thinking differ from those of word-thinking. A sight-thought of a bridge is evanescent; it flashes on our consciousness, then fades. Also, it is comprehensive, including all visible aspects of the bridge at one and the same instant, whereas a word-thought about a bridge has to be accumulated gradually by adding words together. Finally, and most importantly, the sight-thought of a bridge is specific, not generalized. We can sight-think an individual bridge, or even a group of individual bridges; but we cannot sight-think a generalized abstraction of bridges.

Just as there are sight-thoughts, there are also feel-thoughts, smell-thoughts, taste-thoughts, and sound-thoughts. The terms may sound odd and unfamiliar, but we all know the realities to which they refer. With a little effort we can think the feel of a cold beer can in our hand, and think the taste of the metal as we drink from it. And we know that these other sense-thoughts, like sight-thoughts, are evanescent, comprehensive, and specific.

These sense-thoughts share, then, a significant property

that differentiates them from word-thoughts. They are specific, not generalized.

They also share a significant limitation, as compared to word-thoughts. They cannot be arranged in logical or syntactical patterns. The kind of direct and specific awareness we derive from sensory thoughts, unlike the awareness we derive from word-thinking, cannot be communicated symbolically to others in conventional forms that can be easily recorded, memorized, and reproduced in identical copies.

Yet, if we trained our capacities for sensory thinking, instead of discouraging them as our educational system customarily does, it would be clear that this limitation is an asset, rather than a liability, if only because the non-discursive properties of sense-thoughts can serve as a check on the discursive thinking we do with words. The editors of that scholarly symposium on American civilization mentioned earlier concluded their preface with a wistful reference to the possibility that "if there were more unity in modern man's total view of himself and his world," the symposium itself might have produced a more consistent and unified image of our culture as one part of that world. What interests me in that conclusion is the implied assumption that there could be (or should be) a unified total view of the sort described. The very idea of such a unified and consistent view is, I suspect, a verbal illusion. It is an illusion we could not entertain if we had not become habituated, by our schooling and long practice, to accept words —unhitched from particulars—as the ultimate realities. Such terms as "modern man himself" and "modern man's world" are only remotely affiliated, if at all, with any of the infinitely diverse individual existences to which the terms pretend to refer. Who on earth, the reader should ask, is "modern man himself"? To what, if any, specific reality do the words refer?

But that is the very question we do *not* ask. Because we are educated as we are, we expect to find in actuality the unity and consistency that verbal symbols can be arranged to express, forgetting that the unity and consistency are properties of a system of verbal symbols, not of the multifarious particularities that are averaged-out in our nominative generalizations. Because we are educated as we are, we too readily assume that in the realm of speculative discussion, as in the realm of faith, "in the beginning was the word."

In American Studies, as in the humanities generally, we have been largely preoccupied with records left by those "who had the habit of scribbling" (and more recently, thanks to the "oral history" projects, by those who had the habit of prattling). And it is chiefly from this verbal evidence that we have happily or gloomily deduced the lions and unicorns (as logically demonstrable and as non-existent as Sir John Hawkins') about which we theorize and argue. If there are no unicorns hereabouts, let's stop arguing about them. Our primary allegiance, as sentient creatures, is surely not to the creations of our verbal ingenuity, but to the particular sights, tastes, feels, sounds, and smells that constitute the American world we are trying to discover.

An "Eye" for America

WARREN FRENCH

WARREN FRENCH, Associate Professor of English at Kansas State University, has contributed the volumes about John Steinbeck, Frank Norris, and J. D. Salinger to the Twayne "United States Authors" Series. He has also edited (in 1963) a "Companion" to Steinbeck's *The Grapes of Wrath* and contributed frequently to the publications of the National Council of Teachers of English. Work in progress will stress the role of motion pictures in the development of American Studies.

IT HAS BEEN SAID THAT A STUDENT DOES NOT REALLY NEED teachers and classes at all; by ransacking the library, he can learn for himself all that there is to be known. What is less frequently pointed out about such rugged intellectual individualism is the kind of narrow, anti-social creature those few who ever manage thus to educate themselves are likely to become. We don't need many Colin Wilsons and Henry Millers to illustrate the vast wastefulness of self-education programs, and we need attend only a few "Great Books" sessions to learn what is accomplished by the blind leading the blind through Professor Adler's maze. Fortunately most of the delusions about the self-made man went out with the oil lamp by which he studied. Today we rarely need to be told that a conspicuously successful individual is not college trained; his behavior speaks for itself.

Actually, as Emerson emphasized, neither books nor experiences are enough in themselves to produce a well-educated man, and such a variety of both is now available that one needs some kind of seasoned guide through both if he is not to consume his energies rediscovering the obvious. Even when it has been recognized, however, that teachers are not just baby-sitters or policemen, American education has tended to be too largely verbal. The sciences long ago learned the need for laboratory training, but the humanities and most of the social sciences have been slow to profit from science's example, even though it is possible that it is not just the lure of money and prestige that draws many of the better students into the sciences. Preoccupied with training (if not simply indoctrinating) the mind, we have neglected the training of the senses.

Americans have made great progress in recent years in developing an "eye" for the past; but this progress has not always been reflected in our educational system. One of the most effective ways to develop some sense of the past, for example, is to participate in its reconstruction; yet the idea of restoring the past—particularly in the United States— is a relatively new one. It originated scarcely more than a century ago when a group of persons became alarmed about the dilapidated state of Mount Vernon and Independence Hall, shrines which today it seems impossible could ever have been neglected, even though the latter has only within the last decade received the kind of setting usually given a priceless jewel.

We were slow to learn, too, from these precedents. Old Williamsburg was allowed almost to disappear before its reconstruction was begun, and the preservation of structures of historical and cultural interest is still haphazard and uncertain, especially in New York City. The conditions at even the most successful restorations have not, furthermore, been especially propitious to study, since the emphasis not only at Virginia City, Nevada, but even at Williamsburg has been upon the tourist dollar. Actually, I have felt more success in recapturing something of the past in the tiny and unostentatious collection of restorations at Harvard, Massachusetts, and in the quiet streets of Concord, Massachusetts (but even Walden Pond has been threatened recently) than in the thronged thoroughfares of Williamsburg where the camera constantly clicking to capture too gleaming period costumes and undisciplined brats sporting about the stocks too often illustrates contempt rather than respect for the past. In many ways, slapdash Virginia City with its grotesque slot machines and piles of tourist-tempting baubles more nearly suggests the vulgarity that animated the city in its heyday than does the carefully staged production at Williamsburg, which gives us the past not as it was but as we would like to think it was.

An eye for the past is certainly, however, not best developed in self-conscious restorations, for the average tourist is attracted by either snob appeal or bad taste and most of all by such a happy combination of them as the Hearst Castle at San Simeon, California, or New Orleans' French Quarter. What is distressing about what Pat Hazard brilliantly calls the "Kodacriminals" is that—since many of them are college trained—our schools have failed to produce Americans sensitive enough to their past (and present) so that touring means more than simply hurrying from one well insulated Holiday Inn to another, leaving the swimming pool only to sop up quaintness or alcohol.

I certainly do not wish to appear to suggest that American Studies programs should settle themselves down in quaint, pseudo-colonial villages, where their proprietors shall be known by their syllabub. Students could best learn to achieve a sense of the past not by being herded through existing reconstructions and restorations, but by being posed with the problem—in their home community and elsewhere —of determining what truly merits being preserved, restored, and reconstructed. The restoration of St. Augustine, Florida, offers right now, for example, challenging laboratory work to the student; but once the quadricentennial festivities begin in 1965, the student should seek some still undiscovered country. Formulating proposals for preserving the really significant relics of our cultural growth could serve to show concretely the interrelations between history, sociology, and the study of the arts stressed in American Studies programs, while devising programs for the realization of these proposals could provide the student with an often disillusioning but invaluable working knowledge of the realities of present-day American politics, economics, and psychology.

II

We need not wait, however, for programs that may truly put our students "on the road" to learning to develop a better "eye" for America. We can begin right now in our classrooms to stress the significance of pictorial media in the development of American culture. We need here especially to recognize that today's students have throughout their lives been much more extensively exposed to eye-catching devices than were previous generations. The vast improvements in color reproduction in magazines and advertising signs, and, most of all, the omnipresence of television, assure us that students today will be experienced, sometimes even discriminating, viewers. We ignore these pictorial media at the risk of wasting our time by failing to refine skills that the students have already developed.

Like everyone else, academicians find such security in their stereotypes that they fail to recognize that the once predominant specimen that "doesn't know much about art, but knows what he likes" is becoming as freakish a bird as other arrogant boobies. While these cultural John Birchites still sully the air with their raucous cries, the sound is out of all proportion to the size of its source. While vast crowds

were certainly lured to the Metropolitan Museum to see the
Mona Lisa and the fabulous Rembrandt only by the much
publicized millions of dollars the paintings represented, one
needs only attend less publicized events like recent exhibitions of Van Gogh and the German Expressionists in
Kansas City to discover that serious art is attracting increasingly sizeable and serious audiences. Indeed one is as
likely today to encounter a traffic jam at an art exhibit as
at an athletic event or a bargain sale. It is no longer surprising to find reproductions of serious works of art and sometimes even originals in students' quarters, and we can hope
that these students will carry this taste away from the
campus with them.

The American response to fine art is especially encouraging because for years so little was done to develop it. Anyone familiar with the dull black-and-white and fuzzily
registered color prints that shrill old maids used in an
attempt to instill into squirming schoolchildren a "respect"
for arts that should really be loved will little wonder that
American eyes rarely turned to the art treasures of the
ages. Anyone predicting even a generation ago that a brisk
trade would develop in this country in reproductions of
famous works of art would have been considered addled
by his own addiction to culture; but improvements in color
printing and the daring of publishers who have supposed
that Americans might have an eye for something besides
muddy sentiment have shown that painting has charms like
music when it is allowed to soothe the savage on its own
terms.

Despite the sympathetic efforts of a few outstanding art
historians, however, painting has not yet occupied the place
that it should in American Studies programs. Nor can we
expect extensive help from scholars who are generally and
properly concerned more with the great artistic achievements of Europe and Asia than with America's spotty pro-

duction. The United States has so far produced few truly universal masterpieces; but we have produced a great many works that are of inestimable value in documenting and highlighting the history of our social growth. Probably the American dream has never been given more impressive visible form than in the monumental canvases of Thomas Cole. The conflict between the agricultural past and the industrial future of the country is nowhere more ominously if unintentionally epitomized than in George Inness' "The Lackawanna Valley," a visual testimony to the often frustrated hopes of men of good will that the claims of nature and the machine might be reconciled. What more vividly communicates the often remarked "loneliness" of American city life than the paintings of Edward Hopper? The shrill cheapness of pleasure seekers breaking the bonds of Puritanical restraints than the canvases of Reginald Marsh? Even if we cannot send our students out to discover the United States for themselves, we can bring them the pictorial record of the nation's agonizing growth.

A special problem that arises in this transitional period (as old suspicions of the artist as Sybarite or sycophant to the detested aristocracy are fading) is that students' taste in art is sometimes better than their mentors! It is difficult for the young admirer of Klee to communicate with an artistically naive professor enamored of Salvador Dali's concept of the Last Supper. Nor do "home seminars" in pasting postage-stamp sized reproductions into prepared pamphlets do much to bridge the gap, since, even if we could, we do not need to teach students how to appreciate paintings so much as how to integrate the study of the visual record of our past with readings in American literature, history, and sociology.

Fortunately recent developments have vastly facilitated the study and teaching of American art even by those comparatively uninformed about the visual arts. Collecting

American "primitives" has become almost a mania, and reproductions of specimens in the Abby Aldrich Rockefeller collection at Williamsburg and in other museums abound in the wake of the enthusiasm for Grandma Moses. None of these efforts to preserve specimens of our folk and early commercial art, however, equals in its value to the student of American culture the remarkable collection known as the Index of American Design, housed at the National Gallery in Washington. The faithful reproductions of paintings and artifacts that form this Index have been drawn upon for most recent studies like the impressive volume *America's Arts and Crafts*, sponsored by *Life* magazine.

The professional artist in America has not been entirely ignored as a result of this recent enthusiasm for naivete. The Detroit Institute of Art is assembling a research collection of materials relating to American painting that will bring together long scattered information and greatly facilitate the reconstruction of American art history from the Peales to the present. This history has already recently been told several times in elegantly illustrated volumes, one compiled under the auspices of *Time* magazine from color plates that had appeared in this widely circulated journal, which has long sought to increase Americans' art consciousness.

One need not journey even to Washington or Detroit, however, to deepen one's acquaintance with our native arts; nor need one assemble from diverse sources his own collection of slides to develop his own approach to the teaching of these arts. The recent formation under the auspices of the Carnegie Corporation of a collection of thousands of slides illustrating all aspects of American art makes adequate material of the highest quality available to any institution with the vision to invest in this remarkably versatile and reasonably priced collection, examples of which have been provided to universities in several sections of the country.

Indeed the principal problem today in the study of American painting is no longer that of finding adequate materials for vivid presentation, but of encouraging schools and teachers to make adequate use of the material that is becoming available. The resources, like the students, have often outstripped the teachers; but it is to be hoped that the rising generation trained at schools conscious of the fine arts will soon be in a position to insist upon furthering the American student's acquaintance with his artistic heritage. Those interested at every institution can at least agitate for adequate funds to purchase and care for the Carnegie Corporation collection, as well as for the acquisition of representative works of contemporary American art. While building such a collection for the study of the history of American painting as even that at the University of Kansas is beyond the resources of many institutions in view of today's fiercely competitive market for art works, every school can encourage the training of its students' eyes by small but tasteful purchases of paintings, sculpture, and prints; and in doing so, schools can also encourage the American artist by providing him with a wider market.

III

In another visual medium—the one to which the American contribution has been the most distinctive and in which I am particularly interested—the situation is more dismal than any that I have touched upon so far, because, as far as scholarship is concerned, the materials are neither appreciated, understood, or even available. I refer to the motion picture.

The notion lingers among those implacably opposed to all mechanical media that the motion picture is a diabolical last resort of the teacher too lazy to prepare for class. Nothing could be further from the truth, because the greatest objection to the use of motion pictures in class-rooms is, on the contrary, that choosing and presenting them effectively is a time, energy, and thought-consuming process that is likely to frighten off all but the most energetic and imaginative.

Mentioning motion pictures in connection with educa-tion is, of course, likely to bring to mind those unpleasant sessions in stuffy rooms at which we learned how bread is made in hygienic bakeries or were warned that unhygienic lusts exposed us to venereal infections. The commercial motion picture has been regarded by many high-minded academics as strictly a pleasure device which one pays to attend as a brief escape from the rigors of the educational process. Even though it is a benighted institution that does not today boast some kind of "art film" or "film classics" series as part of its cultural recreation, these programs are likely to be haphazardly planned, unprofessionally managed, and divorced from the academic curricula.

Only a few of our most unconventional critics, such as James Agee, have recognized that the motion picture, even though invented recently, is an independent art form that deserves to be studied on its own merits. It is not merely a teaching aid in older disciplines; it is a medium with a his-tory and an aesthetic theory of its own. If the motion pic-tures have not always fulfilled their promise as an art form, our colleges may be in part responsible because of their neglect of cinema's serious claims.

A few universities, principally in California, have in-stituted film departments, but these are generally devoted, like journalism and radio-television departments, to the pro-fessional training of technicians. Some other schools have instituted courses in the history of the motion picture, but these courses are still uncommon and largely dependent for their existence and irregular offering upon the efforts of one devoted scholar. Even such an outstanding institution as the

University of California at Berkeley, which publishes the distinguished *Film Quarterly*, has not yet stabilized its offerings in the history of the cinema or begun to build the film library such a course would require. Although there is at least one educational film library in many states, its holdings are likely to be confined to documentary films produced by governmental agencies and industrial corporations or to antiquated adaptations of literary classics.

The Winter 1962–63 issue of *Film Quarterly* lists the resources for film scholarship in this country; this survey shows that so far only the New York Museum of Modern Art and Eastman House in Rochester have built collections and developed facilities that make the scholarly study of the cinema possible, and they have not been able to do all that would be desirable. It is fortunate that our colleges have not made the demands that they might upon these pioneering institutions, since such demands could not be fulfilled under present conditions.

Providing for the adequate study of the motion picture is, of course, a formidable task, not to be lightly undertaken by humanities departments already hard-pressed to compete with the better-understood and better-endowed sciences. There is, in the first place, the problem of acquiring a film library. Even if an institution has the money, it cannot go out and buy films as it can books. Some film masterpieces have disappeared altogether: Max Pabst's *Three Penny Opera*, for example, was assembled only with immense difficulty from two fragmentary copies of this outstanding film that Hitler sought to destroy, and Albert Johnson tells me that no copy has been located of the version of *Showboat* in which the inimitable Helen Morgan and Paul Robeson appeared. Even when copies of films exist, studios are reluctant to sell them outright, for fear that they may be used to compete with re-releases or remakes. They must be convinced that universities should be allowed to purchase or should be given copies that will be used for educational purposes only. Before such gifts can even be solicited, however, universities must be persuaded to provide proper repositories for the films and to hire technicians who can handle these fragile materials properly, as well as scholars acquainted with the history and significance of one of the great artistic creations of our own age. They might begin by converting the usually formless series of "film classics" into a thematically planned program, part of either a credit course or at least a series of lectures.

Fears that students and members of the community would shun such a pedantic approach to the motion picture and that commercial exhibitors would suffer from this subsidized competition have been proved groundless by the experience of the University of California at Berkeley where the imaginative film series planned by Albert Johnson (director William Wyler, for example, has visited the campus to discuss his own pictures) are well attended by a paying audience and have served to stimulate rather than destroy audience interest in commercial showings of related pictures.

I have been delighted by the enthusiastic response in Berkeley to my own brief series of films with which John Steinbeck is connected. I would not hesitate to recommend such a program to other schools, and I plan whenever possible to incorporate the showing of such works as Steinbeck's *The Forgotten Village* and Ernest Hemingway's *The Spanish Earth* into the specialized study of these authors. (*Intruder in the Dust*, filmed commercially in Faulkner's home town of Oxford, Mississippi, also provides invaluable visual material for an understanding of the background out of which Faulkner's great fiction springs; any school offering courses in his work—as many do—should certainly possess a copy of this film, one Hollywood product that was a greater artistic than commercial success.)

Some schools have shown commendable initiative in encouraging academic approaches to the cinema. The University of Washington, to cite the most outstanding example, has enabled George Bluestone, author of the invaluable *Novels into Film*, to experiment with motion-picture making. Bluestone's first production is a controversial but undeniably moving film version of Herman Melville's "Bartleby, the Scrivener," that may be rented or purchased by interested American Studies groups or other educational agencies. The spread of educational television is also likely to tempt more universities beyond the occasional production of garish short films extolling the school's assets in a way that it hopes will appeal to high-school students and small town Rotary clubs; but it is hardly likely that many schools will be able to produce worthwhile motion pictures when they cannot even subsidize creditable literary magazines. They can, however, take the problem of building film libraries as seriously as that of building any of the other libraries essential to the education of today's students in the study of the American achievement.

In view of the difficulty of building such collections, however, cautious custodians of closely guarded funds are likely to ask just what motion pictures can be used for beyond "mere entertainment." There are three answers.

First, as I have already stressed, the motion picture is an autonomous art form that deserves study in its own right. We need to study both its comparatively few successes as enduring works of art of universal value and its failures for the evidence that they may offer about the conflicting demands of culture and commerce in the modern world. We need to recognize—especially in American Studies programs —that during the twentieth century the motion picture has probably been more influential in shaping the American dream than any other art form, and we need to know how its formulas have both shaped and been shaped by other forces in our culture. Shifts in American attitudes and tastes have been reflected more clearly by nothing than the American film and the attempts that have been made to censor and control it. Films offer, often unintentionally, an unduplicated record of changing American fashions and ideals in homes, clothing, cars, entertainment; they offer also, by their omissions as well as their commissions, a record of our attitudes toward sex, religion, education, the accumulation of wealth, social discrimination, and every other controversial matter that has disturbed the twentieth century public.

Our students need to see the films for themselves, however, in order to learn from them. Repeating conclusions drawn by others is no more useful in the study of the motion picture than is rote learning in any other subject. To understand the changing nature of spectacle one must see the successive versions of "Ben Hur," "Cleopatra," "Mutiny on the Bounty." To know whether "pre-Hays Code" and "post-Hays Code" naughtiness are the same thing, we must confront Liz Taylor with Mae West. Differences between silent and talking pictures need to be analyzed critically rather than discussed sentimentally. Despite a handful of classic studies of the art of the cinema, film criticism today is in about the same impressionistic state that literary criticism was before the New Criticism began to make its influence felt; and, resentful as film producers often are of academic criticism, it is unlikely that a "new criticism" of motion pictures will develop outside the universities.

Motion pictures, to move to my second point, should not be studied, however, only in isolation, but also in relation to other art forms. Intelligently studied, they can shed much light upon our understanding of literature. I am not talking now about chasing students to see *Henry V* to help the unimaginative envision the scenes that they read or *Miss Julie* to give them practice in listening to Swedish. Students should, above all, be specifically discouraged from thinking about films as enormous pictorial versions of books and plays designed to delight those too lazy to read. As George Bluestone has pointed out, the two arts are separate, and efforts to reproduce distinguished novels on film have produced undistinguished results, while filmed plays are likely to be flat both physically and emotionally. The adapter's difficult task, as DeWitt Bodeen points out in *Films in Review* (June–July, 1963), is not simply to reproduce the original but "to recreate and sustain an established mood" in a medium with unique characteristics. Often, however, the adapter makes changes that are demanded not by the nature of the new medium, but the expectations of a less sophisticated audience and the caprices of producers, stars, and censors. When changes like these are made in the translation of a work from one medium to another, comparative study can help us to understand more clearly than we otherwise might the intentions of the original work.

In my book, *J. D. Salinger*, for example, I discuss the way in which the single movie made from a Salinger story, *My Foolish Heart*, clarifies by its departures the meaning of the original story, "Uncle Wiggily in Connecticut." In the original, the heroine, Eloise, loses her "niceness" after the boy she loves, Walt Glass, is killed in a freak accident in a rest area during the war and she marries a humorless sadist who drives her to drink. In the Samuel Goldwyn film, Walt is killed, not in an accident for which the blame cannot be established, but in a plane crash that makes him the victim of a savage society, and Eloise is forced to steal a friend's fiancé to provide a father for the issue of her pre-marital intimacies with Walt. At the end of the film, Eloise's husband justly deserts her for his original sweetheart.

As I point out, "Salinger's basic contrast between the 'nice' and 'phony' world has vanished. In Salinger's terms, the Eloise of the film has been a calculating 'phony' from

the beginning. . . . Ironically, the film-makers have simplified the situation in just the way that Eloise says she would
if she tried to explain it to her jealous and literal-minded
husband." A poignant account of the defeat of innocence
has, in short, been turned into a conventional melodrama
of virtue rewarded and evil receiving its comeuppance. We
can see the subtle meaning of Salinger's original more
clearly, however, when we compare his story with what
the script writers made of it.

Possibly because of their changes, Salinger has refused
to allow any of his works to be filmed. Samuel Goldwyn
has disturbed other serious writers, too. One of the most
valuable sets of documents for any study of film adaptations of literary originals is the acrimonious correspondence
between Goldwyn and James Thurber over Goldwyn's
production of Thurber's "The Secret Life of Walter Mitty"
as a starring vehicle for Danny Kaye. The correspondence,
which is printed in *Life* (August 18, 1947), is one of the
very few which places the views of the principal parties
to such a controversy clearly before the public.

Since it is difficult to obtain rights to screen Goldwyn
pictures, students may not be able to settle this controversy
for themselves by comparing the originals; but there are
still abundant materials to use in developing their critical
faculties. An especially interesting problem is posed by
John Steinbeck's own adaptation of his "Red Pony" stories
for the film with the same title, since he felt that the tone
of the work should be lightened to make it appropriate for
the different medium. Students are also likely to be especially intrigued by a comparison of the original and film
versions of Tennessee Williams' plays from *A Streetcar
Named Desire* to *Sweet Bird of Youth*. I have found it
provocative also to have even students not especially interested in literature compare Poe's short stories with some
of the vastly altered motion pictures that have been derived

from them. A small literature has already developed that provides models for student analyses: Milton Stern discusses *Moby Dick* in *College English* (May, 1956), and Bernard Knieger talks about *La Dolce Vita* in *College Composition and Communication* (January, 1963). The field, however, remains largely unexploited.

Such comparisons serve to refute that motion pictures simplify things for the teacher. It takes both careful planning and viewing to prepare comparative discussions, and instructors must keep on their toes to be prepared for the observations of perceptive students. Happily the National Council of Teachers of English sponsors a monthly journal, *Studies in the Mass Media*, edited by Joseph Mersand, that facilitates the difficult job by providing materials for the discussion of some outstanding pictures, but even this useful guide can only point a way. The alert teacher will also wish to read the discussions of motion pictures in magazines like the *Hudson Review*. By far the most helpful source of material, however, especially for planning thematic programs of motion pictures is *Films in Review*, published ten times a year since 1950 by the National Board of Review of Motion Pictures, Inc. (31 Union Square West, New York 3). Besides reviews of current films, this unique magazine features articles listing the pictures in which particular performers have appeared, which famous directors have made, or which deal with particular themes and subjects. The issues for 1961, for example, described the pictures made by Paul Muni and Ingrid Bergman, pictures made from the writings of Poe and Mark Twain and from the Sherlock Holmes stories, and pictures about Lincoln. There are also many fine books on the cinema, but most instructors will benefit not so much from reading about movies as from looking at them and thinking about the ways in which they can be used to carry out the basic aims of American Studies programs by showing the relationship

between motion pictures and other subjects that we study
—history, literature, psychology, and even—though artistically minded film critics may object—sociology.

Such careful study of the motion picture, to progress to
my third idea of the benefit of studying films, can even aid
the student who is not interested in the arts. I do not mean
simply that it will encourage him to think about an important force shaping his environment—although it will—
but that an awareness of the clarity, precision, and acute
editing demanded for success in the visual arts may make
him more aware of fuzziness and sloppiness in his own
thinking and writing.

Teachers and businessmen have frequently decried the
inaccuracy, longwindedness, and confusion of even many
college graduates' writing. Few have speculated, however,
about the effect of too many attempts to wrestle with uncongenial abstract subjects upon students' expression. Nothing fosters exactness in writing like attempting to explain
clearly and briefly what one has seen. Learning something
of the techniques of the visual arts and then describing examples of these techniques may help prevent students'
getting lost in a fog of words because they cannot "see"
what they are talking about. Surely anything that might
eliminate even a little of the abstruseness, clumsiness, and
dullness that afflicts much contemporary writing should be
encouraged.

Thus although color printing and artistic films may at
first seem only casually related, we may be able to develop
the vision to perceive that all offer to American Studies
programs means of opening students' eyes to the true variety
and wonder of their nation and its culture. Whatever else
American Studies programs may do in the future, I hope
that they will open participants' eyes not only figuratively,
but also quite literally.

America as an Underdeveloped Nation

PATRICK D. HAZARD

PATRICK D. HAZARD is Chairman of the English Department at Beaver College. In addition to teaching American literature and journalism, he is co-chairman of American Civilization. Recently he founded Triptych Productions, a firm seeking to add eloquence to insight in the popular media. His first assignments are TV documentaries on Hawaii and the erection of the Washington Monument.

MY TITLE IS NOT MEANT TO CONCEAL A TRICK, BUT TO REVEAL a truth. The United States, which spends millions to help "underdeveloped nations" is herself, in important respects, immature. The paradox became apparent when I served as the first Director of the Institute of American Studies at the East-West Center for Technical and Cultural Exchange at the University of Hawaii. An old pedagogical saw holds that one never understands a novel until he tries to teach it. I found out that the principle is even truer applied to one's own country.

Our real weakness is that we don't know what America means in human history. We have not developed a deep or broad historical understanding, having enlarged our know-how much more fully than our know-why. This imbalance is crippling us. It could destroy us. Too many Americans have highly idealized, essentially nostalgic images of what has happened in the course of American history. This naive innocence is our single most debilitating influence in helping the world modernize. Why?

53

At the East-West Center a most interesting discovery was that the Asian grantees were greatly frustrated by the American grantees' superficial understanding of American institutions and traditions. Asian students know much more about their cultures than we do about ours. Though deplorable, this is due to several factors. American grantees are younger. But theoretically we are the best informed nation in the world. What this cliché really means is that Americans are bombarded by more and diverse messages than any other nationals. It may also mean that our minds are the most cluttered and the least coherent. Information does not necessarily lead to wisdom. Indeed, sociologist Paul Lazarsfeld and Robert Merton have argued, in their theory of narcotizing dysfunction, that a surfeit of knowledge tends to paralyze people as information intake becomes a substitute for outgoing decision.

American ignorance of the enduring values in life also stems from their enthronement of the entertainer over the past generation. We all know the most intimate details of Bing Crosby's family; but did we read the Federalist papers? We all recall Bob Hope's latest gag, but how many of us here have re-read Emerson lately? We all know who Elvis Presley is (or was, already), down to the last wiggle, but how many have heard of Philip Booth, one of the finest contemporary poets America has produced?

In a pre-industrial, tradition-ruled society an individual needs little sense of history to become empathetic enough to sustain change. Tradition is the best guide because generations have been through the same experiences. In a modernizing society, not even father can always be counted on to know best. Unprecedented conditions confront everyone with equal freshness. Tradition not only often doesn't work well; it can be a positive impediment to a rational solution of difficulties. Experience must replace tradition as a guide to behavior.

History in our kind of society is not a luxury but a necessity. In totalitarian societies ancestor worship may do; but not in a society where men are free to choose their own styles of life. A sophisticated awareness of the past prepares one for the uncertainties that are the only certain thing in our world today. Keep the majority from achieving this kind of self-understanding, and you deprive a formidably complex machine of most of its lubricants. Today many Americans do not have a valid sense of where they have come from. This lack is the most serious challenge facing our historians today.

Deprived of the resilience a mature historical sense would provide, we seem destined at the moment to become another kind of *ancien regime*. Big labor, big capital, and big agriculture and a complacent middle class seem content in the cocoon of suburbia—willing to ignore deteriorating conditions of urban life and unwilling to internationalize abundance fast enough to abort the appeal of competing totalitarian systems. It is when one measures the depth and breadth of our historical awareness that he sees that we may indeed be an underdeveloped nation.

One deep-seated reason for ignorance of our past and its living traditions is that America is a future-centered country. We know too little about our past partly because many came to America to get away from an oppressive or stultifying past—whether it was the rigidity of a fixed class position, the affront to conscience of an established church, or the frustrating conscription into a noble's private wars. America, the poet Archibald MacLeish reminds us, was promises. We came to *make* history, not to *revere* it. That is a sense in which Henry Ford's pronouncement about history's being bunk is true. One has to be free of the burden of the past to create a River Rouge. By the same token, you inevitably end up wallowing in the nostalgic irrelevance of Greenfield Village if you have a shallow sense of your country's past.

A defective sense of the past is endemic in our country. Instead of making our people more resilient to the stresses of accelerating social change as choice replaces tradition in the full modernized society, popular history is a psychological safety valve for escaping into some Golden Age. Instead of insight into the future's complexities, instant nostalgia pretends to revere a past that never existed. It provides the patriotically lazy, say, with the easy alternative of visiting attractive Sylvan Valley Forge instead of accepting, as Peace Corps volunteers do, the contemporary equivalent of no shoes in the snow. The summer soldier of today apotheosizes Founding Fathers instead of flattering them with substantial imitation of their own virtues in new circumstances. These, after all, are the times that try men who still know they have souls. Only the sunshine patriots are Polyannas enough to hope the fighting is long since over.

Why has our revolution stalled? Precisely because we have so inadequate a sense of our national past. Asian, African and Latin American countries are displaying the same sense of over-compensated inferiority complexes that we showed towards European aristocratic travelers who came to America to reassure themselves that our democratic experiment wouldn't work—they hoped! For if it did, they would have to change their status quo in Europe as the American good news spread among their peoples. Americans who don't "understand" the neutralism of Nehru and Sukarno have forgotten George Washington's Farewell Address as well as the Monroe Doctrine.

There are other ways in which it would be easy for us to sympathize with the "new" underdeveloped nations since we so recently threw over colonialism ourselves. Take Brasilia, for example. Americans grumble about all that elegance the economically strapped Brazilians are erecting in the middle of forests hundreds of miles from centers of population. Does it sound familiar? It should. Washington City was founded in a swamp in the early 1800's for precisely the same reasons: to give a new country some architecture to live up to in spite of the fact that economically we couldn't afford it at the time. The truth probably is that psychologically we new Americans probably couldn't afford *not* to aspire to such compensating elegance given the gap between our ideals and reality. Or take the tendency of every country to want its own airline. I'm less sympathetic with this penchant for global public relations; but American history has an important lesson on this score too.

John Adams reacted in an interesting way to the smug comments of European aristocrats about how little culture Americans had when he was president. He said it was the responsibility of his generation to insure the political stability of the United States (and how enduringly those architects of our Constitution did build). Andrew Jackson followed John Quincy Adams as president in 1828, announcing to the world with every muddy western boot that followed his Tennessean footsteps into the White House that there could be no turning back politically. Property, literacy and sex qualifications would eventually be abolished—as they almost are in America today with the exception of the Southern Negro.

Adams thought it would be the responsibility of the next generation to insure economic growth—and Charles Francis Adams, a generation or two late by his forbear's schedule, was a railroad tycoon. Charles' brother Henry was the original alienated American intellectual, with qualities literally too fine to be of use in that shoddy post-Civil War era. This brings us to the third phase in John Adams' prophecy. Once politics and economics matured, culture would flourish. He predicted that his grandsons would reap the artistic harvest from the careful political and eco-

nomical cultivation at the grass roots that the two generations preceding had taken care of. That cultural revolution
is now transforming America.

I want to relate the problems of the cultural revolution
to our policies towards the underdeveloped countries.
American intellectuals have suffered from a cultural inferiority complex ever since Sydney Smith made his insult-
ing sneer heard round the world about who ever read an
American book, or saw an American play, or gave a hoot
and a holler about American culture with a capital "C."
For a century we've been trying to mass produce artists to
keep Europe from laughing at us. When we try to understand why Asian students are not interested in the arts
of America but in the small "a" arts of agriculture, politics
and economic development, John Adams' model of how a
society develops becomes most helpful to us. Asians are
in the earliest stages of his model of how a society matures.
Literally and figuratively, the Institute of American Studies
had to re-orient itself to the needs of Asia, Africa and
Latin America; as indeed I believe the American Studies
movement on the mainland United States must do and as all
of us in America ought to do if we are to revitalize our
revolution.

Carl Rowan, then in the State Department and now the
U. S. Minister to Finland, made a brilliant speech at the
University of Washington's Communication Week held
as part of the Seattle World's Fair. What we do at home, he
said, is more important than what we pretend to be abroad.
If we can't meet our own racial, industrial, and social
problems in a humane way, all our libraries, jazz combos,
and international road shows will avail us little. Instead, our
own headlines will undermine our pretense.

Consider the Sydney Smith syndrome. Too much energy
in American Studies is devoted either to explaining away

cultural impoverishment or in arguing that our Jackson
Pollock is as good as your Michelangelo. American Studies
is excessively esthetic in emphasis. This is a defect in an
anthropological sense. What we need is more "culture" and
less anxiety about "Culture." One result of our century-
long inferiority complex, vis-a-vis Europe, is that we have
turned out thousands of articles and monographs on trivial
and irrelevant figures in pre-industrial genres. Meanwhile,
our new institutions such as television drama, advertising
graphics and photo journalism have achieved substantial
bodies of significant material that has not been recorded, let
alone analyzed and criticized. Mass communication, for all
practical purposes and in spite of the pioneering work of
men like Gilbert Seldes, is *terra incognita*. We keep shuffling
a worn deck of minor nineteenth century literary figures
while Saul Bass and his peers have never even entered our
minds, let alone our curricula. We busy ourselves with
huge projects on the collected papers of every old president; yet our ignorance about the achievement of photo-
journalism remains abysmal.

A related area of darkest ignorance is mass production.
Despite seminal work (like John Kouwenhoven's *Made in
America*) the tradition of vernacular art remains something one must stumble upon. Our contention that humanists are helping students see life whole and see it steadily
is a travesty. Contemporary industrial civilization is a life
almost totally unexamined in our humanistic curricula,
slighting the whole area of how automation and mechani-
zation have transformed our environment. These are not
things which should be admitted grudgingly into the curriculum in one final lecture. They ought to be the very warp
and woof of our intellectual concern. Sydney Smith's sneer
has had devastating effects; it has taken the limited resources we have had available and whipped up enthusiasm
for appreciating or creating the elite arts of Europe, when

we should have been concentrating on civilizing the new institutions of mass communication and mass production in industrial America. That remains our central task.

Why have so many obviously intelligent men so mis-allocated scarce energies? The only explanation I would have is what might be called the new Adam tradition. De Crevecoeur exulted in "this new man, the American" as he toured the post-revolutionary Atlantic seaboard of small but sturdy yeoman farmers. Later Frederick Jackson Turner closed the book on American character development, at the World's Fair in Chicago in 1893. Four hundred years after Columbus discovered America, Turner discovered that America was no longer a "new land" and shuddered at the disintegrative possibilities. Thinking of the 1893 "Great White City" as a form of architectural escapism from the brutal realities of the Chicago stockyards, we may begin to comprehend why professional humanists and laymen Americans alike have not grasped the meaning of their own urbanization. The hard fact is that America is no longer an Eden. It is an *ancien regime*. Not the *ancien regime* of 18th century France, with its rigidities of class, established church, and royalty, but *ancien regime* nevertheless. It is long past time for us to look at how the very virtues of the democratic experiment have become its characteristic vices. Like the 18th century *ancien regime*, ours too is one of complacent privilege, more widely diffused privilege admittedly; but also with medians of responsibility significantly lower than those of the best European aristocracies.

Equality, liberty and fraternity parodied become rigidities of the mind, much more difficult to overcome than mere property ownership. Egalitarianism, for example, has led to the fear of the superlative, to rationales about giving the public anything it wants, anything it can be made to crave. Liberty has declined into contempt for order and discipline. Everyman's flipping his expended beer can onto nature becomes a paradigm of democratic man following his own collective whims. This wantonness, multiplied throughout the entire range of daily activities, poisons the very atmosphere.

Fraternity has deteriorated into the packaging of amiability. Toothy clowns, like Jack Bailey, promise those who have not fulfilled their dreams that they can at least be "queen for a day." This is a marginal consolation prize indeed when one looks at the *ex parte* rationalizations that big capital, big labor, big agriculture and the big middle give for their various impediments to fulfilling the American dream of opportunity. For all, one gets an oppressive sense of the inertia of the middle class as an *ancien regime*. These fat-cats of mass America, satisfied with the height they've been able to reach, are ill-prepared to fulfill the American dream of a qualitative revolution in which excellence will be the keynote.

What the American Studies Movement ought to be doing domestically is preparing the way for such an intellectual revolution instead of wishing it were really as respectable as the literary scholars or as scientifically sophisticated as atomic physicists. A book like that edited by Daniel Lerner, *The Human Meaning of the Social Sciences*, is more humanistic, though written by social scientists, than most of what we write. Lerner and Lasswell have elsewhere established their definition of what they call the policy sciences; that is to say, objective knowledge which clarifies decision making in politics, economics, and social relations. The humanities ought to assume a somewhat analogous role with respect to establishing the quality of American life.

Most American Studies curricula have been patchwork affairs reflecting the prior commitment of their planners either to history or literature. American Studies seems like an easy way to pull our methodological chestnuts out of the fire. But the anthropologist's culture concept can be no better than the materials it has been using to organize or the sensibilities of the organizers. We must look afresh at the American Studies curriculum. It ought to be more than just a way to put literature into context or give esthetic richness to history.

My proposal would be to study the United States in both domestic and international aspects. Let me suggest a sequence of courses which would provide a four-year undergraduate experience.

First Semester: The European Roots. (In this introduction America as the beneficiary of the excess intellectual and economic energies of Europe, which could develop free from the rigidities of the *ancien regime*, would be studied.)

Second Semester: The Two Americas—North and South. (This would explore "the road not taken" by South America. It would be a comparative study of how Europe's memory represented by Spain and Portugal created the cultures south of our border, while the North American development was going in a new direction based on northern Europe's dreams.)

Third Semester: America and Africa. (This would study the differential acculturation of African immigrants to the Caribbean and to southern United States and the adjustment of the African Negro to the plantation economy and later dispersal through urbanization. This would examine historically the most destructive dilemma now facing American civilization.)

Fourth Semester: America and Asia. (This would examine the first contacts between America and Asia, the Chinoiserie imports of 18th century New England ship captains and the interaction with Asians of the 19th century missionaries. It would concentrate on changing American images of Asia from the stereotypes of Charlie

Chan movies to the managed images of today's Red and Free Chinese.)

Fifth Semester: America and Russia. (This would explore the Cold War's tensions at a high intellectual level, with particular emphasis on the uncommitted two-thirds of the world's unwillingness to accept either Russian or American ideology as the only ways of organizing human behavior.)

Sixth Semester: America Today. (This would be an analysis of the qualitative revolution now under way in America.)

Seventh and Eighth Semesters: These would be devoted to original research designs submitted by seniors in consultation with their advisors. I can already hear the charges of Utopianism reverberating dully throughout committee rooms. And it may very well be that some no longer have the will or way to respond freshly to the challenge of events. This perhaps is the most discouraging part of America as an *ancien regime*: the really shocking timidity and time-serving which keeps American Studies and other humanistic enterprises from fulfilling their potential.

The internecine warfare that characterizes most college communities may not permit the creation of an ideal American Studies curriculum; the college is not the best place to introduce innovations in curriculum today. The National Broadcasting Company, and later the Columbia Broadcasting System, have shown with "Continental Classroom," "Sunrise Semester," and other video-taped courses how to create a "national university." This dream of Thomas Jefferson and John Adams may actually come into being through the newest and "most vulgar" medium in American mass communication. TV makes a national democratic university possible and practical.

If we were to have the boldness to create a really new American Studies, rather than a jerry-built accommodation to insecure disciplines, we might then go on to learn that our fear of eloquence in the newer media is the second most debilitating influence in our academic endeavor. What is needed is a wholesale re-definition of our concept of publication. Most of us know that much of what passes for scholarship is so dull and irrelevant that it is a blessing that it remains mercifully unknown in the vast wasteland of academic quarterlies. I would say that we ought to publish more of our results in photo-journalistic, filmic, and broadcasting forms to test the relevance of what we are researching. If what we are digging up cannot be made significant to the general audience, perhaps it shouldn't be dug up. I look forward to the day when graduate schools will approve of a student's presenting his thesis in an hour-long documentary. The research done behind television series such as "The Twentieth Century" and "Project XX" no longer makes it possible for academicians to dismiss the world of popular culture as beneath contempt. It would be liberating for us if we were to train ourselves in one or more of the newer media, not simply to be eloquent, although that is no mean ambition, but to meet the responsibility of putting what we learn into circulation.

By leaving North America I discovered that I did not really understand the unique characteristics of American civilization; its so-called bread and butter institutions, political stability and economic development, social intercourse. I was forced to explain them to Asians who come to American institutions with an entirely different set of expectations from ours. They forced me to see the excessively esthetic bias of the American Studies Movement. This bias can be understood historically, as I have tried to show in a brief summary of John Adams' theory of American growth, the Sydney Smith's sneer heard round the world, and the De Crevecouer-Turner concept of the American as that new Adam. Such an intellectual self-analysis indicates that America is an underdeveloped area, imaginatively and intellectually, oblivious of much of the significance of its past, and therefore unable to comprehend what is happening in the present, let alone establish a sound policy for the future. The only way to continue our revolution is to complement the already largely achieved quantitative one with a qualitative revolution: one concerned with the quality of the American life. We would not only save ourselves much boredom and frustration, but would also have much greater intellectual and imaginative resources to aid those other countries who want to modernize —not necessarily in the way we have, nor at the same cost. The American Studies Movement is not too surprisingly a victim of some of the same assumptions which inhibit the maturing of the larger American society. Even if we expect "saving remnants" to be perfected, or at least perfectible, it should not astonish us that we are not perfect. Were we to commit the same energy to a criticism of our own discipline that we currently devote to criticizing the social sciences, we might be less confused than we now are.

That is why I have outlined, in bare detail, an archetypal American Studies curriculum that is more than a pragmatic attempt to resuscitate literary history or to enliven social and cultural history. Beyond the admittedly difficult problem of studying mass production and mass communication, and publishing these new subjects in new ways through photo-journalism, motion pictures, radio and television, I would say we must commit ourselves in a most energetic manner to the problems of public school reforms. There is a Chinese proverb, "You can't carve rotten wood." Our society will not achieve its needed qualitative revolution until our public schools, particularly the high schools, have humanities programs which are superlative in concept and in execution. The simplest thing one can say about our stewardship is that for the most part the professoriate has completely neglected this responsibility. We now reap the results of that intellectual abandonment.

I think we need to be reminded, with respect to the "two cultures" controversy, that in America scientists have been much more humane and civilized than we with respect to their responsibilities in public schools. Beginning with the biological and physical sciences and going on to mathematics, American scientific specialists have accepted the challenge of new knowledge and the possibilities of new forms of publication. They are making science even more attractive, more sound and significant, to the high school student today. If for no other reason than self-protection (and surely there are better reasons than this), we must do for the high school curriculum what the scientists have already done for their sectors of that curriculum. The growing gap of disaffection between the humanities and the sciences will become even more ominous unless we concentrate on secondary schools. Here is a grass roots problem which no one can ignore.

For many years methodology has been held in contempt by some "intellectuals" and academic people. More and more people are coming to see that this whole matter is neither amusing nor irrelevant. With all their shortcomings and dilemmas, men in American Studies have been willing to talk of methodology, integration, and synthesis. Perhaps we are still an underdeveloped academic segment, paralyzed by just and unjust fears in the special world in which we must operate. But, since these *are* the times that try men's souls, let us not be sunshine patriots. Our fight is well worth waging, and winning.

"Don't Nobody Move!"

JOHN ASHMEAD

JOHN ASHMEAD is Professor of English at Haverford College. His first novel, *The Mountain and the Feather*, appeared in 1961. His articles have appeared in *Harper's Atlantic, American Literature, C.E.A. Critic*, and the *Virginia Quarterly Review*. His third Fulbright, for 1964-65, will take him to Benares, India.

IF WE TAKE A BAFFLING 1913 NUDE ON A STAIRCASE AS OUR midpoint, we can all sense, however intuitively, that in 100 years of American culture from the 1860's to the 1960's we have ranged along a colorful spectrum of style. Talking about the complexities of culture, Ezra Pound once said that in an age when scholars have to know all about minute subjects, "any man who knows where the oil well is, is considered superficial."

And the question comes at once, what shall we call the two most opposite colors of our cultural spectrum? Shall we admit objects such as the Brooklyn Bridge along with Hart Crane's poem on the bridge? Shall we go so far as to compare the strapless bra and the suspension bridge on which its intricate engineering is based? Or may we brood over the bra only in a painted collage, such as Ernst von Leyden's *Birds of Night* (1963)?

"Don't Nobody Move!" warns Leo Jensen's pop art sculpture, one painted hand on that swinging door, the other aiming his trusty six-shooter—aiming at us, the audience. How shall we find the oil well in such a dazzle of sand?

From the art and civilization histories of Burckhardt, Wolfflin, Panofsky, and others, and from the psychological researches of Felix Deutsch, we know that one stimulus or creative impulse may find simultaneous expression in differently mirroring facets of a personality or a civilization. A similar creative style can show itself in scholasticism or in the Gothic cathedrals or even in "Twenty bookes, clad in blak or reed—" that Chaucer's clerk liked to keep by his bed. George Eliot found inspiration in Dutch genre painting. The painter Marsden Hartley wrote poems that match his paintings. As Harry Levin has reminded us recently in *The Gates of Horn*, the painter Courbet on reading *La Terre* called Zola "the foremost painter of the epoch."

Scriabine saw his music as painting, and Kandinsky saw, or perhaps heard, his paintings as music. The novelist Hardy was first of all an architect. Painting has been the other art of the poet E. E. Cummings, the novelist D. H. Lawrence, and the dramatist, Kokoschka. The painter Demuth once painted a poem of W. C. Williams, "I Saw the Figure Five in Gold." Piet Mondrian combined the perforated rolls of a barrel organ and Broadway boogie-woogie music in his last canvases. We may well conclude with Pierre Francastel, social historian of European art, that "All progress in our knowledge of history henceforward demands the correlation of the various disciplines of knowledge."

A memorable advance in this correlation is now possible because of the Carnegie Corporation collection of color slides, *The Arts of the United States*, some 2500 slides (with many supplemental slides available) arranged by periods strikingly similar to periods of American literature, and covering all the arts: decoration, stage sets, photography, the graphic arts and advertising, as well as sculpture, architecture, and painting. With the aid of this notable addition to what Malraux has called "the museum without walls," let us go back to our pivot point of 1913.

To be sure, Henry Adams said of the World's Columbian Exposition in Chicago, 1893: "Chicago was the first expression of American thought as a unity; one must start there." Willa Cather, who with Edith Wharton shared the unenviable distinction of being one of the two good American writers who wrote bad fiction about the First World War, wrote that "the world broke in two in 1922 or thereabouts . . ." But 1913 and the Armory show mark the real break in our cultural century, and not just in reforms of art, for in 1912 the contest between Roosevelt and Wilson had been a battle of reformers in government.

Nor was Teddy Roosevelt completely hostile toward the Armory show of 1913; instinctively he sensed a sympathetic drive towards reform and why should a Rough Rider worry if feelings were outraged. He stopped short only at that nude going downstairs, for the Navajo rug in his bathroom had better art sense than to look like that. But the humorist Irvin S. Cobb, whose customary laughter had failed at the sight of Duchamp's many-headed, many-breasted and many-legged nude descending a staircase, spoke nostalgically of "the Rutherford B. Hayes School of Interior Decoration," which demanded only an oil painting of a dead fish in the dining room, and another of thirsty cows by a brook in the living room where the drinks were served.

Wherever we draw a dividing line between the old and the new in our century of American culture, surely on one side is Rutherford B. Hayes. And equally surely, on the other side is Gertrude Stein, exclaiming in her work *Narration* (1935): "And after that what changes what changes after that, after that what changes and what changes after that and after that and what changes and after that and what changes after that." One of her own characteristic changes had been her *Four in America* (1932-33); in it she transposed Ulysses S. Grant into a religious leader, Henry James into a general, Wilbur Wright into a painter, while Washington received the ultimate distinction—he became a novelist.

Today when *Fanny Hill* has made the short difficult journey from under the counter to display window, we think of all subjects, or even of "no" subjects as possible. But the subject range of creative culture in the early 19th century was still restricted to Joshua Reynolds' hierarchy which put classical epic subjects first, portraits second, and landscapes third. A standard application of this formula was Greenough's George Washington as Olympian Zeus (1833-41). In the second half of the 19th century America had become the leading industrial power of the world, and the rising industrialists and their wives favored a lightly impressionistic, realistic and anecdotal art; a touch of sentiment helped. And so we have the painted anecdote, a static and real moment in time, of Chase's *A Friendly Call* (1895); two women call on each other in a lushly decorated room—only a small Japanese hanging on the wall of this room warns that an artistic explosion is coming.

Henry James, a more powerful artist than Chase, still associated himself with the anecdotal realists of the Barbizon group, and even shared their studio life for six weeks in 1886. There is a small touch of Japonism in Henry James, for he had studied art with John LaFarge, the first American artist to contemplate and write about Japanese decoration in the collection of Raphael Pumpelly—the oldest and sturdiest explorer who ever crossed a desert. Henry James in later life thought that the Japanese had reintroduced "taste" to the western world.

And from Manet's *Zola*, Degas's *Tissot*, Ensor's *Skeleton Studying Eastern Paintings*, Whistler's *Princess du*

Pays de la Porcelaine (1864), to van Gogh's *Pere Tanguy*, a Japanese woodcut hangs in the background, like the hanging cloth in Chase's painting, and whispers "Taste!" Such taste is evident in those realistic American novels which use Japanese decoration, as in Howell's *A Hazard of New Fortunes* (1890). In the studio of its sculptor anti-hero Beaton hang Japanese fans, screens, bronze vases, and even costumes. Whistler's tastefully arranged studio, with its white and yellow walls in the supposed Japanese manner, dealt a death blow, after 1878, to the Victorian wall, which rarely got much brighter than a Gothic dried-blood red.

And what could be more tasteful in actual late 19th century life than the fashionable Japanese nook, loaded with bric-a-brac, and shaded—against what was never made clear—by a large Japanese parasol hung from the ceiling. There was taste, yes, in all this Japonism, but something more; for the Japonism encouraged, if it was not at the heart of, an increasingly explosive shift to modern art. About the time Gauguin was doing a characteristic *Still Life with a Japanese Print* (1889) van Gogh was writing in Arles that he saw things "with an eye more Japanese" —"As for me here I have no need for Japanese art, for I always tell myself that here I am in *Japan*, and that consequently I have only to open my eyes and to take in what I have before me."

Certainly Japonism is the most conspicuous force that stimulates shift along our spectrum, from what we might call realism at one end, to modernism at the other. We can see Japonism completely assimilated in such different works as the later paintings of Winslow Homer, the influential impressionistic prose of Lafcadio Hearn, the drawings and paintings of Mary Cassatt (*The Bath*, 1891), and Pound's "In a Station of the Metro"—that superb encompassment of the Japanese poetic form called haiku:

> The apparition of these faces in the crowd;
> Petals on a wet, black bough.

Characteristically Pound has industrialized—commuterized —this ancient form of nature poetry, and he has given it the sense of motion and speed of the departing train (according to his own interpretation of the poem). The haiku has exerted a powerful influence, and some critics, with apparent justice, find a steadily repeated haiku line in Joyce's *Ulysses*.

The Japonism of Frank Lloyd Wright's architecture is a common-place of architectural history; he had gone to Japan in the 1900's full of the Chicago style and somehow became one of the greatest collectors of Japanese prints we have had—until the modern novelist Michener.

However we weigh the significance of Japonism, we can see here a steady movement of the Japanese object and its template of technique, from a cloth or print hanging in the background, to the foreground, and eventually to complete assimilation and merger. The process is curiously like that by which a virus inserts the template of its DNA molecule into a juicy stranger, and forces the host molecule to manufacture new patterns of the invader.

Theory, as the science historian James R. Newman has said, "shapes our instruments, our methods, our interpretations." For too long we may have accepted a theory of cultural influence, a model as it were, which is essentially that of a mechanical, almost Newtonian die forever stamping out all subsequent cultural coins. Such is the somewhat rigid model behind Ruth Benedict's *Patterns of Culture* or Clyde Kluckhohn's brilliant *Mirror for Man*. But perhaps we are now ready for a model which is something like the biological ones that have set forth so admirably the latest discoveries on the genetic code and how it transmits its messages by its intertwined helices—at once patterning, mutating and recreating. Some such more flexible model fits better the actual infiltration of Japonism into painting, poetry, prose and architecture.

We have said our spectrum's range was from real to modern. Still keeping in mind Chase's *A Friendly Call*, with its dangerous bit of Japanese cloth, let us compare it with Max Weber's cubist *Chinese Restaurant* (1915), which, as Weber once explained, gives you all the sensations of the Chinese restaurant at the moment you enter it. I don't wish to overexaggerate Japonism, but the painting shows traces of the influence of that bird's eye view so common in Japanese scroll paintings. A cubist bird, of course.

What would Henry James, with his love of anecdotal realistic art, have thought of such a painting? In fact, as his notes for his unfinished last novel surprisingly suggest (*The Ivory Tower*, 1917), he was perhaps moving towards a modernist kind of characterization, which he termed, somewhat mysteriously, his law of successive aspects in a character. Weber's openly cubist painting has its own law of successive aspects, or even simultaneous aspects, since it places us simultaneously at the entrance and deep within by means of a reversed perspective. Here we may suggest that narrative technique in the limited sense of point of view can at times be equivalent to painterly perspective. If so, Faulkner's *The Sound and the Fury* (1929), told from four successive points of view (or perspectives), or Pound's *Hugh Selwyn Mauberly* (1920) show a strikingly cubist rotation around fragments of their real worlds.

Chase's *A Friendly Call* and Weber's *Chinese Restaurant* can illustrate the two extremes of our cultural spectrum; on either side we can visualize, pottering about, Rutherford B. Hayes and Gertrude Stein. What about the border line country, the real battlegrounds, of our spectrum? Here we find charges and countercharges ("All artists hate each other," said a modern sculptor recently at an Annual

Awards Banquet)—and always a *Battle of Light*—so Joseph Stella styled his futurist painting of Coney Island (1913). Though literary historians and art historians don't often try to cope with the fact, novelists in particular keep up with new painterly techniques. The Hudson River Valley school of American landscapists had hardly got started before Cooper was placing their canvases inside his novels, and the woods that Deerslayer sees were those painted by Cooper's friends. Cole's *Last of the Mohicans*, a painting which seems to be twice the size it actually is, more than returns the compliment. And so the New York scenes of Dos Passos's *Manhattan Transfer* (1925), especially those at night, are as much American futurist painting as they are anything Dos Passos himself saw. We cannot understand all of either art without the other.

If we go back to the beginnings of the battle of light, we must go to the impressionists, who unlike their sturdy French cousins, were only a weak, small group in America. James in his art criticism cannot be said to favor them, but his practice, as so often and so fortunately for us (witness his novel prefaces, a kind of fiction piled on fiction), was different from what he said he favored. And when we contemplate Childe Hassam's lightly impressionistic *Rainy Day, Boston* (1885) we can see a play of light, a kind of sweeping brush work, that almost inevitably reminds us of James's *Bostonians* of the same year, in which he sketched what he called in the novel, " 'tender' reflections" of the light; his heroine, like an impressionistic painter, liked to observe "the faintest gradations of tone" in the sky. Perhaps we may be permitted to borrow from the art historians and call this kind of work, in literature as well as art, light impressionism.

For dark impressionism we may turn to that vividly named American group of painters called the Ashcan School for their willingness to depict forbidden vistas and subjects—their critics labeled their vitality "horrid or-gasms." Henri, master and teacher of the school, said that "a Hester Street pushcart is a better subject than a Dutch windmill," and the novelist Dreiser quoted him with ap-proval. Dreiser's novel *The Genius* (1915) was about a painter of the Ashcan School—either Shinn or Sloan, with something of Dreiser himself. Of such painting Dreiser wrote: "Bang! Smash! Crack! Came the facts one after another, with a brutal insistence on their so-ness."

The painter George Luks took Eakin's static *Study for Wrestlers* (1899) and converted it into the darkly im-pressionistic *The Wrestlers* (1905), making the wrestling match a fight between two animals. We think of Jack London's *Martin Eden* (1909) in which sex fights, usu-ally two men for a girl, are a feature of his muscular Darwinism. Martin Eden, battling Cheese Face, pridefully observes: "God! We are animals! Brute beasts!" Surpris-ingly enough, even Amy Lowell's "Evelyn Ray" of 1925 has just such a sex fight, in darkly impressionistic color-ing.

Le Corbusier once pointed out that idiotic terms are used for art movements because they are almost always in-vented by the enemy. The simpler reaction of the painter Marin to these labels was to say, "Bah, don't bother us." In his new anthology of realism George Becker has suggested that we give up distinctions between realism and naturalism and use them interchangeably, or just use the term realism. Perhaps light impressionism and dark im-pressionism, or light realism and dark realism, in both the arts and literature, would provide pragmatic difference enough.

By 1913 the realistic *Sister Carrie* of Dreiser, suppressed in 1900, was back in print; she with her vibrant sister in oil paint, Glacken's *Chez Mouquin* (1905) signaled the triumph of the Ashcan School. As subjects in literature and art, city locomotives, snow, breadlines and rain had crossed out forever what Whitman once called the overpaid accounts of classical Greece; Dreiser walked the streets of New York with a painter of the school to sharpen his novelist's eye. These realistic painters did more than any other group to bring about the 1913 Armory Show. At its end, in criticism and in sales, they found themselves elbowed aside by their guests, the modernists, who had come not just for dinner, but to take over the house.

So far as we can find a single cause for the defeat of the realists, it was motion. "Don't Nobody Move!" says Jensen's pop art gunman; but in the best American tradition one hand caresses a hair trigger and the other rests on a swinging door.

The American tradition was peculiarly receptive to a modernist aesthetic based on motion. Long before Marcel Duchamp showed his nude simultaneously descending all the steps of a staircase, Americans showed they favored motion even when seated, in the well-known American rocking chair, as in the graceful design of Cooper (1860) or the more modern creation of Stickley (c. 1910).

Giedion believes these rocking chairs developed from the American Indian hammock which so startled Columbus. The hammock led to the hammock chair or porch swing of the '80's (today's glider is similar in design), to the swingy cantilevered tractor seat, source of so many international chair designs, and to the rocker. Seated on his glider, tractor, or rocker, the American gave the foreigner an impression of motion. Whitman, and the movie director D. W. Griffith, saw the birth of a nation in a cradle endlessly rocking. Gertrude Stein perceptively observed in *The Making of Americans* (1906-08, 1925) that American space was to be "always filled with moving." Sooner or later a character in an American novel collapses into or rises from his rocker, or, as in Henry James's *The Ivory*

Tower (1917), finds a rocker necessary for thought: "There *was* nothing else . . . which . . . could maintain him in meditation for meditation's sake quite as well as a poised rocking chair."

Our late President Kennedy and President Johnson have both preferred this chair, which overseas, at least, is perhaps second only to the eagle as a national symbol of America. Alexander Calder had no need to turn abroad for his mobiles, he had only to sit down. It is no accident, then, when Meyer Shapiro defines the abstract expressionist artist as one who "is alert to qualities of movement, interplay, change and becoming in nature."

And 17 years before Duchamp painted his nude descending a staircase, the American photographer Muybridge, in *Nude Woman* (1885) had shown successive pictures of the same woman descending, if not a staircase, at least a ramp. Muybridge's pervasive influence (on the photos and paintings of Eakins, on Marey's bronze studies of successive positions of a flying seagull, on Boccioni's futuristic *Bottle Evolving in Space* [1910], on the time and motion studies of Frank B. Gilbreth) awaits detailed analysis. Muybridge's work is perhaps the first instance of a major idea which has spread throughout the world by means of a photographic image rather than the written word.

In America a native architectural tradition had also reinforced the taste for motion, in steamboat Gothic, for example, as in Mark Twain's Hartford house which substituted a steamboat Texas or pilot house for part of the porch. And the Wright brothers' biplane affected the design of Purcell and Elmslie's Bradley House (1911). By 1916 the Aeroplane Bungalow with Japanese details was the rage in Los Angeles. The American skyscraper significantly takes its name from the topmost sail of the American clipper ship. The art historian Berenson has suggested that the airplane with its aerial views destroyed all previous perspective in painting. Be that as it may, before the invention of the airplane in America, we can find in Whitman's *Leaves of Grass* balloon perspectives of our land, so labeled.

We must give much credit to newly industrialized North Italy for setting the wheels of our native tradition spinning. "Let's go, say I! Let's go, friends! Let's go!" called Marinetti, author of the Italian Futurist *Manifesto* of 1910. He noted that "A speeding automobile is more beautiful than the Victory of Samothrace . . ." At some time in the next decade T. S. Eliot heard the call for motion; perhaps in an early draft of *The Wasteland* (1922) he had already written:

> He took me out on a sled,
> And I was frightened. He said, Marie,
> Marie, hold on tight. And down we went.

(The sled and the early automobile had much in common.)

Modern American culture is rich in remarkably designed autos. The Type 35 J Mercer "Raceabout" of 1914 was manufactured by C. G. Roebling of the firm of John A. Roebling Sons which built the Brooklyn Bridge. This "most talked-of car in America" in its side view bears a striking design resemblance to the Brooklyn Bridge. It shows no trace of a modified buggy without a horse. The evolution of the Ford from the *Model T* (c. 1924) to the *Lincoln Continental* (1941) sometimes called the most beautiful car ever made, shows the native American ability to give an illusion of motion to an object at rest.

Perspective views whether by balloon or plane, Muybridge's photographic studies, Italian futurism—in short the spirit of modernism itself—enabled the Italian trained Stella in his several canvases of Roebling's *Brooklyn Bridge* (1917-18, and the bridge itself 1867-73) to show the bridge in a dynamism of speed and light. This first great American suspension bridge seems to exhibit what the poet

Sidney Lanier, combining the science of Helmholtz and the poetry of Emerson, called the rhythm of the universe, "a great flutter of motions."

Statues and fictional characters show this modern flutter of motions as no solidly static and realistic figure ever does. William Zorach's *Floating Figure* (1922), a beautifully carved woman, rests on air, but so do Daisy and Jordan in Fitzgerald's *The Great Gatsby* (1925). They first appear "buoyed up as though upon an anchored balloon. They were both in white, and their dresses were rippling and fluttering as if they had just been blown back in after a short flight around the house."

Once we have established the importance of motion for the modern side of our spectrum, other related hues become visible. But first let us follow the example of George Becker in disposing of confusing distinctions between naturalism and realism by accepting both terms interchangeably. I suggest that we adopt interchangeably practically all the isms of modernism—except of course the term modernism itself. We have suffered too long in art and literature from a Balkanization of terminology. A recent survey of the novel added activists, anti-realists and double novelists to an already burdensome list. Whether we need such terms in art as machinists, immaculates, and abstract impressionists is a question.

Two remaining qualities of modern culture have found significant outlets in a variety of arts. These are simultaneity, first associated with so-called cubism, and the self-expressionisms which gave the movement termed Expressionism its sometimes misleading name.

In his attack on realism in the 1910's—that great decade of cubist modernism—Proust concluded that literature was not intended just to show us a cabstand. Its true function was to show us what the cabstand meant to us in the past, now, and in the future; for artistic time is simultaneous. We have already tried to show the presence of simultaneity, of simultaneous time, in Weber's cubistic *Chinese Restaurant*. But the impulse is equally present in Stella's futuristic notion of Brooklyn Bridge. Simultaneous time is used in Wilder's play *Our Town* (1938) and in Faulkner's fourfold *The Sound and the Fury* (1929). Cubist distortion of the perspective plane shows a more than metaphorical resemblance to fictional distortion of the narrative plane by means of complicated narrative positions and by extensive chronological looping back and forth in time.

Most recently, in Arthur Miller's *After the Fall*, the hero Quentin is able to talk freely and simultaneously to Louise, his first wife, to his suicidal wife Maggie, and to his latest love, Holga. Quentin's privilege has more to recommend it in modern art than in life.

Where cubism took liberties with the chronology of the arts, expressionism, initially at least, took liberties with surface appearances in the arts by adding to those surfaces an expression of the artist's feelings about them. O'Neill, America's first expressionist playwright, said: "We have suffered too much from the banality of surfaces." The Emperor Jones brought on stage his little formless fears, and in *The Hairy Ape* (1922) Yank the stoker is crushed to death by the simian ancestor he wishes to free. Marsden Hartley's *Portrait of a German Officer* (1914) spreads out on the canvas all those attributes of a German officer which in 1914 aroused lack of enthusiasm. Expressionist novels have a strong element of autobiography, of *Ich Roman*, as in Wolfe's immense six-part novel, which began with *Look Homeward, Angel: A Story of the Buried Life* (1929) and ended only with Wolfe's own life.

As Matisse well put it, for the expressionist spirit in modern art, there is no way to distinguish between the artist's feeling for life and his way of expressing his feeling. Such a spirit is almost the direct opposite of that of a realist such as Flaubert, who said in 1852 that he did not want "a *single* movement or a *single* reflection of the author."

Probably self-expression can go no further than the point it has reached in American abstract expressionism, as in the activist loopings of point after point in a Jackson Pollock canvas, *Autumn Rhythm* (1950). The emotionally related American dramatic form, the theatre of the absurd, finds a striking example in Albee's *The American Dream* (1959-60), of which he wrote: "Is the play offensive? I certainly hope so." In this play a superfluous grandmother must be disposed of not by gun or axe. Instead she is to be carted away in that symbol of American mobility, the moving van.

Now that we have ranged along our spectrum from realism at one end of our century to modernism at the other, what remains? Writing of the 1913 Armory Show, the pivotal point in our century, Robert Henri said of the modernism which had replaced his own Ashcan realism: "There always has been a new movement, and there always will be a new movement."

Recently a new museum rejected the proposed name of museum of modern art. So as not to seem old-fashioned it called itself a museum of contemporary art. From time to time new houses are now advertised not as modern houses, but as contemporary houses. There are small erratic signs of something stirring—new moiré pattern art; room size pop art hamburgers; self-destroying sculpture good for one viewing only; Bill Cushenberry's asymmetrical Hot Rod; a novel whose pages come in a box so that they may be arranged in any order by the reader; sculpture that moves and makes noises; magnetic reliefs that the spectator must rearrange; attempts in New Wave fiction to do away with ordinary characterization. Is there a new contemporary art movement slowly gathering shape?

"Don't Nobody Move!" warns our pop art guardian. But the culture typified by this carved wooden statue moves on, expressing itself equally in objects (any objects) and in words (any words), always duplicating, mutating, and recreating.

Do Good Fences Make Good Scholars?

SIGMUND DIAMOND

SIGMUND DIAMOND is Professor of Historical Sociology at Columbia University. His former works include *The Reputation of the American Businessman* (1955) and *The Nation Transformed: The Creation of an Industrial Society in the United States* (1963). He is currently working on a comparative study of colonization in North and South America in the sixteenth and seventeenth centuries.

THERE MUST BE FEW PERSONS WHO DO NOT KNOW BY NOW that they live in a world divided between two cultures. Those dismayed by the fact may take consolation in knowing that their macrocosm, even so, is a third less complicated than the microcosm of the university; for the university, like Gaul, is divided into three parts—humanities, social sciences, and natural sciences—the partisans of each attacking the others as though they were Amalekites to be smitten hip and thigh.

In 1892, when he assumed the chair of economic history at Harvard University, William James Ashley warned that a spectre was haunting, if not all mankind, at least the historical profession:

> The general cultivated public . . . wants to know how individuals and episodes are related to some large whole, and what the significance of it all has been. If scholars competently trained will not try to satisfy this natural and laudable desire, incompetent writers will. . . . The historian and the economist may expel Nature with the fork of the

Seminary and the Deductive Method; but Nemesis stands very near the shoulder of 'Pure Economics' or 'Pure History'—and in America it usually calls itself Sociology.[1]

As a historian in a department of sociology I have dwelt in Rhamnus for nine years, gazed upon Nemesis and yet have returned unscathed; and I bring you the encouraging word that the journey is not as fearful as has often been thought. Indeed, I sometimes feel that I have never been away.

This does not mean that I have returned with the answers to the questions that troubled Ashley and continue to plague all of us. Much of the displeasure vented against the social sciences today arises from the inevitable frustration produced when expectations are pitched at too high a level because the hucksters have oversold their product or because dissatisfaction with the state of affairs in one discipline leads its practitioners to believe that things cannot possibly be as bad in another. I am sure I speak no treason to my discipline when I say to you, ask not what the social sciences can do for you; ask rather what you can do for the social sciences.

Speaking of the connection between artistic styles and the forms of social life, the distinguished art historian Meyer Schapiro insists on the propriety, even the necessity, of inquiry into the social nexus of artistic productions and yet admits the impossibility, in the present state of knowledge, of solving the question he poses:

> The idea of a connection between these forms and styles is already suggested by the framework of the history of art. Its main divisions, accepted by all students, are also the boundaries of social units—cultures, empires, dynasties, cities, classes, churches, etc.—and periods which mark significant stages in social development. . . . In many problems the importance of economic, political, and ideological

conditions for the creation of a group style (or a world view that influences style) is generally admitted.

But no adequate comprehensive theory of style has been produced, Professor Schapiro continues, because scholars friendly to inquiries into the social determinants of art are fearful of being accused of reductionism and, even more, because such a theory of style must "wait for a . . . unified theory of the processes of social life in which the practical means of life as well as emotional behavior are comprised."[2] Concerning the first of Professor Schapiro's two caveats, it may need to be said that I recognize that art is multivalent and is in a sense always in the process of renewing itself. To say something about it is not to exhaust all that may be said about it, yet that one thing may be very much worth saying. Concerning the second of his caveats, it does not at all need to be said that I do not have that "unified theory of the processes of social life" which is a prerequisite for special theories of artistic production. A theory of society, however, is not to be confused with social science. My purpose is to state the claims of the latter. If that is less dazzling than the presentation of grand theory, it has at least the merit that preposterous claims cannot be made for it.

Liu Hsieh, the fifth-century Chinese literary historian and critic, tells us that in earlier times the emperors had two historians at court, "the left-hand historian, who kept records of what was done, and the right-hand historian, of what was said."[3] Though Liu Hsieh is silent on the subject, it is not difficult for us to visualize what sharp jurisdictional disputes—masked behind the elaborate ceremonial of court etiquette—must have occurred between recorders of the word and recorders of the deed. We attempt to deal with the complexities of our subject by dividing it differently from the Chinese, but the special characteristics of our historiography, no less than the Chinese, are artifacts of our mode of inquiry. We speak of "fields of study," and the agrarian metaphor exercises a powerful influence on our style of work. Cultivators of our own academic garden-plots, we till our soil, harvest our crop of conclusions, stay strictly within the territory the surveyors have staked out for us, and often grow resentful of what we feel to be the intrusions of our neighbors. It may well be, in the world of the poets, that good fences make good neighbors; it remains to be seen whether good fences make good scholars. At the very least, there is considerable evidence that the existence of the fences has been responsible for a yield less rich than would otherwise have been the case.

In view of the widespread perception that any product of human thought and labor, no matter what the cubbyhole in which we place it for reasons of convenience, must be seen as inextricably enmeshed in the full range of human experience, it seems odd that academic recognition of the same fact is often expressed so grudgingly. In his commentary at the conclusion of a chapter entitled "Literary Development and Time," Liu Hsieh writes:

> Against the background of ten dynasties,
> Literary trends have changed nine times.
> Once initiated at the central pivot,
> The process of transformation circles endlessly.
> Literary subject matter and the form in which it is treated
> are conditioned by the needs of the times. . . .[4]

Alexis de Tocqueville, observing that superior works of art do not flourish in modern democracies, concluded that men "engaged either in politics or in a profession" have no inclination to do more than "to taste occasionally and by stealth the pleasures of the mind" which are felt only "as a transient and necessary recreation amid the serious labors of life." The predispositions conditioned by the means of earning a living, give rise to a need for excitement in leisure time to offset the boredom of the job; modern man, therefore, needs "strong emotions, startling passages—truths and errors brilliant enough to rouse them up and to plunge them at once, as if by violence, into the midst of a subject."[5]

When so implacable a foe of the use of biographical and historical considerations in literary studies as Leo Spitzer analyzes the advertisement:

> From the sunkist groves of California
>   Fresh for you

"in the same unbiased manner as I have attempted to do in the case of a poem of St. John of the Cross or of a letter of Voltaire, believing . . . that this kind of art . . . offers . . . a 'text' in which we can read . . . the spirit of our time and of our nation,"[6] then surely we are justified in accepting the dictum that the social basis of art might be overlooked, but it can hardly be disputed.[7]

Whether these observations about the content and style of literary productions are in fact true is not of great importance. What is important is that the attempt to prove or to disprove them would necessitate the examination of a body of evidence and the use of certain procedures generally considered to be outside the limits of traditional literary history.

Dissatisfaction created by traditional definitions of the proper scope and method of literary and historical studies has prompted a number of efforts to alter the shape of the disciplines so that significant new questions might be properly investigated. The pioneering role of the Johns Hopkins University History Department in raising standards of scholarship is well known. But few have noticed that one of the first serious efforts at participant-observation in this country—John Johnson's *Rudimentary Society among Boys*, a study of the organizations, attitudes, and behavior of boys at a private school near Baltimore—was published in 1884 as a Ph.D. thesis in, of all places, the Johns Hopkins Studies in Historical and Political Science. What matters here is not Johnson's simplistic evolutionary scheme, now thoroughly out-moded, but that their conception of history forced the members of the Hopkins seminar far beyond the traditional limits of the proper subject matter of history. "When the publication of the Johns Hopkins Unversity Studies began," Herbert Baxter Adams wrote in his introduction to Johnson's work, "it was not anticipated . . . that any contributor would descend lower in the scale of institutional subjects than Towns, Parishes, Manors, etc. . . . Modern students are finding historical and sociological materials in such imaginative writings as Plato's *Republic*, More's *Utopia*, and Bacon's *Nova Atlantis*, but there are few scholars who have thought it worthwhile to utilize the wealth of fact and illustration for institutional history which lies at our very doors."[8] If the "wealth of fact and illustration . . . which lies at our very doors" is, by definition, preempted by the practitioners of other disciplines, there is no mystery why it should have been overlooked. In Johnson's work and in many other products of the Hopkins seminar, much was achieved and a promising program was suggested. The accomplishment, however much we may disparage it today because of our greater stock of information about the subjects they studied, came about not because they attempted self-consciously to define the scope and method of the discipline they practiced. It occurred because they explored problems with which the conceptual and methodological apparatus of their *own* science was inadequate to deal, and in the undertaking they made findings and raised questions that became the common property of all. The promise inherent in their program was in the conscious use of theory to suggest problems for investigation and in the explicit design of research to demonstrate the adequacy or inadequacy of that theory. The merit of what they attempted is independent of what we think of the theory that guided them. That theory might, from the standpoint of 1964, be entirely outmoded; but the conscious search for the kind of knowledge that would provide a critical test of its adequacy revitalized history at the turn of the century and was in the best tradition of scientific inquiry.

In this same spirit the economic historian Guy S. Callender, depressed by the limitations imposed by the narrow range of human behavior comprehended by the assumptions of economic theory, called in 1913 for a rapprochement between history and sociology. Historians, he wrote, are coming to have a broader conception of their field. "It is not difficult to make out in general what this conception is. . . . Perhaps the best way to describe it in a phrase is to call it the sociological view of history. As a rule historians will object to this term. It does not seem possible to them that any body of theory composed so largely of somewhat loose generalizations as sociology, can have anything in common with careful scientific history. Even more than the economist, the sociologist seems to them prone to play fast and loose with the facts. He is an utter stranger to the chastening influence of 'source materials.' . . . Nevertheless it is to sociology that the new conception of history is most akin and it is with the sociologist that the historian is coming to have most in common." Not that Callender was willing to exonerate sociologists from the indictment he levelled against the historians. "The failure of historians to recognize this kinship with sociology is matched by the indifference of sociologists to history," he continued. "The institutions of the 'Todas and the peaceful Arifuras' continue to receive more attention at their hands than the German kingship, the village communities of medieval Europe, or the feudal system. Few students of sociology in our universities are ever advised to take such an admirable sociological course as the early constitutional history of England."[9]

This dissatisfaction received perhaps its sharpest expression in France—in the attack on *histoire historisante*, the notion that history concerns itself not with the life of man in society but with the explication of documents in archives. In the first volume of his *Revue de Synthèse Historique*, Henri Berr, in a way reminiscent of Ashley, warned of the approach of Nemesis:

> Now if we consider the nature of historical work in this last third of the century, this cautious and intentionally limited effort, this preoccupation with a 'good method' to be applied rather than sweeping results to be arrived at, we are better able to understand the rapid advances of sociology and the popularity that it enjoys. There are doubtless many reasons for this success: by far the most important is the soundness of the idea that there is something social in history, that society is a factor in the interpretation of history.[10]

Though it might seem from this brief review of the relations between historical studies and sociology that the dominant attitude toward the situation suggests hyenas snapping and snarling for their share of the carrion, it would be surprising—especially in view of the length of time during which the debate has raged—if all that we had to show were exhortations to do and warnings not to do. Sir Lewis Namier, one of the great historians of the twentieth century, was, in these matters, willing to go far beyond most of his fellow-historians, insisting upon the indispensability of that bogeyman of humanist scholars, team-research. "No one would expect a contemporary survey of the life and work of the people or of political behaviour to be undertaken other than by teams," he wrote. "Why then for a past period? The low productivity of historical research in this, and even in many another, direction, is due to antiquated concepts and methods—

'always scribble, scribble, scribble! eh, Mr. Gibbon?'
—but the questions now asked and the materials to be
mastered would have baffled even that greatest and most
industrious of eighteenth-century historians. Unless there
is concerted research, history cannot deal with aggregates
otherwise than in vague generalities: to treat them as
entities in which each person retains his individuality requires a new technique."[11]

Namier specified a number of problems concerning which
historians know all too little. "Even worse than our position
with regard to the psychology of individuals . . .," he wrote,
"is that regarding groups, the masses, the crowd in action.
We are as yet merely groping for an approach to mass
psychology. . . . We do not even know some of the means
whereby men communicate thoughts and emotions to each
other. I remember a remark which in 1911 I heard from Sir
Reginald Wingate: he said that after all the years in the
Sudan it remained a mystery for him how news travelled
among the natives. . . . *La grande peur*, the panic which
seized the French countryside in July 1789 and consolidated
the Great Revolution, is the outstanding example of a
nation-wide psychological upheaval; but smaller tremors
of that kind can be traced in almost every revolution."[12]

It was Namier's complaint that historians had no substantial answers to these questions—the importance of communications for political development and the explanation
of irrational mass movements. I should not like to give the
impression that *everything* is now known about these questions; but I should like to emphasize that much is now
known about them, that much of what is known appears in
the work of social scientists, and that historians interested in
these questions ignore such work at the peril of making
their own appear trivial. In *Communication and Political
Development*, Lucian W. Pye, turning directly to the

question Namier raised about communications in traditional societies, writes:

> Traditional systems lacked professional communicators, and those who participated in the process did so on the basis of their social or political position in the community or merely according to their general ties of association. . . . People turned to opinion leaders to learn what could be made out of the limited scraps of information received in the community. The skill of opinion leaders was not one of sorting out specialized information but of piecing together clues and elaborating, if not embroidering, upon the scant information shared possibly by all present. Thus the traditional system depended upon the role of the wise man and the imaginative story-teller who needed few words to sense truth and who could expand upon the limited flow of messages.[13]

Concerning the second of Namier's problems—the explanation of irrational mass political and social movements —it is significant that three of the best recent studies, Peter Worsley's of the cargo cults, Norman Cohn's of medieval millenarian movements, and Eric Hobsbawm's of primitive rebels in southern Europe in the nineteenth century, were written by an anthropologist, a historian, and an economic historian as products of a seminar participated in by sociologists and political scientists as well, and presided over by the distinguished anthropologist Max Gluckman.[14]

No one has done more in recent years to commend the social sciences to historians than Thomas C. Cochran. Writing ten years ago in Bulletin 64 of the Social Science Research Council, *The Social Sciences in Historical Study*, Professor Cochran called for a new synthesis to replace the presidential motif in American history and designated a number of important problems toward which research should be directed, including the changing character of family relations and of family aspirations. "Perhaps some day," he wrote, "it will be possible to guess widely at the degree to which group aggressions, political radicalism, or instability in mass reactions were due to the stresses and strains of a family conditioning that became unsuited in varying degrees to the changes in surrounding society." He called on scholars to study the conflicts created by the fact that patterns of family socialization—the process by which an individual learns how to become a member of a particular society—which may have been appropriate for a pre-industrial society had been outmoded by social and economic change.[15]

Even at the time Cochran made his appeal a great deal more was known about the subject than he was aware. The relation between family socialization and political movements and social tensions may have been a closed book for most historians; it was a matter of lively interest to other scholars. Let me cite only two students of the subject, whose observations were already nearly twenty years old at the time Professor Cochran made his appeal.

The change from a stratified to a fluid society, Professor Solomon Diamond stated in *A Study of the Influence of Political Radicalism on Personality Development*, has meant that man's place in society is felt to be a measure of his individual worth, rather than a function of his membership in a particular social group. "This change . . . has had tremendous psychological significance. . . . It has changed even the child's world, not only because the competitive atmosphere of the adult world has been reflected in his games, but also because it has led families to place added demands on children, to appraise them in terms of their ability to get ahead, to train them from an early age for the later competition. . . . Under these conditions, feelings of inferiority come to play a major role in the lives of both children and adults. . . . The individual is being at all moments appraised by society, in terms of his chances of advancement, and he learns in consequence to appraise himself."[16]

Considering the relative weight of various factors making for radicalism or conservatism, another investigator noted in 1938 that in a sample population the influence of the home was noted forty-five times; of friends, forty-one times; of books, two times; of prominent individuals, six times; of dramatic incidents, five times; of school service and of fellow employees, once.[17]

If interest in the effects of family socialization on other aspects of social life had produced some findings before 1954, when Professor Cochran's article was published, it has produced a veritable jungle of findings in the years since. Indeed Professor Herbert H. Hyman has written what in effect is a guidebook to the literature of only one of the consequences of socialization—its influence on sheer involvement in politics and on the selection of political goals or policies.[18] Browsing through the pages of a recently-issued inventory of findings on human behavior, I noted a number of conclusions relevant to Professor Cochran's query:

1. Parental pressure for and reward of early achievement, when coupled with a high ratio of successes to failures, results in a high need of achievement in later life.
2. The earlier the parental demands for achievement, the stronger the subsequent drive for achievement.
3. The family patterns of the lower classes change more rapidly under industrialization than do those of the upper classes.
4. Within a society, a stress on achievement in certain kinds of imaginative literature appears to be associated with the subsequent rate of economic development.[19]

My purpose in citing these findings is neither to suggest that scholars who disagree are incorrect nor that the social scientists have discovered all that needs to be known about these matters and that historians need only follow in well-worn paths. Quite the contrary: I believe that historical investigations of the effects of family socialization are indispensable to determine the degree of generality of the conclusions reached by the social scientists and the genuineness or spuriousness of their correlations—issues which must always remain moot so long as the evidence derives from a narrow span of time in the immediate present. Still, no historian, no student of culture can afford to ignore such findings if he is interested in the effects of different modes of socialization on political and economic life. The work of David McClelland and his students suggests the existence of a rich tapestry in which the strands of family socialization, folk literature, and political and economic development produce different patterns in different cultures and even in different social strata of the same culture.[20] They may be right, partly right, or wrong; but historians interested in the problem must consult their work unless they are willing to cut themselves off from a line of inquiry which promises to impose order on a wide variety of recalcitrant and seemingly unrelated phenomena and unless they are willing to forego the possibility of bringing the kind of knowledge they uniquely possess to bear on testing the adequacy of current theory.

A false impression would be conveyed if one were to suggest that no substantial accomplishments have yet been made in our work as historians through knowledge derived from the social sciences. The fact is that a veritable revolution has already occurred. Macaulay once wrote that "the history of the government and the history of the people" ought to be "exhibited in that mode in which alone they can be exhibited justly, in inseparable conjunction and intermixture. We should not then have to look for the wars and the votes of the Puritans in Clarendon, and for their phraseology in Old Mortality; for one half of King James in Hume and for the other half in The Fortunes of Nigel."[21]

Social analysis does not concern itself with a particular subject-matter—in which case we would have still another category of books in which to seek the truth about the Puritans and King James—but with a way of looking at all social organizations and the relationships they impose. One has only to consider significant recent changes in American historiography to realize what an immense transformation has already taken place. Collective biographies of the occupants of particular statuses; studies of the social origins of elites; investigation of the impact of social and economic change on the locus of decision-making; the effects of social mobility on political participation and the choice of political objectives; more sophisticated studies of public opinion and the creation and extension of influence; the importance of non-economic variables like family structure, conceptions of time, and attitudes toward social status in explaining different rates of economic development; the rediscovery of the importance of ethnicity—did not much of the stimulus for investigating these problems come from concepts, findings, and methods in the social sciences?

Literary studies have not been influenced as markedly, but here, too, there has been change and there is promise. Eleven years ago Hugh Dalziel Duncan published a seventy-one page bibliography on literature considered as a social institution;[22] since then investigations to correlate changes in the content of literature with other social phenomena, to determine the intentions of the producers of literature, to study the effects of different types of communications on the audience, to relate different forms of patronage to the creation of new genres and styles have increased rapidly. In this country, in contrast with Europe, such studies deal more with popular literature than with belles-lettres; but the one is as much a part of our civilization as the other and, it ought to be pointed out, one by-product of this interest in the popular culture of our own period has been the increase in scholarly attention to problems of literacy and different reading publics in other times and cultures.

What the sociology of knowledge—the study of the effects of social life on the content of mental productions—has to offer at the moment is an orientation toward our subject matter rather than a theory about it. The importance of the orientation cannot, however, be easily disregarded. Considering how occupation influences outlook, the poet W. H. Auden addressed himself directly to the problem of the impact of social environments on mental constructs:

> Who when looking over
> Faces in the subway
> Each with its uniqueness
>   Would not, did he dare,
> Ask what forms exactly
> Suited to their weakness
> Love and desperation
>   Take to govern there.
>
> Would not like to know what
> Influence occupation
> Has on human vision
>   Of the human fate:
> Do all the clerks for instance
> Pigeon-hole creation,
> Brokers see the Ding-an-
>   sich as Real Estate?[23]

When the poets themselves take account of the sociology of knowledge, it may not be too much to suggest that the poets' glossators can hardly afford to do less.

If, in discussing the relationship between the social

sciences and historical studies, I have not proceeded by staking out the claims of each discipline to a particular subject-matter or to a particular method, it is because I feel that progress is less likely to be made by attempting a synoptic view of the relations between them than by concentrating on specific problems whose solution requires the use of knowledge and methods relevant to those problems, not to the particular disciplines we happen to practice. Sometimes this useful convergence is achieved by illuminating data accumulated in one discipline by concepts existing in another; sometimes, when hypotheses in one discipline suggest new problems for research in another; less often, when a technique of analysis developed in one discipline is applied to the solution of a problem in another.

To the solution of a problem—this is the crux; for if we remember that our concern is not this or that body of data, this or that method, but *the life of man in society*, then both the search for the solution to unsolved problems and the discovery of new problems will tear us loose from familiar moorings and require us to venture out for relevant knowledge and methods wherever we may find them. "To pose a problem," Lucien Febvre wrote, "is precisely the beginning and the end of all history. No problems, no history—only narratives, compilations. Now remember, if I have not spoken of 'the science of history,' I have spoken of 'studies scientifically pursued.' . . .—the formulation implies two operations, those that are found at the basis of all modern scientific work—to pose problems and to formulate hypotheses."[24]

We seek, all of us, to transcend the limitations imposed upon our knowledge and understanding by distinctions that have their origin less in the subject-matter we study than in the assumed requirements of professionalism. In his last book, the great French historian Marc Bloch wrote:

Are we then the rules committee of an ancient guild, who codify the tasks permitted to the members of the guild, and who, with a list once and for all complete, unhesitatingly reserve their exercise to the licensed masters? ... Pasteur, who renovated biology, was not a biologist—and during his lifetime he was often made to feel it; just as Durkheim, and Vidal de la Blache, the first a philosopher turned sociologist, the second a geographer, were neither of them ranked among the licensed historians, yet they left an incomparably greater mark upon historical studies at the beginning of the twentieth century than any specialists.[25]

Shortly after writing these sentences, Marc Bloch was executed by the Nazis. It would not be the least of the triumphs of humanism were we, in our work, to keep his words alive.

1. William James Ashley, *Surveys: Historic and Economic* (London: Longmans, Green & Co., 1900), p. 30.

2. Meyer Schapiro, "Style," *Anthropology Today*. ed. Alfred Kroeber (Chicago: University of Chicago Press, 1951), pp. 310-11.

3. Vincent Yu-chung Shih (trans.), Liu Hsieh's *The Literary Mind and the Carving of Dragons* (New York: Columbia University Press, 1959), p. 84.

4. *Ibid.*, pp. 244-45.

5. Alexis de Tocqueville, *Democracy in America* (2 vols.; New York: A. S. Barnes and Co., 1855), II, 61.

6. Leo Spitzer, *Essays on English and American Literature* (Princeton, N. J.: Princeton University Press, 1962), pp. 250, 252.

7. Harry Levin, "Literature as an Institution," *Criticism—The Foundations of Modern Literary Judgment*, eds. Mark Schorer et al. (New York: Harcourt, Brace and Co., 1948), p. 546.

8. Johns Hopkins University Studies in Historical and Political Science (Baltimore: Johns Hopkins University Press, 1884), II, No. 20, 5.

9. Guy S. Callender, "The Position of American Economic History," *American Historical Review*, XXIX (1913-14), 81, 82, 85-87.

10. "Sur Notre Programme," *Revue de Synthèse Historique*, I (1900), 3-4.

11. Sir Lewis Namier, "History," *Avenues of History* (London: Hamish Hamilton, 1952), p. 10.

12. Sir Lewis Namier, "Human Nature in Politics," *Personalities and Powers* (London: Hamish Hamilton, 1955), pp. 3 f.

13. Lucian W. Pye (ed.), *Communications and Political Development* (Princeton, N. J.: Princeton University Press, 1963), pp. 4, 24, 28.

14. Peter Worsley, *The Trumpet Shall Sound* (London: Mac-Gibbon and Kee, 1957); Norman Cohn, *The Pursuit of the Millenium* (London: Secker and Warburg, 1957); Eric Hobsbawm, *Primitive Rebels* (Manchester, England: University of Manchester Press, 1959).

15. Thomas C. Cochran, "The Social Sciences and the Problem of Historical Synthesis," *The Social Sciences in Historical Study* (New York: Social Studies Research Council, 1954), p. 166.

16. Solomon Diamond, *A Study of the Influence of Political Radicalism on Personality Development* (New York: Columbia University Press, 1936), p. 11.

17. Bernard Breslaw, *The Development of a Socio-Economic Attitude* (New York: Columbia University Press, 1938), p. 61.

18. Herbert H. Hyman, *Political Socialization: A Study in the Psychology of Political Behavior* (Glencoe, Ill.: Free Press, 1959).

19. Bernard Berelson and Gary A. Steiner, *Human Behavior: An Inventory of Scientific Findings* (New York: Harcourt, Brace and Co., 1964), *passim*.

20. See, for example, David C. McClelland, "National Character and Economic Growth in Turkey and Iran," in Pye, *op. cit.*, pp. 152-81; McClelland, *The Achieving Society* (Princeton, N. J.: D. Van Nostrand Co., Inc., 1961); N. M. Bradburn and D. E. Berlow, "Need for Achievement and Economic Growth," *Economic Development and Cultural Change*, X (1961), 8-20.

21. "History," *Edinburgh Review*, XLVII (1828), 365.

22. *Language and Literature in Society* (Chicago: University of Chicago Press, 1953), pp. 143-214.

23. "Heavy Date," in *The Collected Poetry of W. H. Auden* (New York: Random House, 1945), pp. 106 f.

24. Lucien Febvre, "Vivre L'Histoire," *Combats pour l'histoire* (Paris: A. Colin, 1953), p. 22.

25. *The Historian's Craft* (New York: Alfred Knopf, 1953), pp. 21, n. 1, 21-22.

Change and New Perspectives

RALPH H. GABRIEL

RALPH H. GABRIEL, President of the American Studies
Association, had a long and distinguished career at Yale University before his retirement in 1960. Since then he has been
associated with American University, and has held several special lectureships at home and abroad. His publications include
The Course of American Thought (rev. ed. 1956), *Religion
and Learning at Yale* (1958), and *Traditional Values in American Life* (rev. ed., 1963).

AMERICANS HAVE BEEN ON THE MOVE SINCE MIGRANTS FROM
Europe came ashore in the seventeenth century from the
Susan Constant and the *Mayflower*. The newcomers built
simple habitations between the shore and the forest. In the
eighteenth century clusters of houses beside the beach
evolved into thriving seaports and inland farmers pushed the
outer edge of their fields westward to the Appalachians
and northward to the White Mountains. Toward the end
of that century the farmers and the townsmen of the seaports threw off colonial subordination and embarked upon
the hazardous adventure of independence. In the nineteenth
century the sons and grandsons of the signers of the Declaration of Independence, turning their backs on the Atlantic,
moved on foot, on horseback, by river boat and by covered
wagon westward to the Pacific. They founded homes and
established enterprises in an area as large as Europe. The
historian of the American people, looking back over three
centuries and a half, observes, first and last, change—a

people on the march behind moving boundaries; a society passing from a limited to a complex ethnic composition and from enslaving a race toward the reality for that race of equality of opportunity; an economy evolving from a simple agrarianism to an advanced industrialism; a nation, beginning as a weak confederation of states on a continent remote from centers of Western civilization, achieving strength and finally surging into world leadership to become the protector of that civilization threatened by a ruthless power and by a materialistic philosophy and system. From the beginning of their history accelerating change has been the massive fact in the culture of the American people. In this phenomenon lies America's uniqueness.

Change approaches a climax in the middle decades of the twentieth century. To gain a clearer understanding of the conditions of life for the present generation of Americans it is useful to inquire into the factors which have been important in bringing about change in the past and are still significant. Three emerge: the accelerating increase in the body of knowledge, especially scientific and technological knowledge, which undergirds our civilization; the ever shifting cultural configurations and power manifestations in the world outside our borders, a societal environment to which we make adjustments; and a cluster of values within our civilization which have been so long and so tenaciously held as to amount to a national faith. These three, operating in the middle of the twentieth century, provide the essential perspectives for the present generation.

The *Susan Constant* and the *Mayflower* crossed the Atlantic in the century which saw in Europe, and particularly in England, that break-through in knowledge and thought which has been called the scientific revolution. From the beginning American annals paced forward synchronously with those of modern science. But until the twentieth century was well advanced the great centers of scientific learning remained in Europe. With the exception of the solitary Josiah Willard Gibbs and one or two others science in the United States remained primarily derivative. At the same time, however, in days when technology was relatively simple the ingenuity of American tinkerers brought about extraordinary advances in the artifacts of their civilization. As the twentieth century opened, the historian, Henry Adams, sensed the emergence of new scientific understandings. He pointed out to his countrymen the phenomenon of acceleration in man's acquisition of scientific knowledge. He noted the marriage of science and technology and the dynamism born of that union speeding up innovation continuously, remorselessly. In a disturbing metaphor Adams tried to drive home his conclusion, namely, that advance in knowledge and evolution in technology bring and must continue to bring profound changes in society. He saw, even in his own day, modern man grasping a live wire which made him dance to its pulsations but which he cannot let go. Events confirmed the accuracy of Henry Adams' insights.

Then the United States took its place beside Europe as a center for scientific advance. Laboratories in universities, in industry and in governmental agencies turned out an ever increasing volume of research findings. The simple technology of the nineteenth century was left behind as new materials and new machines transformed the life of society, harnessed the energy of the atom and made possible the systematic exploration of inner and outer space. The government of the United States made science the cornerstone of national defense. In a world which survived because a nuclear stalemate had been achieved the United States government pushed research and development, the union of science and technology, to innovation and more innovation. In this context the perspective of Henry Adams becomes further clarified. We see the mid-twentieth century American at the same time bending his efforts to push forward innovation and, summoning what wisdom he can, to adjust his life and society to swift, continuous and compelling change.

Within this larger picture two details stand out. One has to do with the fact that natural science has brought into being a body of knowledge staggering in extent, and the accumulation accelerates. The social sciences have added to the total. Inevitably the specialists emerged. The preoccupation of the specialist with the problems and tasks of his particular area of interest tended to generate in him parochialism both in loyalties and in outlook. Parochialism expressed itself in walls between intellectual disciplines. C. P. Snow in England discovered what he considered a deeper and more fundamental dichotomy. He pointed to a polarization between the sciences and the humanities which took the form of two cultures.

But the conditions of the modern world increasingly demand the wisdom and leadership of men who can transcend the limitations of a specialty or even of what Snow calls a culture. Perhaps because History as a discipline has a foot in both the camp of the social sciences and of the humanities it was an historian who brought to the attention of teachers the importance of bringing the sciences and the humanities closer together. It had been achieved in the eighteenth century. The eighteenth century man, such as Benjamin Franklin or Thomas Jefferson, had been a generalist in a simpler civilization and in an age when the body of scientific knowledge was small. His twentieth century successor is, at the same time, more difficult to create and more needed by the times. The historian, Joseph R. Strayer, aware of the importance of science and of the specialist for mid-twentieth century life, has pointed out to members of his guild obligations they have to students and to the general public. "The post-Civil War period," Strayer remarked, "also gives an opportunity to take up a topic that is somewhat neglected even in our college courses—the emergence and growing importance of the scientific point of view. This should be more than a listing of scientific discoveries and theories, more even than a discussion of the impact of science on our way of life. What should be done, difficult though it may be, is to give some feeling for the scientist's way of looking at the world; some idea of the scientist's presuppositions and expectations. Thus perhaps a start could be made in bridging the gap between scientific and humanistic cultures about which C. P. Snow has written so eloquently." (*The Social Studies and the Social Sciences*, sponsored by the American Council of Learned Societies and the National Council of Social Studies [New York: Harcourt Brace and World, 1962], p. 32.)

C. P. Snow dramatized a fault zone in modern Western civilization at a time when other men were becoming increasingly aware that such a separation of the humanities from the sciences is not only unnecessary but poses dangers to society. Strayer's charge to the teachers suggested an emerging new perspective. Human knowledge, in spite of all the boundaries which Balkanize it, is an interrelated whole. "Something there is which doesn't love a wall," wrote Robert Frost many years ago and then proceeded in poem after poem to translate the insights and understandings which he had received from science into lyrics. More recently a chemist, Harold G. Cassidy, remarked: ". . . it is my thesis that the sciences and the arts, though different in many ways, are not mutually exclusive or fundamentally contradictory. They are complementary parts of our culture; loss or injury to one is a damage to others and the whole; neither the scientist nor the humanist need fear to respect the other. In fact in their mutual understanding lie the possibilities of unimagined cultural advances." (Harold Gomes Cassidy, *The Sciences and the Arts, a New Alliance*

[New York: Harper and Brothers, 1962], p. 2.) Cassidy, Frost and Strayer speak each from the background of his own specialty, science, the humanities and history which combines both. In a civilization where change is far-reaching and swift they warn against schism. If the modern American is to live by reason, he must fuse the understandings and outlooks of science and the humanities. Dichotomy and mutual suspicion between them represents the failure of reason.

Mid-twentieth century developments require the modern American to consider one especially among the "scientist's presuppositions and expectations." Within the corpus of the natural and the social sciences cybernetics has emerged. The name may be freely translated as steersmanship. The steersman must have at command reliable information about the constantly changing effect of control measures. Feedback provides such information. "The brain, the sense, and the nervous system constitute a physiological cybernetic device. Fire directors, autopilots, computers, telephone networks, regulators, and a host of other engineering devices constitute examples of inorganic cybernetic instruments. There are basic laws of these devices which do not depend upon whether the apparatus is made of metal or protein molecules, and cyberneticians seek these laws." (Marshall Walker, *The Nature of Scientific Thought* [Englewood Cliffs, N. J.: Prentice-Hall, Inc., 1963], p. 95.) Cybernetics has made possible the machine to control machines. Only when the inanimate steersman fails, as it did for Gordon Cooper on the eve of his re-entry into the atmosphere, does man take over. Whereas formerly machines displaced the muscles of men and animals now the robot governor displaces the mind of man. The "thinking machine," already powering changes of the greatest moment of American society, represents a dazzling triumph for its human creator. But the present generation asks: "What price automation?"

Automation, displacing men at practically all levels of skill, has become a challenge to the human spirit. To cope with it and to keep it a beneficent force requires all the wisdom and the compassion which can be garnered from the sciences and the humanities together.

But cybernetics may be moving into other activities. The behavioral sciences, following the practice of the natural sciences, have begun to develop models in social science. Mathematics has been applied to economics and games theory to strategy in military operations. The psychologist, B. F. Skinner, believes that enough knowledge about the means of manipulating and controlling human behavior exists to make possible a last utopia, a Walden II, where science brings peace and happiness. More important, cybernetics, the science of steersmanship, is an undertaking congenial to the materialistic philosophy of the communist Soviet Union. It is common knowledge that the Russians are far advanced in the study and use of cybernetics. According to a preliminary announcement they will announce at the Twenty-second Communist Party Congress a twenty-year plan for bringing into being a "second and higher" phase of Communism. This plan, apparently beginning in the schools, appears to envisage the psycho-political automation of their society—the creation of a gigantic communist Walden II. Perhaps Khrushchev had this plan in mind when, during his visit to the United States, he boasted: "Our system will bury your system." Cybernetics provides a perspective for the mid-twentieth century American from which to view and to take account of the changes in the world about him.

Automation, whether it be actual as in the machine, or suggested, as for society, throws into relief the gap which C. P. Snow described between science and the humanities. The lore of the humanist includes the deposit left by the succession of vanished generations—art, literature, philo-

sophical inquiries, ethical searching, worship. The vision of
the humanist focuses on the individual person as a unique
center of value, possessed of dignity when freed from external control, aspiring to ever further ranges in the development and expression of his powers. The lore and vision of
the humanist exist in mid-twentieth century American civilization beside the knowledge and understandings and techniques of the scientist. The two are parts of a single whole.
In the words of Cassidy "in their mutual understanding lie
the possibilities of unimagined cultural advance."

Science brings about another quite different change which
affects all the civilizations of the world. Since the time when
homo sapiens become also *homo faber* mankind has created
a profusion of differing cultures. The variety among these
cultures attests to the creative capacity of the human spirit.
In such a world modern science, originating in the West,
spreads over the globe from laboratory to laboratory and
from university to university. With science goes the technology created from the knowledge produced by research.
Inevitably the spread of science with its associated technology makes toward uniformity in a multi-cultural world.
This strain toward uniformity in cultures, when seen from
the long view of history, has only begun. But great cultures
and civilizations have their own peculiar genius. They resist
change in core institutions, attitudes and values. So the
Japanese have put their own stamp on industrialism in the
face of the similarity of its technology to industrial technology everywhere. In spite of the toughness of individual
cultures, however, science opens new channels of discourse
between peoples. The university, which includes the humanities along with science among its responsibilities, widens
these channels. Whatever their particular tongue university
men and women speak a common language in the shop talk
of their specialties. No matter in what country the university may be, the traveling scholar, when he sets foot on its

grounds, feels at home. Universities over the world, sharing in the task of adding to a common body of knowledge and joining in the work of passing it on to generations of students, are moving toward what at some distant time may evolve into a new civilization. Already within the world-wide community of universities the vision of Socrates has validity for the scholar. "My country is the world," said the great Athenian. "My countrymen are all mankind."

Not only many cultures but many organized nation-states comprise the societal environment of the United States. These are power structures of varying strength and stability. Back of the present relationships of the great nations lies a long historical record of the coalescing and dissolution of power units, the aggrandizement, diminution and conflicts of nations. In mid-twentieth century a great company of new and hopeful nations has appeared. Nationalism remains a primary force in the world. Over the globe men look to the nation-state as the chief instrument with which to effect their purposes. Changes in this societal environment have compelled changes in the United States.

World War II brought to maturity the concept and the practice of total war. Since 1945 total war has, in spite of the cessation of large-scale shooting, become continuous war. The appearance of the absolute weapon in the possession of the two greatest among the powers deflected the struggle to confrontations which did not threaten mutual massive destruction. Since World War II the American people who, in the nineteenth century enjoyed an extraordinary sense of security, have had to learn to live with insecurity. A nation of tinkerers has made science the cornerstone of national defense. A people who in the nineteenth century maintained a small standing army primarily to police the sparsely settled frontier have given the military such budgetary support and such a place in the councils of the nation as the Founding Fathers never dreamed of. The foreseeable future offered no prospect of a lessening of the tension of the cold war.

In the twentieth century Americans were also forced to adjust to a new understanding of the limitations on national power, that of their own and of other nations. At the turn of the century Alfred Thayer Mahan had advanced and developed the concept of a fortress nation whose ramparts must be manned by an army and guarded from the sea by a navy. President Theodore Roosevelt went a long way in translating Mahan's theory into policy. He saw the great powers with whom he dealt as fortress-nations and looked to the fortifications of the Republic. The appearance in the mid-twentieth century of the nuclear bomb in the warhead of an intercontinental missile signified that the time had come when ramparts could be over-flown. Moreover the Nazi Fifth Columns in nations marked for conquest in World War II and the outward spread after the war of organized and skilled subversion from the power centers of communism demonstrated that national ramparts can be infiltrated. Mahan's once precise and persuasive concept became a period piece. The changed situation brought changed policies of government. The efforts to achieve a moratorium in nuclear testing, the lone American soldier ambushed and killed in Viet Nam and the Internal Security Act of 1950 were all consequences of the obsolescence of national ramparts.

But nationalism did not go to the scrap heap. On the contrary it burgeoned. New, small and, for the most part, weak nation-states sprang up in Asia and Africa out of the ruins of once famous empires. At the same time the polarization of power between the two great land empires, the United States and the Soviet Union, became the primary fact in the international relations of the world. A logical consequence of the magnitude of the power possessed by these two giants appeared in a movement in Europe for smaller nations to coalesce into a power structure of comparable proportions. But in spite of logic, nationalism, French nationalism, interposed what seemed to be insuperable obstacles. The new African states met in conclave in Addis Ababa where they projected a dream of a united and powerful Africa. Then the delegates adjourned with pious words to resume the cultivation of the parochial nationalisms which, for the moment, they had laid aside.

What of the United States? National interest, of necessity, directed policy. Europe remained the front line for the forces defending the United States and in a nuclear world Washington kept the decision as to the use of the bomb. In the world arena the United States supported the United Nations, even to making it into a limited power structure, primarily because so doing served the national interest. United Nations troops in the Congo made it possible for the Republic to avoid a confrontation with the Soviet Union in central Africa. Nationalism primarily determined the response of the United States to the conditions of the mid-twentieth century world.

But the power brought into being by national needs brought commensurate responsibilities. Mid-twentieth century Americans whose forefathers for generations had, for the most part, cultivated their gardens with small heed to peoples beyond their borders were compelled to reorient and enlarge their world view. They came to understand that they must take account of and do something about the grinding poverty of a terrifyingly large proportion of the world's population. Especially they became aware that History had made them not only the protagonists but the ultimate defenders of that tradition of humanism and freedom which had been the great achievement of Western civilization and the genius of their own culture. Almost from the time of their Revolution Americans had had a sense of mission. In the nineteenth century they thought of themselves as witnessing before what they considered to be a monarchical and corrupt Europe to the fact that free men could govern themselves. In the twentieth century the continuing and deadly challenge of a materialistic and totalitarian system made the mission crystal clear. The understanding of and the assumption of the responsibilities of power stands out as a major change in American life.

This change is closely linked to one which goes on within the borders of the nation. The revolutionary Continental Congress spelled out in the eighteenth century the inalienable rights of men to life, liberty and the pursuit of happiness; declared that government exists to protect and ensure these rights; and insisted that rule be by the consent of the governed. These values moved the men of 1776 to action. In the nearly two centuries since the Declaration they provided the core values of a free and open society. They became measuring rods with which to assess political action. They brought about the extension of suffrage to all adult males in the first half of the nineteenth century and to women in the twentieth. They called into being the Emancipation Proclamation in 1863. Threatened by external dangers in World War I and World War II, they galvanized American men and women into action. Since these values were first proclaimed in 1776 they have functioned as the conscience of the American people and nation.

In the middle of the twentieth century the power demands for change in social and political patterns are so far reaching as to approach in certain communities of the nation the dimensions of a social revolution. The Negro minority has called upon them. These values have stirred that minority to the burdens and perils of nonviolent action. White Americans have recognized that the colored minority strives to translate American ideals into social and political realities. The nation which understands its mission to be to defend freedom and human dignity against a ruthless totalitarianism struggles to make the dream of freedom and human dignity come true throughout its entire extent. The adversary is the most deep seated prejudice known to mankind. In the present struggle for American civil rights within the United States the Revolution of 1776 comes to its climax and the nation to a great test.

Evolving science and technology, shifting forces in the society of nations and dynamism of old ideals and standards converge and synchronize to bring change to the life of the American people. The stirring and movement of no former age in our history can be compared with that of the middle decades of the twentieth century. Hurricane winds sweep across the American landscape. What the end will be only the future can disclose. But, as for the present, it is one of the supreme moments in history.

II

ON TEACHING AMERICAN STUDIES

A Bridge for Science and Technology

BROOKE HINDLE

BROOKE HINDLE, Professor of History at New York University, is the author of *The Pursuit of Science in Revolutionary America, 1735-1789* (1956), and of a biography of David Rittenhouse now in press. He is currently engaged in a study of the transit of technology to the United States.

MORE THAN GOOD WILL IS REQUIRED TO FIT THE STORY OF science and technology into its due place in American Studies. It belongs; it belongs at the very center. Our conceptual world rests upon what science permits us to believe, and our physical world has been altered almost out of recognition by technology. Yet, we still talk in outmoded terms. We still proceed—albeit uncomfortably—in the illusion that American Studies can remain a compound of literature, conventional history, government, and a few sprinkles of economics, sociology, philosophy, and fine arts.

Not that there is any objection or resistance to admitting science and technology within the scheme of American Studies courses, programs, and writings; on the contrary, responsible scholars are all too anxious to welcome these disciplines within the fold. Indeed, the importance of science in our society is so generally recognized that the problem is rather to turn the enthusiasm to effective use than to generate it.

The trouble is that there are too few bridges between a receptive attitude and a fulfilled understanding. How, in fact, can a scholar fit science and technology into the center of his picture of American civilization? Where can he find descriptions of the relationships between science and the more familiar aspects of the landscape? Where can he even find explanations of science that are adequate to his needs?

An immediate difficulty is the language barrier—or perhaps, mental curtain. C. P. Snow's concept of "the two cultures" provoked so much denial, so much comment on the admitted compartmentation of learning, and so many other smoke screens that we may forget the reality behind his observation that literary and humanistic scholars often experience difficulty communicating with scientists absorbed in science.[1] We need not count noses to perceive that most students interested in American Studies are drawn from the humanistic and social studies fields—and when a scientist wanders in, he seldom is any clearer about how his special knowledge of science can be related to the general objective. He, too, needs a bridge.

The bridge analogy has often been applied to the history of science as a connection between science and the humanities, but it is likely also to be the most effective bridge by which science and technology can be introduced into American Studies. The historians of science and the historians of technology seek a synthesis strikingly similar to our own. It is proclaimed even in the titles of their journals: *Isis, An International Review Devoted to the History of Science and its Cultural Influences* and *Technology and Culture*.

Perhaps this breadth of view is a consequence of the historical approach, for all true history is a synthetic or composite study. Indeed, some observers have suggested that if historians had done their job, if the "new history" of James Harvey Robinson had ever been written, there would be no need for American Studies or area studies of any sort. History would then include the insights of all the scholars of all the disciplines; American history would represent a chronological survey of American Studies. That this objective has been and must remain unattainable should not obscure the central relationship history retains to any success in the American Studies approach. It is not the only means of integrating diverse fields but offers unique advantages.

Most important is the perspective history provides. To the "flat," two-dimensional understanding we can gain from current studies of our own society, history offers a third dimension: the dimension of depth in time. This third dimension is especially useful for those aspects of current life that are hardest to comprehend and hardest to relate to the composite picture of American civilization; it is especially useful for an understanding of science and technology which in their present complexity defy easy analysis. What they are sometimes yields more readily to the question how they came to be that way.

But answering this question involves the historian of science in difficulties that do not equally confront other scholars using the historical approach. Nineteenth century science, or eighteenth century science, is unquestionably less complex than twentieth century science but it remains inaccessible to the humanistically oriented whose knowledge stops at the doors of mathematics and the physical sciences. There is no way around this bitter fact.

Many years ago, George Sarton established the dictum that no one should consider working in the history of science until he had first become a scientist. To use his metaphor, science is as essential in the history of science as chicken in a chicken pie.[2] He felt, moreover, that science must become a part of him early in a man's career, while the tools of history, by implication, might be picked up at any time.

Recognition of the fundamental need for facility in science is now widespread. The better graduate programs in the history of science seek students with the equivalent of an undergraduate science major and the capacity to pursue graduate work in at least one field of science. At the same time, since these programs are carried on within established history departments or within specially constituted departments of the history of science, the historical sense is equally cultivated. Some of Sarton's followers are better historians than he was.

This accomplishment has had some undesirable "side effects." Excellent scholarship and a dramatic rise in the market value of the history of science have contributed to an esprit de corps and to some impatience of attitude. The study of the central story of the development of science is so exciting and so demanding that comparative studies and efforts to relate science to other fields are sometimes neglected or denigrated. A part of the reason for this is that among those who have interested themselves in inter-disciplinary studies and the "social relations" of science are two tarnished groups. The first is the Marxists who are led by their dogmas to emphasize these aspects of science, but they are less influential than they were just a few years ago. The second, which continues to be important, is made up of scholars who attempt generalizations and comparisons without adequate grounding in or understanding of science. Even beyond the identification of such shortcomings, some express the fear that insufficient work has been done on the internal life of science to permit anyone—however well qualified—to make meaningful generalizations or significant interdisciplinary comparisons.

American Studies students must come to grips with this ambivalence on the part of historians of science, and to a lesser degree, of historians of technology. They still carry at their masthead the goal of the large generalization and the relationships of science. At the same time, many prefer limited and detailed studies within the bounds of science.

American Studies will benefit from progress in both directions. Our own synthesis of American civilization will lack authority until the specialized studies of the sciences which are a part of it have provided a firmer foundation than we have now. But, it is not necessary to abandon interdisciplinary studies while this work continues. Indeed, they must proceed concurrently for each feeds the insights of the other. Moreover, the large scale generalization and comparison possess advantages which are especially well known to the American Studies scholar and which he is in a position to impress upon the historian of science.

But, in addition to these difficulties, the study of specifically American science carries with it an additional load of complications. The very idea of "American science" must be rejected at the outset. We can speak meaningfully of American literature, American music, or American painting and certainly of American politics and American economics because, in each case, the product is demonstrably marked by its American environment. Each constitutes a valid story in its own right. It cannot be divorced entirely from parallel and preceding activities in other parts of the world but it can be viewed in a measure of isolation.

Not so with science! American contributions to science do not constitute a connected, coherent, or viable story in themselves. They are fragments which take on meaning only when fitted into the main structure of western science. We may speak, of course, of American natural history, American ethnology, or chemistry *in* America, but there is no American chemistry or American mathematics. There is nothing American or un-American about the equilibrium of heterogeneous substances or the conservation of electrical charge. Historians have agreed that instead of "American science," the preferable term is "science in America."

This is not a peculiarly American limitation. Even in those nations which have enjoyed scientific creativity during a longer period of time, the international character of science predominates over local variability. The late F. S. Bodenheimer liked to point out that scholars wrote the general history of science with great overemphasis upon the episodes which took place within their own national boundaries.[3] Whether this is the hazard or whether the American problem is primary, everyone who works in this field must keep the mainstream of science in full view.

The student of the American scene must always play a difficult dual role; he can write of American science only from a deep understanding of the major course of international science. With this necessity in mind, Donald Fleming decided a decade ago that only those capable of contributing to the understanding of the history of science in general might be presumed qualified to write fruitfully of science in America. On his part, he took time out from his specifically American studies to write two articles demonstrating that he possessed the qualifications required. He wrote of Watt's steam engine and Galen's concept of the circulation of the blood, subjects only elliptically related to his major interest in American science.[4]

Conscious of the same difficulties, John C. Greene urged a different solution for intellectual history in general and the history of science in particular. He counselled against the acceptance of a Monroe Doctrine in this area, asserting that the American scholar must study developments on both sides of the Atlantic simultaneously.[5] Otherwise, his interpretations can have but little value.

He too then set out to fulfill the objective he had set. He studied the development of several late eighteenth and nineteenth century sciences in both America and Europe with special reference to the rise of the evolutionary idea within them. When it came, however, to putting the fruits of this research together, he found it more practicable to publish two differently oriented books rather than one comprehensive synthesis. The European study, which has already appeared, is his highly original *The Death of Adam: Evolution and Its Impact on Western Thought.* The American volume, dealing with science in the "age of Jefferson," is in preparation.

It is altogether unlikely that many students of American science will hold themselves to the discipline of looking for a discovery to be made in ancient science—as Mr. Fleming has done—or of writing a book on European science for each book written on American science—as Mr. Greene has done. Yet, the underlying necessity cannot be escaped. Work in American science demands both facility in the basic sciences and knowledge of the development of western science during the period studied.

The recognition of these necessities only opens the door to other gnawing problems. One that is not amenable to individual solution is the spotty chronological structure of the history of science which is least complete in precisely the period of maximum American accomplishment. Good work has been done on episodes of ancient history, in much of the medieval period, on the scientific revolution, and, recently, on the eighteenth century. Work is proceeding on the nineteenth century and the pivotal Darwinian story has received concentrated attention. But the recent past is relatively barren of careful investigation or acceptable generalization.

The problem is so serious that many responsible instructors have established a "cut-off point" at 1870 or 1885, beyond which they decline to carry courses in the history of science. This is documented by the content of most textbooks and by Charles C. Gillispie's exciting *The Edge of Objectivity*, based upon his undergraduate course, in which he places everything after Maxwell in a brief epilogue.

This is a more serious deficiency when regarding the American scene than it is for the ancient seats of scientific creativity. America did not exist during the longest course of the history of science, and during the seventeenth, eighteenth, and nineteenth centuries our contributions were occasional and irregular. If we use Nobel prizes as a yardstick, American participation in the advance of science became respectable only in the 1930's, and not until the Second World War did we become eminent in most of the fields of science and preeminent in some. In short, during the period of maximum American attainment in science, our ignorance about science is deepest.

The chronology of technology in America is somewhat different. The United States began to make major contributions to technology early in the nineteenth century and, at least that early, technology became active in altering the bases of life in America. Its importance has been recognized and recorded by a variety of interested students although careful scholarship is relatively recent. More important, the technology of the first railroads and canals was but little more dependent upon science than the notoriously non-intellectual technology of the middle ages. Today, it is very different; it is often difficult to distinguish technology from science. Science began to swallow technology at just about the point when our knowledge about it becomes untrustworthy. Of the recent past, our knowledge of technology is equally poor and the need, for all who seek to understand American civilization, almost as great.

Most historians of science and technology would prefer to bring their accounts down to the present; some argue strenuously in favor of doing so. The problem, however, is qualitatively different from that faced by political historians who know that they may have to wait twenty or thirty years until enough monographs appear to provide specialized knowledge. No such passage of time will automatically supply us with the information and the interpretations we need.

Science has altered so dramatically in the past seventy-five years that the methods used successfully to interpret the science of the Middle Ages cannot cope with the twentieth century. It is now physically impossible for a historian to read all of the papers written on even a relatively small topic in science, but the sheer increase in the volume of scientific activity—which continues to rise on a logarithmic curve—is a minor part of the problem. How can any scholar become sufficiently expert in one discipline alone to evaluate the major accomplishments of each of its divisions and subdivisions? If this partial task is insuperable, how then can we speak of a synthesis of the general history of science in which we seek to make sense out of the entire complex of sciences? Moreover, if there be degrees of impossibility, we can only anticipate that the informed evaluation of science will become increasingly impossible.

Fortunately, the human character seems to refuse the possibility of impossibilities, and frequently as we contemplate them, their impenetrability diminishes. Gerald Holton is a physicist and historian of science who had much to do with the resounding success of the interdisciplinary journal, *Daedalus;* he suggests that an aspiring historian of science might prepare himself for research in recent history of advanced physics in the same time he would need to acquire the languages and history required to study medieval science. Strikingly, current sessions on the history of science show a large increase in the number of papers dealing with very recent science—most of them by men who have recently entered the profession. It is too early to predict just how these problems will be solved—only that they will be.[6]

Meanwhile, those who feel the compelling need to include science and technology in their understanding of American civilization must recognize the limitations of the research that can so far be offered them. They must recognize, too, the magnitude and difficulty of the work required to provide more. This helps to explain the touchiness of some historians, intent upon their study of the internal structure of science, to questions about its social relations, but we should not be deterred.

Of this area, as of all others, we must insist upon asking the big questions, for the answers we receive can never be better than our questions. The narrative development of thoughts and concepts within a branch of a science is not one of the big questions, however difficult to attain it may be. We should be encouraged by the greater breadth of view American historians bring to their studies of the general course of science than is usual in Europe—as, for example, the programs of the International Congresses of the History of Science demonstrate.[7] Nevertheless, there is a continuing danger that man in science and science in man's life may not retain the dominant role in all our inquiries that it should.

This is what George Sarton had in mind when he spoke, ecstatically, about the study of the history of science leading to a "new humanism."[8] Whatever else science is, it is a great human achievement—probably man's greatest achievement. A cumulative development, we no longer imagine that it grows like a seed or a crystal to preordained forms. It is built by a succession of creative acts, which can be added together, and multiplied, in a way that other creations of man cannot.

By any standard, the human relations of science are, ultimately, its most important aspect. They are also the aspect of primary value to the American Studies approach. We must concentrate upon these relationships of science in full knowledge of the need to know the internal structure of science, its European course, and its intellectual imperatives.

Fortunately, the tools are being provided. Societies, journals, graduate programs, libraries, financial support, and all the underpinnings for effective advance in the history of science and technology have been established and are being constantly improved. The fruits are already appearing in the form especially of better knowledge of the internal growth of science. Inevitably, this will increase at an accelerating pace. Foundations for similar advance in knowledge of American science have been laid in university programs and in several projects for collecting and making available source materials on American science. Nathan Reingold leads a growing drive to provide a means for preserving the manuscripts of American scientists. Richard H. Shryock and Whitfield J. Bell, Jr., in developing the American Philosophical Society into a repository of materials bearing on American science, are including photocopies of significantly related European materials. Robert L. Schofield is developing an archive of American technology at Case Institute.

Recent studies of American science have sought to focus attention upon various relationships of science while at the same time they give careful attention to the internal structure of science. This is perhaps best achieved in I. Bernard Cohen's *Franklin and Newton,* a brilliant relationship of Franklin's electricity to one aspect of Newtonian thought. My *Pursuit of Science in Revolutionary America* seeks to relate science and scientific aspirations to the social and political setting. William Stanton's *The Leopard's Spots* relates scientific knowledge of race to a complex of social attitudes about it. Most widely useful is A. Hunter Dupree's *Science in the Federal Government,* the first volume of which has appeared; the volume treating the period since 1940 is in preparation. Also in preparation is a multi-volume survey of science in America by Donald Fleming. These beginnings all point to a vast panorama of work yet to be done.

American scientific biography occupies a peculiarly important position in this stage of development, because it serves two functions. It must carefully evaluate the internal structure of those sciences which the subject of the biography touches. At the same time, if indeed it is to be a biography at all, it must concentrate attention upon the man and portray him in the wholeness of his life. *All* of his relationships must be probed. Through the study of a man, the relationships of science can emerge out of detailed analytical research.

Of course, it is possible and often extremely useful to study only a man's thought and the intellectual relationships which bear directly upon his creative writings. This is what Perry Miller does in his *Jonathan Edwards*, reducing the man to outline scraps of "external biography." His approach is followed by George F. Frick and Raymond P. Stearns in one section of their *Mark Catesby*, but in another section, they supply also a full biography of the man.

Most successful of the recent American scientific biographies are A. Hunter Dupree's *Asa Gray* and Edward Lurie's *Louis Agassiz*. These both represent very careful examinations of the subject's science and the result is two contributions not only to our knowledge of science in America but to our understanding of the mainstream of scientific development. Yet, this is accomplished by bringing the men to life: Gray's science unfolds as a part of the man we come to know and Agassiz's strange attitudes are made explicable in terms of his character and his environment.

Historians usually shy away from predictions, but the future of science and technology in American Studies is now so clear that it ought to be proclaimed. Barring global catastrophe, science will grow at an increasing rate and technology, dependent upon it, will determine more and more of the dimensions of our life. All aspects of our culture will be increasingly influenced by science. In consequence, those who seek to understand American civilization will have no alternative—whatever their tastes in the matter—but to include science at the center of their synthesis.

The end is inexorable. We should approach it with the best understanding we can find and the best key we have is offered by the history of science. Despite occasional indications to the contrary, historians of science and historians of technology have a fundamental dedication to an interdisciplinary view of civilization which provides firm groundwork for cooperation with those committed to the American Studies approach. Opportunities for such cooperation will increase and they should be exploited.

Recognizing the necessity for understanding the internal structure and development of science, we must not limit our quest to that understanding alone. We must always ask the big questions. We must know how science relates to man and to man in society. Enough scholarship has already been applied to this objective to demonstrate that it is not an unattainable goal. Enough foundations have been laid that such demonstrations will become increasingly satisfying.

The study of science and technology for the purpose of enriching our synthesis of American civilization is demanding. It cannot rest upon a broad view alone; it requires knowledge in depth. But, it has almost limitless rewards to offer; it will lead not only to a re-evaluation of our own culture but, perhaps, of man's role on earth.

1. C. P. Snow, *The Two Cultures and the Scientific Revolution* (New York: The Macmillan Co., 1958).

2. C. Doris Hellman, "George Sarton, Historian of Science and New Humanist," *Science*, CXXVIII (1958), 643.

3. F. S. Bodenheimer, *The History of Biology* (London: Dawson Publishers, 1958), p. 74.

4. Donald Fleming, "Discussion of Values and Limitations of the Study of the History of Science," November 28, 1953, Meetings of the National Council for the Social Sciences, Buffalo; Donald Fleming, "Latent Heat and the Invention of the Watt Engine," *Isis*, XLIII (1952), 3-5; Donald Fleming, "Galen on the Motion of the Blood," *Isis*, XLV (1955), 14-21.

5. John C. Greene, "Objectives and Methods in Intellectual History," *Mississippi Valley Historical Review*, XLIV (1957), 76-88.

6. Gerald Holton, Conversation September 3, 1959, IXth International Congress of the History of Science, Barcelona.

7. Especially Program of History of Science Society, April 5-6, 1963, Bloomington, Indiana, and Program of Section L, American Association for the Advancement of Science, December 27-30, 1963, Cleveland.

8. George Sarton, *The Life of Science* (New York: Schuman, 1948), p. 57.

The Problem of Synthesis

JOHN A. HAGUE

JOHN A. HAGUE took his doctorate in American Studies at Yale, and is now Head of the Department of American Studies at Stetson University in Florida. His articles have appeared in several academic journals; and his essay on "American Character in American Literature: An Acceptance of Experience" in *Essays in Modern American Literature* (1963).

IN 1959 SIR CHARLES SNOW DESCRIBED BLUNTLY A SEPARATION of cultures which existed "all over the western world." He suggested that the scientists who were in the process of constructing the culture of the future and the intellectuals who were dedicated to the task of preserving and transmitting the traditional culture were not only the victims of a serious breakdown in communication, but were often positively contemptuous of one another. The lack of interchange between the two groups, he thought, could spell disaster for the free world, and he saw the situation as getting worse, not better. Sir Charles felt that the only way out of this predicament lay in rethinking our education.

If we educators are to rethink our curriculum and methodology, we need to analyze with some care the factors which have impaired our ability to communicate effectively with one another. Perhaps in the process we will discover that the breakdown is both more extensive and profound than even Snow's analysis would lead us to believe. We may also gain some insights which will be helpful to those who feel that all intellectual efforts, at their best, must be related to the whole range of human experience.

From the vantage point of those who are concerned with the preservation of a rich and complex cultural heritage, effective communication appears to be hampered by several developments. The rapidity with which the world is changing and growing makes it hard for such men to keep standards of critical analysis and inquiry relevant to the needs of their contemporaries. In short, the historian and the humanist are today likely to find themselves on the defensive in much the same way that the classicist has in the last hundred years. Secondly, the growing body of knowledge with which these scholars must deal forces them to become specialists at the very moment that both science and current events are urging them to cope with a universe whose vastness almost defies imagination. The student of nationalism, for example, who now must come to grips with movements of people in Asia, Africa, and South America, may well wonder whether he possesses an intellectual structure which is sufficient for his task. Finally, the awakening of "the masses" has called forth new elite groups while isolating and destroying many of the old ones. Many of the new elites, however, are paralyzed by their fear of failing to maintain the approval of the very groups that have brought them to power. Anyone, therefore, who tries to communicate standards and values may find himself cut off from the support of an elite or an aristocracy which in previous generations might have undergirded his efforts.

On the other hand, the scientist, even though he feels an identification with the culture of the future, is also apt to worry some about the problem of communication. A physicist recently told me that he thought all of the major contributions in his field were being made today by people under 35. He thought that the discipline was growing so rapidly that the older members of the craft, whose graduate training was a dozen or more years in the past, had little chance of keeping abreast of current developments. Moreover, many of the striking advances now involve bridge areas, so that the struggling physicist, for example, must keep up with a variety of developments in chemistry and biology. The scientist is therefore likely to feel that he does not have sufficient time to communicate effectively with those whose research is directly related to his own, let along bridge the gap of which Snow complains.

Such factors are, however, somewhat misleading. By concentrating on conditions which explain the divorce between the scientific and the humanistic cultures, we may be tempted to ignore other causes which have disrupted communication among virtually all branches of inquiry in the modern world. Moreover, these additional causes may tell us even more than Snow's analysis about the gaps which must be closed if we are to educate people to live in the twentieth and twenty-first centuries.

In 1919 Sherwood Anderson published *Winesburg, Ohio*, one of the seminal books in the development of modern American fiction. Winesburg was a small town caught between the traditions that had shaped the older agrarian America and the forces which were creating an urban, industrial society. Anderson called his book "the book of the grotesque," and explained that individuals who tried to possess truths became grotesque. As the stories unfold it becomes clear that one of the things that makes the characters grotesque is the fact that they can't communicate with each other. The hero's mother hopes that her son will not accept his father's rather conventional and shabby definition of success but she cannot tell him what she wants him to be. Over and over again individuals in the book struggle to communicate a truth and find that they have not the strength or the imagination to do so.

A story by Thomas Mann, "Death in Venice," sheds

some light on the awkward silences which pervade *Winesburg*. In the Mann story a middle-aged writer sojourns in Venice and becomes enamored with a teen-aged boy. He does not actually converse with the lad, but he worships, from a distance, the boy's youthful beauty. When a choleric plague strikes the city the writer stays, thereby choosing death, rather than forsake the opportunity to view once more his young idol. An air of decay hangs over the tale, and the reader feels pity rather than compassion for the plight of the writer. The artist lacks the strength and the self-discipline to accept the transitory and perhaps foolish aspects of his romantic infatuation. He is hypnotized, not by fate, but by his own capacity for idyllic dreams and fantasies. The sojourn, which was supposed to refresh and invigorate the writer, led instead to a gradual sapping of his will and capacity to live.

"Death in Venice" appears to make two significant comments about nineteenth-century romanticism. The romantic movement insisted upon a turning inward; upon the necessity of exploring the inner world of one's own spirit. As a consequence it often discounted or even repudiated the allegiance to form and tradition which characterized the rationalism of the Enlightenment. The romantic artist proclaimed the necessity of relying upon eternal forces which gave life and breath to man's soul. Men like Thoreau deplored the tendency of individuals to rely unduly upon social and political institutions, and they applauded Emerson's assertion that "Every spirit builds itself a house, and beyond its house a world, and beyond its world a universe." Mann, I take it, recognized the source of the romantic's productivity; it was the self-discipline born of the vision which he relentlessly pursued. If for any reason he lost this self-discipline, he was doomed. Dreams keyed to the internal life of the soul and divorced from sustained work brought chaos and death. Thomas Wolfe recognized the accuracy of Mann's insight more clearly than any other modern American writer. Working at a frenzied pace Wolfe seemed to know that if he ever stopped he could never get started again. And indeed, when he finished his novels he died.

Mann's second insight has to do with the substance of the dreams which the romantics pursued. Some, of course, hoped for a radical reconstruction of the social order and committed themselves to various utopian schemes. Others hoped for a radical reconstruction of human nature and hoped for a race of men that would perform heroic deeds and achieve superlative literary and artistic triumphs. Closely examined, the dreams amounted to types of in-fatuations which affected all levels of meaning. The romantic, according to this analysis, was in the end betrayed by his own vision, a vision which offered death rather than life.

At this point the social scientist might well insist upon a few questions. In what kind of an era did the romantic flourish? Did his dreams reflect the era or the society in which he lived? Has the romanticism of the nineteenth century affected in any basic way the capacity of men in the twentieth century to communicate with one another? First, it is obvious that from the standpoint of the western democracies the nineteenth century was a period of enormous expansion. New lands were opening up, industries were developing with extraordinary rapidity, and vast numbers of people were on the move. Small wonder that it was an age of optimism; man seemed capable of attaining new heights of material prosperity and spiritual well-being. Secondly, the newly released energies and the growing productive capacity which society contained gave birth to a multitude of reform movements, utopian visions, and personal ambitions. In short a pluralistic world was coming into being, and the creative efforts of nineteenth-century artists everywhere testified to the fact. Ironically, however, most of the writers and artists who can legitimately be identified with the romantic movement had their roots in communities which retained a strong sense of homogeneity. The pre-Civil War transcendentalists and the post-Civil War regionalists drew inspiration and support from the communities in which they lived and worked. They did not have to search for common things of the mind and heart because they already possessed them. I think it is significant that a twentieth-century writer, such as William Faulkner, prized especially the homogeneity of the South. Finally, it seems evident that many writers were able to communicate effectively in the nineteenth century precisely because they were members of communities which seemed to possess common traditions and common hopes. The fact that the pragmatists thought metaphysics was a waste of time provides further evidence to the reality of a belief in progress which seemed clearly attainable. John Dewey did not need to argue about ultimate truths because they seemed to him as "self evident" as they had at an earlier time to the Sage of Monticello.

This analysis suggests that individuals coming to maturity at the close of the nineteenth century may have failed to recognize the pluralism that was inherent in the very fabric of the exploding culture. Moreover, the extent to which communities retained a sense of homogeneity and shared an implicit faith in a self-evident progress probably obscured for many people the terms upon which effective communication rested. The result was that people who thought they understood each other completely discovered, under stress of war and poverty, that the lines of communication extended only to superficialities. Randolph Bourne's attack on John Dewey when he discovered that Dewey had renounced his pacifism in the First World War is a case in point.

More than he realized, the nineteenth-century writer

had mirrored with great sensitivity and fidelity the conditions of his society. When his search for meaning caused him to hold up a mirror to twentieth-century culture, he saw reflected the hollowness, the anonymity, and the alienation which seemed to bedevil the modern world. At the same time he found himself cut adrift from supporting social structures and in open rebellion against a past which had betrayed him. In defense he became more and more introspective. As a consequence, his writings gave fresh illumination to the tragic and poignant facets of human existence. Men discovered depths beneath depths, but the discoveries did not provide their own cure. Like Mann's writer who went to Venice, we have fathomed the nature of the plague which is sweeping the land, but whether we possess the will and the intelligence to deal with it is another question.

Meanwhile a great many social scientists have recovered from their brief period of disillusionment in the 1920's. They have accepted with open arms the liberation from nineteenth-century absolutes which scholars in a wide variety of disciplines effected. They know that individuals, groups, and institutions must be judged by their performances, and they have found stimulation and excitement through the discovery and refinement of techniques which measure behavioral responses with more accuracy and greater subtlety. The large questions which excite the humanists frequently leave the social scientists cold. They are finding significant answers to more limited inquiries, and they ask no more. They understand that a science of behavior must grow out of the efforts in which they are currently engaged.

The fact that these efforts are frequently described in language which seems to defy intelligibility should not mislead us. Although the social scientist who entitles his articles "Instrumentality and Emotionality in Family Interaction," or "Status Congruence and Cognitive Consistency," alienates a great many potential readers, he is nevertheless attacking important phenomena. His "jargon" is, in part at least, a search for more precise language in a culture grown sloppy in its treatment of words. The specter of bright students who are as "word deaf" as others are "tone deaf" provides sufficient testimony on this point. The social scientist is also conscious of the complexity of his subject matter. He must analyze a great many facets of experience, and he needs a technical language to assist him. Ultimately, he needs a mathematical language which will enable him to communicate with computers, and which will enable him to absorb and correlate the vast bodies of information which his colleagues are producing.

The social scientist might do well to remember that the past is rarely a definitive guide to the future. Even a perfectly programed computer can only provide adequate predictive data to the extent that the past provides direction for the future. Nevertheless, it seems clear that we are in the midst of a large-scale revolution which will vastly enlarge our understanding of power structures, group dynamics, social stratification and mobility, and a host of related developments. The fact that Washington University of St. Louis has established a project to translate significant research in the social sciences into English should remind us that social science "gobbledygook" is not simply "much ado about nothing."

The Washington University project testifies to another obvious breakdown in communication. The breakdown is serious because there is no guarantee that additional knowledge will provide more extensive or effective involvement for educated citizens in their society. The difficulties which the President of the United States has encountered in trying to give the public an elementary education in economics prove that knowledge must be communicated on many levels to be effective. In *The Mind of the South*, W. J. Cash stated that never before had so many Southerners known so much about the South, its problems and its needs, and never had they experienced greater difficulty in communicating their knowledge to the grass roots of society.

C. Vann Woodward, in an article written for *The New York Times Book Review* on July 28, 1963,[1] observed that mid-twentieth-century historians have not yet offered us new syntheses to replace the old ones. They have pointed out fallacies in previous generalizations, and their work has, according to Woodward, paved the way "for more positive contributions," but they have not inspired men to accept new responsibilities. As a result we see our past more clearly and we are probably more familiar with a larger segment of it, but this understanding does not always lead to an acceptance of or involvement in the struggles and hopes of present-day society.

Clearly enough, there have been many significant interdisciplinary studies in recent years which have involved effective communication among the various academic disciplines. What has been lacking, however, is the kind of synthesis that relates a knowledge of present day society with a comprehension of its heritage and an understanding of man's inner torment in a world which finds itself cut adrift from the moorings that have structured existence for previous generations. The result is that we find it hard to see life whole. We do not wish to accept our past, which is to say our limitations, nor do we wish to accept our future, which is to say our death. Therefore the present frightens or bores us. Joseph Heller, in *Catch 22*, has caught perfectly his aspect of modern existence. One of his characters, who knows that he must die, does everything which utterly bores him in order to prolong his existence. And the central protagonist offers a point of view involving personal courage but rejecting an involvement in the ordinary society of selfish mortals.

Robert Penn Warren's *All The King's Men* attempts the kind of synthesis which I think offers hope for the future. Jack Burden is a student of history who finds himself in the middle of Louisiana politics. His doctoral dissertation involved the study of an ante-bellum southern family, but he could not complete the thesis because he could not accept his own past. As long as he rebels against the past he is, paradoxically, bound by it. Ultimately Burden discovers that one cannot hope for the future until he accepts the past because the future must evolve out of the past. This is a point of view which allows him to accept the ambiguities of the present without being defeated by them. He can forgive those who have compromised with values while understanding what the results of the compromises have been. Understanding himself and his society, he can make sense of history and indeed of life itself.

The type of synthesis which Jack Burden achieved allows him to understand in depth the problems of his society. He thus illustrates an old truism; one cannot achieve real depth without breadth. Too often we have assumed that American Studies, because of its synthetic nature, necessarily sacrifices depth to breadth. Nothing could be further from the truth. To the extent that it forces students to make the right journeys, it will help them to think, write, and act in a responsive and responsible fashion.

What are the right journeys? Ralph Gabriel argues that every individual must face two questions "as a condition of conscious life." He must consider the nature of his relationship to society and also to the "mystery that envelops him." Involved in both inquiries is the task of self-discovery. It seems apparent, therefore, that the serious student must take three related journeys. Moreover, many of the scholarly tools which he needs are now available.

First he must travel inward, exploring the dilemmas and anxieties which confront all men. Literature, the arts, psychology, philosophy, and theology can all help him here. Secondly, he must travel outward, exploring the nature and structure of society and culture. Men *are* culture-bearing animals; they only achieve greatness or meanness in a specific society. Ultimately, therefore, no matter how many other societies the student studies, he needs to come to grips with his own.[2] Finally, modern cultures, at least, are never static; they can only be understood in terms of their history. In order to move forward one must first go back. The third journey must involve a search for an understanding and acceptance of one's cultural inheritance.

No one can guarantee where the journeys will lead, or indeed that the roads will meet. One can hope, however, that students who travel this way will at least acquire a measure of self-discipline; that they will become articulate; and that they will base their hopes for the future on a mature understanding of what the past will permit. Detachment *and* involvement may then characterize their ongoing search for wisdom and understanding. In a society which has premised many of its understakings on the assumption that the search for truth is never ending, this would be no small achievement.

1. C. Vann Woodward. "Our Past Isn't What It Used To Be," *The New York Times Book Review*, July 28, 1963.
2. An interesting experiment in this direction is the recently published volume, *Sociology through Literature*. Lewis A. Coser (ed.), (New York: Prentice Hall, 1963). For example, the problem of "Anomie" is studied through selections from John Donne, William Butler Yeats, Alfred de Musset, Denis Diderot, Fedor Dostoevski, F. Scott Fitzgerald, Charles Dickens, and Ambrose Bierce.

The Culture Concept as Keystone

RICHARD E. SYKES

RICHARD E. SYKES is a Unitarian Universalist minister and candidate for the Ph.D. degree in American Studies at the University of Minnesota. He has previously published in denominational journals and in the *Sociological Quarterly*. He is presently working on "The Effect of Rapid Social Change on Unitarianism in Massachusetts Between 1800-1870," and other aspects of the sociology of American church history.

AMERICAN STUDIES IS YOUNG, UNSURE OF ITS GOALS AND methods. Many have suggested theories and methods. Others feel that it is best to avoid dogmatic definition of content or method; to wait for the discipline to define itself through practice. Henry Nash Smith writes "Method in scholarship grows out of practice, or rather out of repeated criticism of practice intended to remedy observed shortcomings."[1]

While those who suggest that practice must come before theory deserve our respect, especially because of their outstanding practical successes, it seems doubtful whether anything can be gained from the neglect of theory, provided that theoretical suggestions are treated as suggestions, and not as dogma. Theory and definition have the value of clarification, of suggesting useful distinctions and possibly fruitful hypotheses. There comes a point when the justification of a new field must exceed a reaction against the narrow perspectives of either the New Criticism or purely quantitative social science. Nor are the suggestions

that the defining characteristic of American Studies is "the
effort to view any given subject of investigation from
new perspectives," or to view it from an interdisciplinary
standpoint adequate.[2] Hopefully the student of any discipline will attempt to look at his subject from new perspectives; an increasing number of studies in both the sciences
and humanities are interdisciplinary.

What then is American Studies? It is the study of American culture. Culture is the key concept, the unifying concept, the root word which suggests both theory and method.
Being a branch of culture studies, it is closer to the social
sciences theoretically than to the humanities. It is a specialized branch of cultural anthropology.[3] The materials
studied may be literary, but the approach will be that of
the student of culture, not the specialized critic.

If American Studies is essentially a culture study, how
does it differ from other such studies? Are there special
defining characteristics? Of course the obvious unique
characteristic is America itself. A culture can be defined
according to certain spatio-temporal dimensions. In the
long run this will be its only distinguishing characteristic.
If American Studies fulfills its promise, similar investigations will be taken of other national cultures. The subject
will be but a branch of culture studies of modern literate
societies.

Most studies by anthropologists have been of non-
literate cultures. In primitive societies culture is usually
communicated by oral, not written means. Even in high
civilizations only a small minority of the population was
capable of reading or writing until after the invention of
the printing press. Systems of universal free public education organized to transmit culture have been created only
in modern times.

To the student of the humanities culture is becoming
even more important. To the anthropologist the written

and artistic expressions of modern literate societies are of increasing significance. We need a discipline which combines special knowledge of both culture and humanities. The student of modern literate societies requires training in the use and interpretation of written artifacts—not only such things as government documents, personal diaries, and other historical resources, but also literature. To the student of culture, as contrasted to the historian, literature is more useful in discovering cultural significances than merely descriptive documents.[4] The understanding of works of fiction, as of other documents of art, requires knowledge, not only of content, but of craft and form. They are documents, but in a very special way. The student of modern literate culture must master the techniques of the high arts as well as of popular culture and mass communication. American Studies as a branch of modern literate culture studies requires a general theoretical orientation to culture study, and additional special knowledge of the written artifacts which are a defining characteristic of modern life.

The necessity of knowledge of literary technique is especially evident in historically oriented culture research. Unlike the anthropologist who observes the natives of an existing primitive culture, students of historical American Studies must use the surviving documents of a past era. This requires knowledge of many disciplines. Thus far most effort at inferring the psychological states of past natives of our culture has been centered on written documents. The American Studies student has often confused his concern with written evidence—especially with great American literature—with American Studies as a whole. The artifacts from which a culture is inferred include not just written documents (certainly not just literature) but the creations of other arts and the products of technology and science. Hence the true reason why American Studies is interdisciplinary becomes evident—not because we need to look on an event from several angles, but because the culture concept cuts across and includes the content of other disciplines. These disciplines are, in fact, the means our society uses to communicate a knowledge of culture, and are thus primary sources for a student.

Students of culture have been by no means agreed as to the precise meaning of the word. In *Culture: A Critical Review of Concepts and Definitions*, A. L. Kroeber and Clyde Kluckhohn include and comment on 164 definitions. Culture is a concept, an abstraction—not a thing. Culture is an abstract description of *trends toward* uniformity in the words, acts, and artifacts of human groups. Culture is not generally considered actual behavior itself; nor need the actual products or artifacts be considered as culture itself. Culture is that which is constructed by inference from behavior and artifacts. No two novels are exactly the same; yet they are enough alike to be labelled "novels." The form exists only in its specific embodiments. The novel form is a culture pattern, a construct, inferred from all its specific embodiments. Ralph Linton makes a similar distinction when he differentiates between real culture patterns and culture construct patterns. Real culture patterns are all the actual novels. Culture construct patterns are the average patterns, the generalizations which describe the mode of specific actual occurrences.[5]

All cultures are characterized by certain patterns of behavior, learned and passed on from generation to generation. They regularize all areas of life important to the existence of that culture. They involve eating, housing, earning a living, rearing children, marrying, burying, and worshipping. There is always variation of custom along a continuum. No one event is exactly the same as another, but we can describe what most people do most of the time in most areas of life. From their behavior we infer meanings, values and ideas. From sermons we derive a kind of pattern of what preachers and congregations expect in a sermon. That which is inferred from behavior or the products of behavior is a *culture construct pattern.*

In speaking of such patterns we can distinguish between *avowed, masked,* and *metapatterns.* An *avowed pattern* is publicly practiced and expressly recognized. Usually legal and openly approved, it is not necessarily a majority pattern; many minority culture patterns are avowed. A *masked pattern,* seldom openly discussed or publicly sanctioned, may be admitted in intimate groups. It may be masked because people do not realize that it is a generally shared pattern. Virtually all members of a culture may be unaware that any pattern exists—not because it is consciously hidden, but because it is too habitual to be noticed. A pattern may be masked because it is repressed. Feeling anxious about a particular danger or threat, men may fear to admit their anxiety. They may be unable to verbalize an unmet need. Often a masked culture pattern contradicts an already avowed one. Masked patterns must often be isolated by indirect means.

In American culture, where there are many culture-detectives employed full-time, it is unlikely that a great many patterns will be completely masked. In primitive societies much of the culture is masked simply because it is taken for granted. A pattern is avowed or masked according to the attitudes toward it, or the degree to which it is self-conscious among those who practice it.

A *metapattern* is one shared by two or more patterns. The structure of language is a metapattern, shared by all participants in a culture possessing a common language.

The search for masked patterns and metapatterns is intriguing and difficult. Avowed patterns are usually obvious, though they differ in subtlety. An avowed pattern in contemporary American culture for Christians is to go to church on Sunday. So is a politician's attack on another politician or political party in terms which would not be allowed in another context. In the South segregation is an avowed pattern. Such patterns are publicly practiced; expressly recognized and sanctioned. They are mostly ideas about action, though certain value patterns, sometimes masked, are implicit in them. It is an avowed pattern to seek profit in business or a higher wage for labor. But certain ways of making a profit are not avowed. We know they exist, but they are masked, like discrimination in the North. If Mr. Kinsey is correct there are many masked sexual patterns. Four books will provide us with fine examples of the search for patterns in American culture.

(a) *Railroad Leaders, 1845-1890; The Business Mind in Action* (1953) by Thomas C. Cochran. From an analysis of the business letter files of some sixty-one presidents of American railroads between 1845-1890 the author abstracts norms (patterns) for social role, that is, for "a shared expectation of a general type of response to certain situations." "A primary aim . . . was to establish some norms of thought and attitude for American railroad presidents of the period . . ." Before the study the author drew up a list of attitude categories including such headings as: expansion of business, competitors, social problems, and innovation. In content analyzing the letters every significant expression of the writer's attitude toward those items included in the list was recorded. Some of these patterns were avowed and others masked.

(b) *Popular Religion: Inspirational Books in America* (1958) by Louis Schneider and Sanford M. Dornbusch. This is a carefully designed study of forty-six best sellers of inspirational religious literature (non-fiction) in America between 1875-1955. The authors composed a lengthy list of religious ideas. General headings in their list included: functions of religious faith, God, man and nature; changing the self and the world; salvation; wealth and health; ways of salvation. One sub-item, for instance, was "religion brings physical health." Whenever this idea appeared in a paragraph of a book analyzed it was recorded. When the analysis was completed the proportion of the book devoted to that particular idea could be estimated.

Popular Religion locates certain patterns and trends in the minds of many Americans about religion, patterns not at all similar to the formal theology of traditional churches. Many ideas found in these books are like those found in *New Thought and Christian Science*. Certainly these patterns are avowed in the sense that many of the authors of these books were well-known clergymen. On the other hand they have a masked quality in that no major denomination and very few responsible theologians would advocate "the power of positive thinking" and similar ideas. Nevertheless these ideas are popular among a large proportion of the American middle class.

(c) *The American Adam: Innocence, Tragedy, and Tradition in the Nineteenth Century* (1955) by R. W. B. Lewis. The author locates in certain images used by several mid-nineteenth century writers the clue to a masked pattern in American literature, and by implication in American culture in general. ". . . the image contrived to embody the most contemporary ideas was that of the authentic American as a figure of heroic innocence and vast potentialities, poised at the start of a new history." Presumably the discussion among American artists over the validity of such an image is the key to understanding everyone from Whitman to Melville. Obviously this is an attempt to isolate a masked pattern.

(d) *Virgin Land: The American West as Symbol and Myth* (1957) by Henry Nash Smith. Through a wide variety of high and popular art, as well as purely descriptive documents, Smith finds myths and symbols which existed in the minds of many Americans during the nineteenth century. "Myth" and "symbol" are ". . . words to designate larger and smaller units of the same kind of thing, namely an intellectual construction that fuses concept and emotion into an image." The author has isolated a pattern in American thought. His emphasis on the two-dimensional aspect of "myth" is also important. His presentation gives depth that is lacking in ordinary intellectual history. The patterns found were in some cases avowed; but as an influence on behavior they were often masked. Americans may not have realized the extent to which they were influenced. In fact the resistance to some of Smith's insights may be an index to the power which this masked pattern still has in the American consciousness, and which some may not wish to examine critically.

If myth becomes vital in a culture it is because it expresses an avowed or masked pattern of values. These were the values to which American agrarian culture has given expression many times. The Myth of the Garden is but one pattern of images which expresses this generally avowed value pattern. It becomes interesting when taken into an urban industrial situation where it no longer applies. A myth is simply a pattern of values which has real force in the life of a people and which has received metaphoric expression, as contrasted with values and ideas which have only intellectual appeal. The use of such words as "myth" and "symbol" tends to obscure rather than emphasize this distinction.

These four books are all attempts to discern patterns in American culture. Each book hypothesizes certain culture construct patterns. The problem of theory and method in American Studies is especially evident in the last two, particularly because of the complications of dealing with imaginative literature. But if the theory informing research is carefully worked out in advance it should aid and clarify. One reason a concern for precise definition is important is that it helps avoid confusion such as that over just what covert and overt culture patterns are.

* * *

American Studies method involves three stages of approach. First one perceives a pattern. Probably the original perception will be an insight or intuition. This will then be stated clearly and explicitly in the form of a hypothesis. The second stage involves proving the hypothesis. Scholarship is an undertaking that requires cooperation of many; the evidence must be public and convincing. The third stage is that of presentation of findings to other scholars. Roy Harvey Pearce is referring to the method of presentation when he writes:

> It may well be that one of the main achievements of the American Studies movement will be its contribution toward a new kind of historiography, in which intellectual history becomes not a matter of ideas analyzed but of ideas dramatized, ideas so placed in their cultural matrix that they are shown to be possible beliefs.[6]

This is what imaginative anthropologists have been doing for some time when writing about primitive cultures. Pearce's suggestion succinctly describes the work of Perry Miller, Henry Nash Smith, and other scholars. The great virtue of their work is that it communicates a kind of sympathetic inner understanding of historic American culture. But their weakness is that they tend to depend too much on their own authority, on what might be described as impressionism. Another scholar, using the same documents, might come to very different conclusions. How can a hypothesis of a culture construct pattern, avowed or masked, be proved in such a way that the evidence, so to speak, will speak for itself to anyone who examines it? How can an undue amount of subjectivity be avoided in research?

There are two problems involved. The first, in the terminology of social science, is sampling. One can substantiate almost any hypothesis if the statements used as evidence are taken out of context or are not representative. Generalize about Orestes Brownson, or Theodore Parker, or Emerson; the words may be almost meaningless, unless some indication is given of the period meant and the documentary basis. In searching for patterns which characterize several writers how does one equate stages in the lives of different persons? Even when one is making studies of a somewhat more impersonal nature in the realm of popular culture what sampling procedures does one use? At least the scholar should state what his sample is and how he took it. It is not enough to say that one is familiar with all the literature of a particular period. Even if this is true one must deal with selections from it and justify one's selection. Usually a sample should be representative, and if it is not the reader should be warned. Further study needs to be given to the problem of the representativeness of samples used in American Studies.

Besides the sampling problem itself, it must be shown that the hypothesized pattern exists therein. One way is by content analysis. Some argue that this is only useful in studies of mass communication, not in high art, but this is only partly true. Content analysis cannot do justice to high art in its totality; but it can provide a useful protection against unsubstantiated generalization. If a particular image or pattern of values is especially significant in a writer or writers, it is possible to use content analysis to discover the frequency with which it appears as well as the author's attitude toward it. Content analytic techniques are constantly being refined to accommodate more complex and subtle problems. Besides *Popular Religion* and *Railroad*

Leaders, already mentioned, two briefer examples are "The Image of the Scientist in Science Fiction: A Content Analysis," and "The World of the Daytime Serial."[7] What we have here is a method to help establish patterns and guard against over-objectivity. Men in American Studies will want to understand and use it.

What I have tried to sketch in this essay is an approach to American Studies based on the culture concept, and utilizing new terms and methods. I contend that it is truly interdisciplinary, uniting many disparate methods used so far. Those employing it would concentrate in three areas: concept, method, and content. Basic to any curriculum should be a course in the meaning and development of the culture concept and its application to American Studies. In the areas of method, besides training in general approaches to culture, courses should impart the special knowledge of technique necessary for the study of written artifacts of modern literate societies—historiography, communications analysis, the craft of fiction, methods of social research, and one in the projective techniques used in contemporary psychological testing. Content courses would be concerned with whatever "American" it is in which the student wishes to specialize. Thus the American Studies curriculum would not be interdisciplinary, possessed of methodological unity. New vistas would be opened to us.

1. Henry Nash Smith, "Can American Studies Develop a Method?" in Joseph J. Kwiat and Mary G. Turpie (eds.), *Studies in American Culture: Dominant Ideas and Images* (Minneapolis: Univ. of Minn., 1960), p. 14.

2. Smith, *op. cit.,* p. 3; and Richard M. Huber, "A Theory of American Studies," *Social Education,* XVIII (October, 1954), 267.

3. This is recognized by William Randel when he writes that "of all established disciplines, cultural anthropology, more specifically social anthropology, is the closest to American Studies in governing purpose." In "Toward a Method in American Studies,"

Quarterly Journal of the Florida Academy of Science, XXIII (Spring, 1960), 67.

4. See below for a fuller consideration of the use of literature in culture studies.

5. Ralph Linton, *The Cultural Background of Personality* (New York: D. Appleton-Century Co., 1945), pp. 30-54.

6. " 'The American Adam' and the State of American Studies," *Journal of Higher Education,* XXVII (February, 1956), 106.

7. Walter Hirsch, *American Journal of Sociology,* LXIII (March, 1958), 506-512. Rudolf Arnheim, *Radio Research 1942-43,* P. F. Lazarsfeld and Frank Stanton (eds.) (New York: Duell, Sloan and Pearce, 1944). There are a number of useful and suggestive articles on "qualitative content analysis." Among them is Siegfried Kracauer's "The Challenge of Qualitative Content Analysis," *Public Opinion Quarterly,* XVI (1952-53), 631-642.

The Historical Fallacy

ROBERT J. COOKE

ROBERT J. COOKE, a member of the faculty of the Maxwell Graduate School of Citizenship and Public Affairs, Syracuse University, holds a dual appointment in American Studies
and Education. He is the author of a forthcoming book on
Eleanor Roosevelt during the post White House years and
occasional articles in professional journals. Professor Cooke
has been Director of Syracuse University's Chautauqua Center
and the Leadership Training Institute. His academic area is
American intellectual history.

IN 1802 PRESIDENT THOMAS JEFFERSON WROTE TO GOVERNOR
Hall,

> The event of our experiment is to show whether man
> can be trusted with self-government. The eyes of suffer-
> ing humanity are fixed on us with anxiety as the only
> hope, and on such a theatre for such a cause we must
> suppress all smaller passions and local considerations.

The genius of Thomas Jefferson's statement lies in the
eager generality with which he gave expression to the
American dream, and in his wise and prophetic identification of the forces against which American democracy must
contend. If he were to return to the scene of his labors
today he would find that those with "smaller passions and
local considerations" had, in important areas of public
concern, diverted America from the main purpose of its
experiment.

Early in the nineteenth century most Americans were sensitive to the future of America. It motivated and activated men in the practical shifts of everyday life; it restrained extreme action, encumbered with self-imposed responsibility, united idealism and practicality; and mediated between cooperation and individualism. The American of the early years had an identity that was readily articulated in terms other than physical existence in a geographical location. As America came of age the dream was lost. It was dissipated in the extremes of vaporous idealism and self-interested practicality. The former was expressed by the baccalaureate sermon and Fourth of July oratory, the latter by the impassioned plea for economic license in the name of free enterprise and freedom from restraint.

During the twentieth century, American civilization has become a primary scholarly preoccupation. Judicious critics have been too few and those less restrained have invariably been predisposed to indict. George Santayana considered his stay in America as a time of "camping in the desert"; Harold Stearns, after editing *Civilization in the United States* (1922), suggested that the wise thing for young men to do was to leave; and today, with humorous cynicism, Jules Feiffer chides us for pompous banalities.

These are the expressions of an American intelligentsia whose judgments are apt to be the products of selective perception rather than any inclusive insight. The critic does not write, as on a balance sheet, scrupulously compensating each vice with a corresponding virtue, nor should he. The counter argument should come naturally from those with differing views. But we have "viewed with alarm" far more often than we have "pointed with pride." It is not surprising that our generation is burdened with a pervasive sense of gloom. Futility seems characteristic of our age and in our day, far more than in Thoreau's, "the mass of men lead lives of quiet desperation."

Although the relation between critical appraisal and secular activity is tenuous, they are, in general terms, compatible. The attitudes, habits of thought, values, and normative response to these values cannot help but find expression in a literate minority who deplore the state of things. Thus we have convinced ourselves that the brawny virtues of frontier America and the delicate refinement of nineteenth century New England are quite beyond our reach; we are hell bound in a jet propelled market basket.

In 1918 Van Wyck Brooks spoke of the dream and the necessity of Young America:

> To live creatively, to live completely, to live in behalf of some great corporate purpose—that is its desire. A national faith we had once, a national dream, the dream of the "great American experiment." But if it had not been sadly compromised, would the younger generation find itself adrift as it is today?[1]

A good many volumes have been written in agonized reappraisal of education for another younger generation since World War II. It has failed, we are told, in both descriptive and analytical areas. Little, as yet, has been said of the failure in attitudinal education. That we have failed to communicate the best of our culture from one generation to another is self-evident. That our generation and the coming one hold attitudes inimical to the democratic process we profess to cherish is equally evident. And that we have difficulty reconciling the content of the Declaration with the extension of citizenship to minority groups is amply illustrated by the continuing crisis over civil rights. Indeed the Declaration itself is often considered a museum piece, the charming memento of a glorious past.

In 1958 the National Council for the Social Studies published a report, submitted by the Committee on Concepts and Values, which has since been widely circulated among educators. Its opening statement sets forth a sweeping and ambitious rationale for social studies:

> The most inclusive aim of social studies as a part of general education in the United States is to help young people learn to carry on the free society they have inherited, to make whatever changes modern conditions demand or creative imagination suggests that are consistent with its basic principles or values, and to hand it on to their offspring better than they received.[2]

This mission appears to be sufficient reason for the social studies to occupy a major sector of school curricula and to account for a significant portion of the college students' general education requirements. But when we reflect that the major instrument used to pursue this aim is the American history course it becomes evident that the goal is a promise to the ear, to be broken to the hope.

If we have failed to transmit an American tradition it follows that we have failed to fulfill the stated goals of the American history course. History, as a subject, is the *one* institutionalized and relatively uniform source of knowledge about America to which most students are exposed. We have had the uneasy feeling for many years that a familiarity with history is not readily distilled by magical process to an essence that it is the *geist* of America. Recent evidence confirms our suspicions. Our Peace Corps volunteers must be introduced to the realm of American Studies before going overseas as casual diplomats, Americans traveling in foreign lands have invariably been mines of misinformation, and the most insightful commentaries on the American scene, from Tocqueville to Myrdal, have come from the pens of foreigners.

History, enjoying traditional sanction in American education, has long been used as the key to the transmission of our culture from one generation to another. (Historians disagree with this usage but unfortunately cannot control their product once it is on the market.) For all the genius of Wertenbaker, Perry, Turner, Beard, Commager, Nevins, Hofstadter, or Schlesinger, their product, when translated for classroom use, is like a condensation of a great novel: the plot remains but the richness and density is gone. Students march reluctantly several times across the plains of America during their formative years but there is little evidence that they are impressed by the experience.

As Martin Mayer pointed out in a recent work on social studies, the American history course doesn't work:

> At best, the result is a vague flow essentially homogeneous with recognized raisins, the knowledge of a few dates and a few names. There is almost no feeling of the texture of life as Americans have lived it, or of the residue of history lying all around.[3]

American history suffers from a conventionality of both content and structure that inhibits its ability to describe reality or to enable the student to reconstruct vicariously events of the past. The pedantry for facts placed in precise chronology has also established a reputation for being dull and colorless. But the failure of history to fulfill our hopes is only one aspect of the problem. A capsule presentation of any great pageant is inherently misleading. We have misled generations of students with the notion that our history obeys the Aristotelian rule in having a beginning, a middle, and an end. Rather than being a continuum (which it is), history comes in chunks, neatly packaged and labeled. When, at the end of the term, the student arrives at the present, the tale ends. The present is something else again and our future, if the student is sensitive to it at all, seems in no way related to what came before.

Apart from the absence of a "sense of history" in the

survey course, the raisins in the dough, those chunks set aside for special treatment, lead the student toward sweeping normative conclusions based on partial evidence. Young people, being prone to think in terms of "good guys" and "bad guys," tend to classify neatly the men and movements of American life. Examples of a "little learning" are presently held notions of students who have drunk none too deeply from the Pierian spring: Jefferson, aside from being identified with the Declaration, usually comes off as something of a hypocrite because he professed to be a "strict constructionist" but afterwards purchased Louisiana. (We call Prometheus a thief.) Jackson is best known for the institution of the "spoils system" which suggests (out of context) government-by-crony. (Not only is this misleading but we also miss the opportunity to illustrate one of the great accomplishments of American democracy: that of peaceful succession and the establishment of the concept of "loyal opposition.") Lincoln remains a benign, homey wit; Grant is a great general and only on second thought identified with the Presidency; Theodore Roosevelt is identified by physical appearance only; FDR is whatever Dad says he is. And so it goes, entertaining in spots but no more relevant than the garrulous reminiscences of an older generation.

When we reflect on our expectation that all citizens of our country understand and agree on the essence of the American experience it becomes evident that we are asking too much of the discipline of history. Unless a program of studies is functionally related to being alive in the twentieth century, in the United States and in the world, there seems little justification for its continued existence as part of general education.

Thus we have fallen prey to a phenomenon which might be dubbed the historical fallacy. In general terms it is this: that a civilization may be understood, appreciated, and propagated by means of the study of its history; that cultural values are implicit in history and are therefore susceptible to being taught via the vehicle of history; and finally, that functional participation in a culture is readily achieved through the study of its history.

The fallacy was not foisted off on American education. It emerged from a set of circumstances peculiar to our national life, an educational lag, as it were. The advancement of learning is not often pursued with an eye to its relevance for general education. Understandably, the scholar, with singleness of purpose, pursues his design without regard for the practical relevance of his studies. On the other hand, educators are hesitant to stray too far from the reservoir of accepted ideas. By the nature of their calling they reinforce the "conventional wisdom" with which the pioneers on the frontiers of every scholarly field must everlastingly do battle. The dissociation of productive scholarship from the more conservative concerns of schools and colleges has always haunted the institution of American education.

This is certainly not to suggest that history be disestablished as a course or to deprecate its value as an academic discipline. It is rather to point out that history is an insufficient instrument to achieve the purposes we proclaim for it. Most historians are highly sensitive to the limitations of history. Indeed, the term "universe of discourse" implies boundaries and therefore limits of both scope and purpose. To suggest to many historians that the purpose of their discipline is to transmit values is to invite argument. History is, by most definitions, morally neutral: but the uses of history in the schools and colleges are highly subjective. When we speak of what *ought* to be taught or what values young Americans *ought* to hold we have both feet in the realm of normative ethics. Beard's *mot* that "history is a damned dim candle over a damned dark abyss" was insightful. We are indeed posed on the brink of a dark abyss and reliance on history alone to save us is hazardous.

Each generation of young Americans begins anew to develop values and perspectives that are often drastically different from the ones held by preceding generations. It seems to be characteristic of American civilization to develop new and unique attitudes toward not only our political, social, and economic institutions but toward the premises underpinning them. We have mislaid our transcendent ideal.

Young America today seems both egocentric and ethnocentric. In the twentieth century when the exigencies of both domestic and international events demand, more than ever, a politically literate and socially liberal population, the cumulative effect of our failure to communicate the best of our civilization is being felt. An understanding of that which is peculiarly precious about America is needed to give direction and purpose to national endeavor and to involve the individual citizen in it.

Attitudes commonly held by Americans which are inimical to the democratic process we profess to revere are numerous. Outstanding illustrations are: a generalized suspicion of the role of government (The government is considered remote, alien to the society, and so complex as to be incomprehensible. There is, it is thought, no hope of effective individual participation.); an ethnocentricity which is the well spring of hostility toward international institutions for the resolution of conflict, such as the United Nations Organization; a provincial attitude which views all foreign aid as idealistic folly; an attitude which holds material affluence to be the measure of all things, and so on, *ad infinitum.*

There is strikingly singular agreement among teachers of history, scholars, and administrators that something must be done. Curriculum revision is in the air. *Social Education* is moved to devote an issue to a symposium on revision in the social studies and another to American Studies and the social studies; the American Political Science Association, the Association of American Anthropologists, the American Historical Association, the Association of American Geographers, represent just some of the disciplinary interests in curricular reorganization; the U. S. Office of Education under "Project Social Studies" and the private foundations as well, stand ready with millions to endow projects and research which seem likely to "do something." The result thus far has been the expenditure of tremendous energy in incoordinate activity. The "interdisciplinary course," "area studies," "non-western culture," "cross cultural studies," and "honors sections" are familiar phrases which illustrate the variety of concern.

At present there is a conviction on the part of educators, university faculty, and the general public that a viable program of liberal education must incorporate forms of instruction which transcend the scope and purpose of the social science disciplines. The accelerated growth of general education is itself evidence of the conviction that instruction must have a philosophical dimension if we are to overcome the cultural parochialism that is considered the residue of specialization.

The problem of revision in the area of things American is particularly knotty. In Galbraith's apt phrase, the American history course is part of the "conventional wisdom." In an area where familiarity is the measure of acceptability, history is acceptable indeed and has, therefore, great stability as an institution. If we can be guided by previous experience, major and revolutionary revision is patently impossible. The number of vested interests that abound in any school or university system preclude rapid change. To quote a current truism, "Changing curricula is like moving a graveyard, you just can't do it."

The last courageous foray by discipline scholars into the realm of education took place during the years following 1929 when the American Historical Association's Commission on the Social Studies was launched. An impressive galaxy including such stars as Charles Beard, George Counts, Avery Craven, Henry Johnson, and Charles Merriam labored between 1929 and 1937 to produce a highly valuable fifteen volume report. In the storm that followed the report was pecked to death largely on the grounds that it used unfortunate terms such as "collectivist" and "social order." Since that time the scholar has had negligible influence on the tendencies of general education.

Educational institutions are highly visible. As such they are at the mercy of the sensitive taxpayers or equally sensitive alumni for financing, the state legislators for direction, lay boards for local policy, and administrators for curricular establishment. Public relations and budgetary matters have become the primary concern of the administrator and change, as in politics, becomes the "art of the possible." No more hopeful is the variety of committees and commissions initiated by scholarly professional organizations which seek to establish courses and units of study, or to furnish materials aimed at establishing the relevance of their academic disciplines in the curricula. The inherent insufficiency of history as a discipline is shared by the other social science disciplines. By definition, they are ethically neutral and do not, separately, speak to basic principles and values of American society except to explain them by tracing them to their causes. They are not competent to answer questions of value. They furnish accurate and descriptive information which is, in the final analysis, only the raw material with which to illuminate the culture and lead students toward functional participation in it. American education needs gifted generalists much more than patriots of a discipline.

What I suggest is that the approach be that of American Studies rather than American history. Since history is an integral part of American Studies, it would be relatively easy (considering the alternatives) to establish such courses as "Backgrounds of American Civilization," "American Institutions," "American Culture and Values," and "America and the Community of Nations." Such courses would utilize illustrative materials from American history and the humanities within a conceptual frame that embraces the relevant ideas of economics, geography, political science, literature, and sociology, thus combining the best of scholarship from both the social sciences and the humanities. To insinuate into the existing patterns the approaches, insights, ways of working, and perspectives of Ameircan Studies would be to reconcile the promise and the hope. This implies abandonment of the "then and now" approach. Chronology would become a simple literary device to place in time and space the great event, the significant turning point, and the influential personality or idea. It also calls forth the courage to exclude. This process is like cleaning an attic. It is necessary to bite one's lip and ruthlessly discard that which is of no consequence, for there is a good salting of the sentimental antiquarian in each of us. We frequently finish with a more tidy attic but with little additional usable room.

The necessary first step is essential agreement on what we are about. This might be a list of expectations in the form of attitudes, values, and concepts derived from the social sciences, history, and the humanities which has been composed by representatives from all these. The next step, and that which gives substance to such an approach, is the logical insinuation of these concepts into the materials: historical, literary, and socio-scientific, of the American experience. The goals determine the selection of materials. The attic cleans itself. Jackson is put to work for economics and political science, the Supreme Court emerges from the shadows, Puritanism moves from Massachusetts Bay to be recognized as an instrumental force in modern America, geography and literature team up to explain the fact and influence of the Great Plains, and the student is introduced to the pleasures of discovery.

1. Van Wyck Brooks, *Letters and Leadership* (New York: Viking Press, 1918), p. 33.
2. National Council for the Social Studies, *A Guide to Content in the Social Studies* (Washington, 1958), p. 1.
3. Martin Mayer, *Where, When, and Why: Social Studies in American Schools* (New York: Harper & Row, 1963), pp. 42 f.

Principled Opportunism and American Studies

HENRY WASSER

HENRY WASSER is Associate Professor of English at the City College of New York. He has been Fulbright Visiting Professor in Greece and Norway, and an active participant in American Studies programs on both sides of the Atlantic. Author of *The Scientific Thought of Henry Adams* (1956), he is currently continuing his research on that distinguished New England family.

AMERICAN STUDIES OFTEN HAS THE APPEARANCE OF SIX disciplines in search of a methodology. The quest has been long and not particularly successful; yet it must continue. American Studies as a viable curriculum will remain vulnerable so long as no dominant method is found.

Experienced scholars have proposed different solutions which have meaning in their particular studies. Henry Nash Smith's *Mark Twain: The Development of a Writer*, for example, as a demonstration of "the interaction between his ideas and attitudes, and the culture that shaped them" is a logical outgrowth of Smith's conviction.[1] Professor Smith is not satisfied with a methodology derived from the social sciences, nor with one from current literary criticism. He complains that the social sciences assume too hastily that all value is implicit in social experience—in group behavior, institutions, or man as an average member of society. Disregarding the exceptional they fail to consider the more complex social values inherent in such a mine of social interpretation as a work of art. He believes that contemporary literary criticism postulates that the values in works of art are outside of society, beyond actual experience. Both approaches, sociological and literary critical, make important findings; neither by itself provides an adequate introduction to the study of our culture as a whole. The aim of studying the *total* culture is at the heart of American Studies. It is justified by the nature, if not uniqueness, of that culture.

In the light of these strictures, what discipline can provide a relevant methodology? Cultural anthropology, often suggested, does not satisfy this want fully because facts are considered more important than values; it is more apt to compare than to coordinate. Some historians would write off the search, saying that American culture should be viewed as cultural history and American Studies as intellectual history. This merely summons forth arguments as to what history is. As the substantive word, history is decidedly limited and narrowing when the scholar weighs the culture or civilization as a whole. Further, history precludes the close analysis of contemporary culture.

The intellectual historian John Higham suggests a partnership between American intellectual history and American Studies, maintaining that the "unequal partnership between intellectual history and a presumably inclusive interest in American civilization will not endure unless intellectual history stays very loose indeed," and that "great historians . . . also need fine control." The combination of looseness and control which Higham sees as essential to intellectual history is even more necessary for American Studies with its substantially greater scope. And the discipline which provides the best clues as to how this might be effected is physics.

"Looseness" and "control" are words for what scientists

might call holoscopic and microscopic observations, total
and fragmentary perceptions, absolute and empiric approaches; and what philosophers might call reason and
nature, unity and multiplicity. Not exactly equivalent, such
terms do express a sense of opposing ways of looking at
data. These polarities might be yoked together in the
complementary harness which would keep the investigation
of American culture moving.

When Smith writes of the limitations of current literary
criticism, he refers primarily to the New Critics' exclusive
concentration on the literary work, with little consideration
of historical or other context. I would also bring into account a group of writers whose most articulate spokesman
is Lionel Trilling—the culture critics.[2] Occasionally they
are dismissed as "Matthew Arnold adjusted to our time."
The Trilling approach is ideological and aggressive in be-
half of a particular analysis which might best be characterized as the operation of the "liberal imagination."
Trilling speaks for an intellectualized segment of a middle
class whose liberal political attitudes have been disillusioned
by current reality. This group, found primarily in the
metropolitan university and the publishing and periodical
world, is more interested in the politics of culture than in
its analysis; more concerned with contemporary implications than with scholarly interpretation. Proper conditioning involves a passing acquaintance with Marx; a deeper
knowledge of Freud; a certain disdain for Max Lerner from
whose simplified (even Philistine) version of their politics
of culture they find it increasingly difficult to disengage;
considerable respect for John Stuart Mill, Henry James,
and especially Matthew Arnold. Although their critiques
are angled from the approach of a clerisy, they scarcely
concede a distinct American culture. Rather, they think
that for a variety of reasons, particularly the locus of power,
Arnold's burden has to be borne in America.

Accepting neither the attack on the culture of humanism by C. P. Snow nor the strictures against the culture of science by F. R. Leavis, they reduce the Snow-Leavis conflict to an instance of bad manners.[3] Finding themselves able to have both Snow and Leavis, they declare that their goals are similar—they too are culture critics of proper moral objectives. This reconciliation, however, does not make necessary close study of what science has been up to; nor does it prompt spelling out what the moral view of culture means.

My major criticism of these "culture critics" is that they reflect the view of a particular middle class culture. If they analyzed American society solely from the vision of the intellectual, a case could be made that such a vantage point brings important perceptions of all American culture. These critics remain, therefore, quasi-intellectuals, interested in maintaining one way of life and in cultivating one kind of sensibility. Consequently they do not attempt to analyze American culture as a whole.

Henry Nash Smith's conclusions permit by extension the formulation of an effective method. He is cautious in conceiving of American Studies as a collaboration among scholars working from within existing academic disciplines but attempting to extend the boundaries imposed by conventional means of inquiry. Students in one discipline would have to make a sustained effort to take account of the others. The scholar of literature would have to weigh carefully sociological, historical and anthropological data and the methods of scholarship in the arts. Thus knowledge would converge on a single topic in American culture past and present.

Although Smith does not give the formal development to his suggestion that warrants calling it a method, this synthesis will have to come piecemeal through a kind of principled opportunism in the daily struggle with various tasks of scholars of American culture. Smith doubts that any one man will be able to redesign the whole enterprise; others hopefully call for the energies and drive of another Frederick J. Turner or V. L. Parrington. As it is probably no longer possible for anyone to survey the field synoptically, the image or model of investigation assumes great significance. Cooperative endeavor can accomplish what one student can no longer do. This cooperation implicit in the construction of the model would resemble that of the scientists. Such a model would consequently influence a long series of particular decisions. It would determine a tendency over a period of time rather than create a new apparatus all at once.

To the social sciences such a mode of investigation may seem of limited value. Specific individual cases would most often be studied since they are usually the result of specifically literary and historical inquiry. But, as Smith asserts, exhaustive analysis or knowledge of a work of art, a particular situation, a problem, or a career may lead to the recognition of aspects which have previously escaped attention. Smith's own interpretation of Mark Twain in terms of a conflict between vernacular perspective and the dominant "genteel" culture has illuminated the complexity of American culture patterns. The literary masterpiece or the exceptionally productive career, Smith concludes, will often turn out to be an expression of the culture in ways beyond the scope of stereotyped examples of the popular, or of an assembly of average life case histories.

Smith's analysis breaks down some barriers erected in previous attempts to find a dominant methodology in American Studies. We might move forward with a flexible epistemology derived from the experience of science, especially physics. The generalized method is an adaptation of the principle of complementarity which has taken on major importance in the contemporary scientific revolution.

John Von Neuman's explanation is lucid.[4] Sciences, he writes, do not try to explain or even interpret: they make models which must correctly describe phenomena and must be simple. "Simplicity is largely a matter of historical background of previous conditioning, of antecedents, of customary procedures and it is very much a function of what is explained by it." The more that has already been explained, the more complicated the model that is acceptable. When only a little has been explained, the model must be very simple and direct. In illustration we may cite Henry Adams. Finding history only partially explained, he set up a model of thirteenth century unity and twentieth century multiplicity with the intervening events seen as the results of motion from controlled unified energy to unrestrained multiple energies. The frontier thesis of Frederick Jackson Turner may also be seen as effectively simple in the light of only a few previous attempts to generalize American history.

Newtonian mechanics, Von Neuman continues, may be both teleological and causal (a complementary relationship). Teleological would mean that by a single optimization or a single maximization the total history between two points in time is determined. In other words a complete historical evolution is developed in a single act by a simple insertion between the known points at the beginning and at the end. Thus Henry Adams in his *History of the United States* seeing the design of American society in the 1870's and 80's studied the data of the early 1800's that went into the making of that design (teleological). The state of the nation being implicit in his mind at the time of writing, he turned to the earlier time of the development and the tempering of the nation to discuss the relation of cause and effect. From the known effects he sought the causes. Causally or in causal theory evolution is developed, progressing from the beginning forward in time. This is the mode of Henry Adams' analysis in his article on "The New York Gold Conspiracy." In it he proceeded chronologically, relating antecedent and immediate consequence in series by which the whole story was told. Relating this analysis to William Faulkner, we see his attitude toward Southern life causally—Faulkner is both an effect and a cause of Southern sensibility—and teleologically for his overriding goal is understanding human nature into which his revelation of Southern sensibility is a partial insight.

The causal and teleological procedures are usually seen as mutually exclusive, as highly antithetical; but in science, Von Neuman declares, it is important and characteristic that there need not be any meaningful difference between these two descriptions. Classical mechanics possesses two absolutely equivalent ways of stating the same theory: one is causal and the other teleological. Both describe the same thing, Newtonian mechanics. Newton's description is causal and d'Alembert's is teleological. All the difference between the two is a purely mathematical transformation. In Professor Von Neuman's words: "In principle such a transformation is no more profound than choosing to say four instead of saying two times two." By mathematical manipulation each of these two ways gives exactly the same results as the other. Things that appear to represent important differences of principle and of interpretation, in this fashion, may be shown not to affect any significant statements and predictions. The lesson of this could be that what are assumed to be roughly antithetical approaches, say the sociological and the literary, may be simply describing data in different ways which do not affect significant statements about American culture and predictions of cultural trends.

A similar situation takes place in quantum mechanics—for example, in that part of the theory which concerns the electronic shells of the atoms. There are two important differing descriptions: Schrodinger's which describes them by an analogue with optics and Heisenberg's which describes them in completely probabalistic terms. The taste among contemporary physicists is for the statistical description, but ultimately the motive for choosing one or the other attitude will be the hope of finding through it a better heuristic guidance which becomes a matter of finding correct formal extensions of the existing theory: of discovering the variant which points the way to explaining wider areas with greater power. The decision will, moreover, likely be opportunistic in the end, for that theory is accepted which shows greater formal adaptability for a correct extension.[5] This is a formalistic, esthetic criterion with a distinct opportunistic flavor.

Applying Von Neuman's version of the method of science to the work of Faulkner, one may construct the following specialized hypothesis. Analyzing Faulkner's enduring Negroes and unmodified aristocrats as a study in sentimentality, one may postulate that Faulkner's sentimentality mirrors a similar, perhaps less altruistic, sentimentality in Southern culture. Sociological study, multiplication of case histories, depth interviews may likely give a rather different profile of Southern Negroes and landowners of the period he writes about. However, this sociological view is not necessarily more true than Faulkner's sentimental one. His sentimentality raised to the level of art quite possibly is a truthful reflection of Southern sensibility which in turn colors and influences data. The point is that Faulkner's artistic representation may contrast with both the historical and sociological but still be neither more nor less true than they are. The complementarity provides the approach that can accept both views emphasizing or giving more weight to the one that explains more.

To follow Von Neuman's suggestion that science makes models which by themselves do not interpret or explain, we may visualize the holoscopic scholar creating a model which encompasses the literary and the sociological approaches and whose mechanism would permit exhaustive description. This model incorporating different approaches to American Studies would change, expanding or contracting, to fit the new data uncovered. Physics does not remain inflexibly committed to one theory. The complementary method expediently responds to the changing set of circumstances. It is always ready to shape a new or transcending theory. This scientific flexibility which Von Neuman calls opportunistic is most advantageous to an interdisciplinary culture study where no single discipline or method has yet become rigidly regnant.

Niels Bohr has elaborated the principle.[6] He believes two approaches to be complementary if they serve to fill out or complete; if they mutually supply each other's lacks; or if they differ from each other in the sense that the more we make use of the one the less we use the other. An illustration of the last definition is K. R. Popper's example of the relationship between political power and sociological knowledge. Power is relatively simple to centralize, but knowledge whose centralization is necessary for the wise use of centralized power is almost impossible to centralize. Unable to ascertain what is in the minds of many individuals (social knowledge), the wielder of power must try to control and standardize interests and beliefs by education and propaganda. However, the attempt to exercise power over minds will destroy the last possibility of discovering what people really think because it is not compatible with the free expression of critical thought. "Ultimately it must destroy knowledge; and the greater the gain in power, the greater will be the loss of knowledge." Thus political power and social knowledge would be complementary in the third sense of Bohr's definition.

Phrasing his definition philosophically Bohr asserts that in the complementary description of quantum physics a further self-consistent generalization is achieved which permits encompassing regularities decisive for the account of fundamental properties of matter but which transcends the scope of deterministic description. The history of physical science is a demonstration of "how the exploration of ever-wider fields of experience, in revealing unsuspected limitations of accustomed ideas, indicates new ways of restoring logical order."[7]

Bohr holds that this epistemological lesson contained in the development of atomic physics is a reminder of similar problems of description and interpretation outside the borders of physical science. In biological research, we find that arguments are based on the full resources of physical and chemical science. They are centered on concepts directly referring to the integrity of the organism and clearly transcending the scope of these sciences—a characteristically complementary relationship. Further, the content of our mind can be complementarily described as conscious experiences and as physical observations. Conscious refers to experience capable of being retained in the memory, like the permanent recordings of atomic phenomena. In this analogy the vagueness inherent in the idea of the subconscious is equivalent to the impossibility of pictorial interpretation of the quantum mechanical formalism.

Bohr also finds possibilities of complementarity in the free will vs. determinism controversy in that the potency of organisms to adjust themselves to environment includes the power of selecting the most appropriate way to make the adjustment. The balance between seriousness and humor in all great works of art may be a complementary instance. Moreover in ". . . the organization of human societies, the description of the position of the individual within the community to which he belongs presents typically complementary aspects related to the shifting separation between the appreciation of values and the background on which they are judged," for "in searching for harmony in human life on the scene of existence we are ourselves actors as well as spectators." Even the relationships between national cultures may be pictured as complementary, although it must be remembered that contact between nations may result in a fusion of cultures, a circumstance somewhat different from complementary descriptions in atomic physics or psychological analyses where invariable or constant characteristics of our situation are dealt with. But any disharmony can only be removed complementarily by an appropriate widening of the conceptual framework.

Perhaps the outlines of what I propose for scholarly investigation of American culture are now coming clear. Conceding that the hard forms of an approach are derived from the experience of those working on cultural topics, whether a problem or a single career, I hold that the hypothesis of complementary relationship promises much for future scholarly study. In this relationship the scholar realizes that there are different but equally or nearly equally valuable approaches. Often in the manner of physics one view does not dominate another but rather explains the same set of phenomena of facts in different ways reaching different conclusions. One approach may supersede another by explaining more. Here the differing disciplines involved in American Studies are each utilized—here at the juncture of the tracks of the sociological, the literary critical, the psychological, the philosophical, the economic, the historical a series of insights are provided. With this hypothesis the whole of American culture is grasped.

A variety of attacks on the problems of American Studies has been attempted with important but limited consequences. "Virgin Land," "Garden of Eden," and "American Adam" are vivid concepts skillfully employed by scholars to show the effective operation of myth in our history, but such studies have given a rather lopsided, distorted view of the complete motion of American society. Similarly scholarly investigations productive within their narrow perspective like those employing the depth interview or an analysis of contextual background, political or economic, do not paint a complete picture. Frequency tests—kinds and numbers of metaphors in a literary text of a certain period—although of some value in heuristic guidance to the culture of the place and time, because of the overwhelming number of statistics collected, rule out the possibility of making relevant generalizations. In like fashion while the Cultural Area file technique has assembled considerable quantities of data for future inductive studies, too often both the compiler and the potential user are swamped by the material. Somewhat wider in scope although still not satisfactory for the over-all look are the psychological analyses showing the broader psychological patterns of society and the "covert culture" search uncovering the hidden assumptions of society. Only slightly larger in perspective are the vision of a cultural dialogue in literary history between intrinsic (all literary values are intrinsic to the work of art) and extrinsic critics (extrinsic values are demanded by continuity in literary expression) and the history of ideas technique (the method of tracing controlling ideas in history). In the first instance an artificial polarizing results; in the second a more or less arbitrary selection of examples of outstanding men and books takes place with both schemes being finally narrowing. The formulation of these praiseworthy but fragmentary approaches simply emphasizes that the effort to comprehend the totality of American culture must be basic to the concept of American Studies.

Considering as a final illustration scholarship concerning Henry Adams, we note that while these studies give necessarily only partial glimpses of American culture, no one has apparently studied all of them with the idea of under-standing as much of the totality of American culture as can be seen through one key figure. No one has judged these studies opportunistically as to which explains more. The complementarity principle is the guiding hypothesis to such a complete view. Whatever the initiatory motive of the various studies, they all "get at" the problem, even if unconsciously, and when these investigations are looked at together, they appear as steps made in the right direction. Moreover, a self-conscious view of cooperation by these different scholars would produce the profit that such co-operation with the objective of comprehending totality constantly in mind has brought to the sciences.

Consequently a coordination of narrow angled studies of major figures, wider angled studies of lesser persons, and different angled studies of the problems and motifs of cul-ture would result in establishing a self-consistent general-ized approach to American Studies. Scholars would attain the shock of recognition that their piece-meal specialized activity has all the while been in the direction of compre-hending American culture. Further, in accord with the tentative approach to American Studies I have outlined, they would adhere to the dictum of science that a theory is corroborated only if refuting facts, which must be searched for, are not found rather than if supporting facts, which are relatively easy to discover, are detected. They would note that it is the public character and the coopera-tive nature of science and its institutions which impose a mental discipline upon the individual scientist and which preserve the objectivity of science and its tradition of critically discussing new ideas.

We need not go so far as Gustave Lanson in declaring that the most important problems of literary history are sociological problems and that the only way to explain literary works is to resolve individual facts into social facts through replacing works and men into social series. This reduction of literary history to sociology is extreme; more meaningfully, literature can at one and the same time be seen as intrinsic (aesthetic) and extrinsic (sociological). Goethe asserted that great works are often dictated by circumstance, and Henri Peyre has elaborated this axiom by pointing out that the creative energy of a writer may be first unleashed by the coincidental request of a publisher, the obtuseness or insight of a review editor, the awareness on the author's part of a potential need in his audience which he wants to satisfy or modify or even contradict. Both the varying circumstantial conditionings and the double vision of the inner, self-sustaining analysis of the literary work of art and the outer, external determination of it may be perceived complementarily.

The continuing discussion and testing of methodologies proposed for investigating American culture and the necessary cooperation involved in realizing that these approaches are fragmentary interpretations are then in a sense scientific. The problem of American culture comes first and determines an interest in data of a certain kind and subsequently such data are collected. The attack on the fortress of American culture will, I believe, in the end be successful. But it should not be forgotten that the approaches must be skillfully utilized and effectively manned. Where such scholars will come from I cannot predict. With analogies, illustrations and generalizations inspired by the complementarity principle, they may grasp the whole of American culture and thus maintain the vigor of American Studies.

1. See Smith's *Mark Twain: The Development of a Writer* (Cambridge, Mass.: Harvard Univ. Press, 1962); *Virgin Land: The American West as Symbol and Myth* (Cambridge, Mass.: Harvard Univ., 1950); and "Can 'American Studies' Develop a Method?" in *American Quarterly*, Summer 1962, pp. 197-208.
2. Professor Trilling's views are summed up in *The Liberal*

Imagination (New York: Viking Press, 1951) and *The Opposing Self* (New York: Viking Press, 1955).

3. See especially Lionel Trilling's article "Science, Literature, and Culture: The Leavis-Snow Controversy," in *Commentary*, June 1962, pp. 461-77.

4. John Von Neuman, "Method in the Physical Sciences," in *The Unity of Knowledge,* ed. Lewis Leary (New York: Doubleday, 1955).

5. Opportunism in the sense of the abandonment of rigid theory to adjust more fittingly to newly uncovered data is significant in the development of modern science; this adjustment, however, is generally within the framework of the existing form or *gestalt*.

6. Niels Bohr, "Science and the Unity of Knowledge," in *The Unity of Knowledge,* ed. Lewis Leary, *op. cit.*

7. *Ibid.,* p. 54.

"ATL" at Michigan State: A Case Study

JOHN J. APPEL

JOHN J. APPEL, an Assistant Professor of American Thought and Language at Michigan State University, East Lansing, specializes in historiography and immigrant history. His work has appeared in *New England Quarterly, Pennsylvania Magazine of History and Biography, American Speech, Jewish Social Studies, Mississippi Quarterly, American-German Review* and similar journals.

"ATL," THE STUDENTS' HANDY TAG FOR THE COURSE KNOWN officially as American Thought and Language at Michigan State University in East Lansing, is a first year course given since 1959 by the University College of the oldest land grant school in the United States. Unlike the other ten divisions of the university which mainly devote themselves to instruction in the vocational specialties for which American universities are noted—and notorious—University College is concerned only with teaching four, year-long, required courses meant to give all students, regardless of vocational goals, a common general education, which is to say the old liberal arts in updated guise.

Along with American Thought and Language is a Natural Science course, another in Social Science and one in Humanities. For seniors who wish to enroll, the college also offers a one-term "Great Issues" program.

According to a brochure published by the Dean's office of University College, ATL has "three principal aims": improve the student's reading, improve his writing, and give him "a sense of the forces which have created American civilization." These aims are to be achieved, the brochure continues, by asking the learner to comprehend and analyze selected "American documents" grouped around "major themes and developments" in the nation's "social, political, economic, philosophical and literary" life and by requiring him to write about these ideas and his reactions to them.

University course descriptions, like Burpee's annual seed catalogues, are meant to inspire as well as to inform. And since the creation of new courses and new names for old ones is a game all colleges like to play, a close look at ATL and its evolution is warranted. First of all, it is a maverick among American Studies programs because, first, it evolved from and has in effect displaced a "skills" course of the traditional freshman English composition variety. Second, because it is one of those American Studies programs singled out by Robert H. Walker in his 1954-55 survey for the American Studies Association as among the least well known because those in charge carry them on "so unselfconsciously" or "consistently subservient to some separate purpose" that they have no particular desire to have their work tagged as "American Studies."

The history of the course begins in 1944. All students then enrolled in the University College took something called "Written and Spoken English." This course was administered by a separate department—the academic progenitor of the present department of American Thought and Language—with its own faculty, supplemented by teachers on loan from such other departments as English and Speech. Despite its place in the general education curriculum, the course was supposed to be a "practical, terminal, functional, service course," centered on "skills" rather than "content." It was meant to teach students *how* to speak and write well without caring too much *what* they talked or wrote about. The full time faculty teaching this course increased from half a dozen in 1944 to about forty-five six years later. In 1952, the department name was changed to "Communication Skills" and the head of the department reiterated the "service function" of the course in a bulletin announcing the new label.

In practice, it seems to have been clear to many—students, teachers, administrators—that the course was trying to do too much. In many classes, to be sure, students under competent teachers learned how to organize a paper and present an effective speech. In others the skills emphasis undoubtedly meant that too much time was spent on fundamentals that challenged neither students nor teachers to the hard thinking or "higher learning" associated with college work. The least able students tended to set the pace. Those who had never read a serious book outside of class, never entertained an adult idea, or whose mental quarters lacked the furniture for such entertainment, tended to hold back students whose mastery of an organized, demanding body of knowledge could be used as a yardstick of progress in learning.

"Skills courses" of this kind are today receiving long overdue critical attention, mainly because they cannot possibly achieve the aims set for them. Good teachers were not at all surprised when the latest comprehensive study of writing practices in American colleges pointed out that the practice and refinement of writing is, like the cultivation of good manners or democratic attitudes, the continuous and unavoidable responsibility of every teacher and every department. (Albert R. Kitzhaber, *Themes, Theories and Therapy, The Teaching of Writing in College* [New York: McGraw-Hill, 1963].) True, some professors may shirk this duty without fatal results for the student's education, but they should not do so thinking a single department or course can do their work for them. It is surprising that it took so long for someone to say, authoritatively, loudly and clearly that writing, speaking and thinking cannot be adequately taught in *any one* course. Since few in responsible positions were ready to announce this basic truth, "communication" courses were offered as a panacea for the patent illiteracy of many high school graduates admitted to our colleges. At Michigan State this mistaken notion came to be gradually recognized as such toward the end of the 1950's. With students referring to Communication Skills as a "mickey mouse" course, the administration decided that a thorough revamping was needed. Speech training was dropped and writing assignments increased. A chronologically organized collection of American "documents" including novels, poems, essays, short stories and plays as well as excerpts from diaries, speeches, letters and political papers, became the basis for study. Students were asked to own and consult a writer's handbook, but assignments were to be firmly anchored in the literary and historical study of selected American topics in American life.

The administrative steps taken to effect the reorganization of the course and the unavoidable frictions engendered by such a process are not here important. It is noteworthy, however, that neither the faculty committee working out the new course content nor the administrators, including the new chairman of the department, had any announced commitment to or, as far as I can discover, extensive knowledge of the American Studies approach. Yet the course as now given, including its present name, certainly has all the earmarks of American Studies.

Like the course from which it evolved, American Thought and Language runs for one academic year—three terms of ten weeks each with classes meeting four hours per week. Until last year, the course syllabus listed twelve topics—four each term—with readings in political, sociological, literary and historical documents suited to each. Beginning in the fall of 1963 it has been limited to a total of nine topics, three to a term. The charge of superficiality made against most "general education" courses is to some extent anticipated by a curriculum that allows almost a month for each of the following:

First Term
I   The Puritan Heritage
II   The Age of Reason
III The Frontier in American Life

Second Term
I   American Renaissance
II   The Emergence of Industrial America
III Literary Currents After the Civil War

Third Term
I   The Impact of Science
II   The Crisis of the Old Order
III An Age of Anxiety

Texts are a two-volume anthology of American political, sociological, religious and belletristic writings, the Student Syllabus and writer's guide already mentioned, and complete editions, two per term, of *The Crucible, Huckleberry Finn, Billy Budd, The Octopus, Babbitt,* and *The Grapes of Wrath.* Also, local bookstores report a steady sale of paperbound copies of supplementary readings recommended by teachers. More specifically, in studying "The Puritan Heritage," for example, students read excerpts from the journals of William Bradford and John Winthrop, selected stanzas from Wigglesworth's *The Day of Doom,* and a typical passage from Nathaniel Ward's justification of intolerance in his *Simple Cobbler of Aggawamm.* They are introduced to the writings and key ideas of the Mathers, sample Edward Taylor's poetry, read descriptions and pages of such New England heretics as the Quakers, Ann Hutchinson, Thomas Morton, Roger Williams. Thomas Morton is represented by a chapter from his *New English Canaan* and shown also as he appears in Hawthorne's "The Maypole of Merry Mount." Hawthorne's "The Grey Champion" is studied, as are selections from the writings of Jonathan Edwards along with William Ellery Channing's "Moral Argument Against Calvinism." Finally, Arthur Miller's *The Crucible* shows a socially engaged dramatist dealing provocatively in a play with early and continuing issues of American life. In addition to these assigned readings, the class is introduced through background lectures to the historical context of what they have read—e.g., the Protestant break with Rome, Calvin's theology, and the social implications of Anglican, Calvinistic and Congregational theology.

This is ambitious! Can the course do all this and still pay adequate attention to helping students improve their language abilities? The answer, undoubtedly, is that the gap between promise and performance is generally, though not always, quite wide.

A recent survey conducted by the department reveals that students agree fairly well on what the course does and does not achieve: a year of "ATL" helped them to read and analyze a variety of American writing, acquainted them with the ideas of some important thinkers, and introduced them to views of American society not found in their high school courses. Faculty members generally feel that this is a fair estimate of what the course does for the majority of students. Like the students, teachers recognize that the course ordinarily does not dramatically change students' writing habits. Indeed, there is no reason why anyone familiar with the results of college composition instruction should find this surprising.

Available studies, often duplicated but seldom implemented, show that unless an entire faculty cooperates in the endeavour to maintain writing standards, seniors will write less acceptably than will freshmen in the composition course. Further, even if instructors in a particular course could markedly increase the number of papers they are able to read and grade, students would still not write enough to change their writing habits decisively. Also, attention to significant subject matter tends to displace attention to language skills *per se*. At MIT the Department of Humanities, present successor to the departments of English and history, offers freshman and sophomore courses in which, as at MSU, original documents and "great books" are used as the basis for writing assignments. Just as at Michigan State, the subject matter tends to "take over" when taught by competent subject matter specialists. As one MIT professor remarked, writing instruction begins to "wither a little." The moral is plain: no solution for the problem of composition is in sight until it can be eliminated *as a subject* because *all* teachers in *all* subjects accept the obligation to recognize good writing and be critical of bad.

It follows that if Michigan State were to adopt the "open door" admissions policy of some state universities a course like American Thought and Language as now taught could hardly be offered successfully. True, the university does admit some students whose writing is very bad indeed, but these cannot enroll in American Thought and Language until they have successfully passed a non-credit course in Preparatory English. The failure rate among those of this group who ultimately are admitted to American Thought and Language is high. Even among students whose entrance tests show them ready for college work, low grades are common. In short, American Thought and Language is best suited for students who can benefit by instruction in writing but whose level of literacy is reasonably high before they arrive at the East Lansing campus.

By substituting attainable learning goals for the generally unattainable ones of the old "skills" approach, the department finds that students can deal responsibly with ideas which can be checked for accuracy and emphasis. Mastery of a body of material is of course no guarantee that a student can arrive at useful generalizations, but without such mastery he cannot write at length or convincingly about anything very substantial.

Because of the size of the ATL operation (five to six thousand students!), it is to some extent possible to group students by ability and use more than one method of instruction. "Standard" sections enroll twenty-five to thirty students while lecture sections may enroll over two hundred with student writing assigned to readers. Students scoring sufficiently high on entrance tests are invited to join honors classes where ideas are explored in greater depth. A few students each year are able to waive the course by special examination.

Makeup of the ATL faculty is interesting. Eight years ago about half were trained in English or American literature and roughly a third in speech, with most of the remainder holding degrees in education. Today, out of forty-seven permanent staff members (all save three or four holders of the Ph.D.), about half are trained in English and American literature, a fourth in speech, drama, and education, not quite a fifth in American Studies and four in history.

Teachers holding appointments in American Thought and Language teach three classes per term and have the same chances for promotion and pay as their colleagues in other parts of the university. Since, however, the man who teaches advanced and graduate classes stands first in pecking order of American higher education, it is not uncommon for teachers in ATL to long for a chance to teach such courses. As enrollments increase and the supply of qualified teachers grows comparatively smaller, more professors of American Thought and Language will doubtless find themselves on loan elsewhere in the univeresity or hold dual appointments in both "general" and more specialized departments.

Some teachers fret over continuous work with undergraduates. Others either honestly enjoy it or feel that teaching but the one course allows them more time to pursue research. The present chairman of the American Thought and Language department has described the ideal teacher for the course as having special competence "in some branch of American studies" and an "active concern with present developments on the American scene." He can "stir students to thought" and cares about the manner of its expression. More than one member of the American Thought and Language staff is convinced that as a "generalist" he is best equipped to meet students at a crucial stage in their development. For him, ATL is "a way of life" which enables him and his students to consider each term "living issues, significant problems, great ideas and values which have involved the best brains in America." Such enthusiasm is contagious.

The American Thought and Language staff is naturally aware of the course's shortcoming, among them large classes, student immaturity (would college seniors be better equipped to benefit from an American studies course than entering freshmen?) and lack of time to explain allusions and historical background. Among the most interesting efforts to overcome these disadvantages have been supplementary programs—i.e, showings of such pertinent movies as *Inherit the Wind* and *Citizen Kane*, television documentaries like *The Real West* and *Mark Twain's America*. Student response to these programs has been favorable. Occasionally, also, there are meetings of an American Studies Club and some members of the staff have prepared video-tapes utilizing fine and folk arts materials for closed circuit TV presentation.

To sum up, American Thought and Language at Michigan State University shows that American Studies have developed in the direction predicted by such men as Robert E. Spiller and the late Tremaine McDowell, associated with its beginnings as an academic movement. American studies, they said, would not become a new "field" or discipline of study and should, in fact, guard against doing so. Instead, they hoped American studies would justify themselves because they encouraged experimentation within the traditional curriculum and explorations across conventional subject matter boundaries. At its best, the product of the American studies orientation would be a more complex kind of intellectual history securely anchored to historical periods and environments, committed to no single method of approach and ready to try out any that promised worthwhile results.

By centering on American materials it was hoped that American Studies would help to overcome the common student attitude that humanities courses are lost in the past. Also, as Professor McDowell emphasized, the American studies point of view would make it easier to strike a balance between the "education in facts and the education in values" invariably named as one of the chief aims of liberal or general education.

Judged by these criteria, the American Thought and Language program at Michigan State University has been a worthwhile experiment of great interest. The course demonstrates, without making the point directly, the inadequacy of any one method or discipline to discover the truth in humanistic studies or for coming to terms with it. Students learn at the beginning of their college years what older and supposedly wiser heads sometimes forget—that neither history nor literature nor the social sciences provide final answers for most questions in life; but that literature and history, like other specialized approaches to knowledge, do furnish important clues for the exploration of reality. The course achieves, at least partially, one of the basic aims of American studies: to gather and bring into focus some closely related data of cultural history, including the ambiguous relationship between belles-lettres and the society with which they deal.

Conversely, those "Americanists" who are pleased to see a course like American Thought and Language validate their approach and point of view must admit there are weaknesses. Because the American studies devotee looks for a distinct pattern in American life, he is likely to find one, often by oversimplifying some of the contradictions of American experience. With freshmen especially, eager to master the "facts" and to know the "truth," even well informed teachers cannot always avoid distortions for the sake of being both clear and brief. Dramatic teaching methods engage even indifferent students but are not always the best vehicles for critical thought. The latest theory, unencumbered by qualifications, is more likely to convince the young than a carefully hedged statement of probabilities. Lastly, emphasis on American issues and American writings may convince all but the most sophisticated students that certain kinds of creative work and thought are reactions to uniquely American conditions.

There is simply not time to show international dimensions of certain issues, or how specialized art forms develop traditions of their own, or how class, regional and ethnic loyalties come into play elsewhere than in the American context. In this connection, the experience of teachers of American Thought and Language demonstrates the need, already recognized for the physical sciences, for greater articulation between college and high school. Students still come to our colleges "knowing" many things about American history that professional historians no longer believe or regard as significant. Social Studies courses leave high school graduates ignorant of the origins of American institutions and how "politics" really works, things basic for study of American literature and history. With high school and college teachers beginning in recent years to talk to each other, perhaps something can be done about agreeing on an appropriate sequence of studies for the high school graduate.

The expected increase in college enrollments will undoubtedly pose new problems for the general education programs of institutions unable or unwilling to resist the clamor of ever greater numbers of students for admission. Courses like American Thought and Language, required of all students during their freshman or sophomore years, will be among the first to be affected by larger classes, more students per teacher, greater reliance on depersonalized means of teaching like television, teaching machines, motion pictures, standardized tests and teaching assistants.

Such a trend need not spell *bad* teaching and learning, but it will certainly change some aspects of the student-teacher relationship valued most by students and teachers today. The teacher's "effectiveness" may indeed increase as measured by many administrators, which is to say the teacher will instruct more students for less money per head. Those who dislike plans for teacher's assistants, lay readers and discussion leaders will probably continue to shake their heads and wish for the good old days. For those interested in American studies, however, the trend should hold few terrors. It will surely mean experimentation with new teaching and learning procedures, new ways to organize the curriculum, and more openings for those with an advanced degree in American Studies.

This is not to say that the evolution of American Thought and Language described in these pages presages a trend toward undergraduate programs of its kind. Nevertheless, the course content and the methods of its organi-

zation show that the once rebellious slogans of the
Americanist are among the presently accepted principles
in American education. Though the strongest support in
higher education still goes to specialization, concern for
the liberal foundations of learning for all students is increasingly being translated into action at the level where
it counts—in the classroom. Where large numbers of students are involved, the difficulties of scheduling and staffing
such courses are formidable. The popularity of Great Books
programs, "core" curriculums, even "communication"
courses are other, perhaps somewhat naive efforts to educate millions without the needed numbers of teachers,
books and dollars. American Thought and Language, together with other University College courses at Michigan
State, is part of this trend to provide liberal education for
the "masses." As an incomplete but vigorous and ongoing
experiment it represents one significant application of
American studies methods. Insofar as it has departmental-
ized the "interdisciplinary" approach, it has gone perhaps
as far as it is possible to go.

An interdisciplinary label like American Studies is no
longer the sign it once was of rebellion and dissatisfaction
with things as they are. The incantation that a course is
interdisciplinary now invariably brings at least a sympathetic hearing and often money from foundation officials
and college administrators. Fortunately, the good sense
of most teachers and administrators will tell them that
courses which, like American Thought and Language,
combine a number of subjects and methods usually offered
in separate courses, are not the answer for the liberal education of students in every kind of institution. In fact, no
one at Michigan State asserts that University College
courses are invariably better for all undergraduates than
a carefully selected, integrated sequence of more conventional courses.

At small institutions, where contact with students is easier to maintain than at the large state university, a more flexible curriculum and a truly inter-departmental faculty rather than a separate department for beginning courses are probably more desirable than a required sequence of courses for all students. Those in charge at Michigan State are not unmindful of the possibility that departmentalization of General Education can lead to uniformity, even sterility, of approach, with a few professors deciding what is good, beautiful and true for all undergraduates. The dean of the College and the chairman of its departments therefore encourage teachers to use methods that work best for them. Insofar as one can generalize about what goes on in the over one hundred and fifty classrooms, some with twenty-five students and others with as many as two hundred, where American Thought and Language is taught, it can best be described as a collection of similar courses with a common end-term examination rather than a rigidly pre-scribed set of lessons. Furthermore, change and reorganization are practically built into the course.

Finally, those in charge of the program believe that the quality of teaching offered to undergraduates compares favorably with that found in any American university when measured by the usual yardsticks of teachers' professional responsibilities and perquisites, advanced degrees, publications, age and experience. This is no small claim and one to which the present writer, who teaches American Thought and Language in East Lansing, subscribes. For the American Studies movement, the history of the course and its present function as a strong link in the general education program of a major state university may be read as an unsolicited endorsement of the soundness of the American studies idea for intelligently conceived courses for American undergraduates.

It is no mere gesture to say that this essay could not have been written without the cooperation of several students, colleagues and administrators at Michigan State University who confirmed or corrected my opinions, supplied reminiscences, and directed me to sources of information which I, a newcomer to the faculty, might have overlooked. I owe special thanks to T. B. Strandness, chairman of ATL, for cheerfully burning midnight oil to read and comment upon several drafts in typescript.

The following books and articles were helpful and are the source of all quotations used except those representing verbatim statements of informants at Michigan State University:

Edward A. Carlin and Edward B. Blackman (eds.), *Curriculum Building in General Education* (Dubuque, Iowa: W. C. Brown Co., 1960).

Bernard F. Engel, "The American Experience at MSU," *Journal of the Conference on College Composition and Communication*, XII (February 1962), 34-8.

Joseph J. Kwiat and Mary C. Turpie (eds.), *Studies in American Culture* (Minneapolis: Univ. of Minn., 1960).

Tremaine McDowell, *American Studies* (Minneapolis: Univ. of Minn., 1948).

Francis Shoemaker and L. Forsdale (eds.), *Communication in General Education* (Dubuque, Iowa: W. C. Brown Co., 1960). Contains chapter on "Communication Skills at MSU" by Frederic Reeve.

Robert H. Walker, *American Studies in the United States* (Baton Rouge: LSU, 1958).

III

ON CONFRONTING THE
WORLD

Anglophobia and Anglophilia

HARRY C. ALLEN

HARRY. C. ALLEN is Commonwealth Fund Professor of American History at University College, London. He has written widely on Anglo-American relations, his main work being *Great Britain and the United States: A History of Anglo-American Relations (1783-1952)*, published in 1955. Recently returned from teaching a semester at Rochester, New York, he is engaged upon a volume for Ernest Benn's "Nations of the Modern World" Series on *The United States of America*.

WE ARE ALL AWARE IN SOME DEGREE OF THE IMPORTANCE of emotion in our individual lives, and, if we are honest with ourselves, of the extent to which it, rather than reason alone, often dictates our actions. We frequently quote Pascal with approval: "La cœur a ses raisons que la raison ne connaît point."[1]

But when we write the history of nations, and especially of their relations with one another, we seldom give these emotional factors the weight that they deserve. There was indeed a period when "diplomatic" historians were wont to produce long accounts—all too often "dry-as-dust"—of all the intricate manœuvres of international negotiations, with scarcely a glance beneath their surface.

Yet patriotism is at once the deepest and most familiar of public emotions: *dulce et decorum est pro patria mori*. Few of us are quite insensitive to the call of our country, although the quality, as well as the quantity, of our feelings may differ not only from person to person but from nation to nation. The love of Americans for their country has characteristically been associated with their belief in liberty and in the contribution which the ever-growing power of the United States will enable them to make to the future of humanity.

> Here the free spirit of mankind, at length,
> Throws its last fetters off; and who shall place
> A limit to the giant's unchained strength,
> Or curb his swiftness in the forward race? [2]

The affection of the British for their native land on the other hand has frequently been linked to what they feel to be the beauty and security of their little island home.

> . This fortress built by nature for herself
> Against infection and the hand of war;
> This happy breed of men, this little world,
> This precious stone set in the silver sea . . . [3]

Some peoples seem to accord a more all-embracing, even obsessive and exclusive, part to patriotism than do others. One observer wrote in 1889, "Patriotism takes the place of religion in France. In the service of *la patrie* the doing of one's duty is elevated into the sphere of exalted emotion. More than any other people, the French make patriotism the source and subject of their profoundest emotional life."[4] On a very different level, nobody who once heard the frenzied and hypnotic baying of a Nazi crowd for their Führer could ever again doubt the often terrifying potency of undiluted emotion in the lives of nations.

But patriotism is an overt emotion, and recognition of this is not enough. During the twentieth century we have most of us come to accept, albeit often with reluctance and in the teeth of strong inner resistances, the fact that our individual actions are remarkably often the result of unconscious motives; that our lives are controlled not merely by reason or even open passion, but also by feelings joined by association with emotions and instincts (with which they have little apparent connection) rooted deep in our unconscious minds. This realization had its forerunners— Carlyle wrote in 1838, "The uttered part of a man's life bears to the unuttered, unconscious part a small unknown proportion. He himself never knows it, much less do others"[5]—but it was essentially the achievement of Sigmund Freud. By 1938 his one-time disciple Carl Gustav Jung could write, "It is incontestable that in every important situation in life our consciousness is dependent on the unconscious."[6]

Even admitting, however, that the unconscious may dominate the behaviour of the individual, can it be said that groups, and in particular nations, act from unconscious emotional motives? Jung for one came to believe something of the kind so strongly that he formulated the concept of the "collective unconscious" as opposed to the "personal unconscious." Historians, and especially perhaps British and American historians with their pragmatic instincts, may be wary of going this far in the direction of the Teutonic idea of the "oversoul," but we may more easily follow the sceptical Freud in believing that groups of human beings— sharing the same instincts, emotions and mechanisms of response and association—may often act in very much the same way as one another. How indeed, looking at the behaviour of modern nations in time of war, can one *not* believe that their inhabitants act from common emotions? As Freud himself wrote in 1915, amidst the first world holocaust, "It would seem that nations still obey their immediate passions far more readily than their interests."[7] And the passions of these aggregated individuals may be triggered off in their unconscious minds by similar and even shared associations.

For if, in seeking to answer the very complicated question of what makes a nation, we had to single out one factor as decisive, it might well be just this existence of a common fund of experience and of the mental associations derived from it. Can it be doubted, for instance, that the following words, from the pen of the greatest of contemporary French public figures, express sentiments not only shared by many of his countrymen but also of the first importance to the history of France and the Western world? They constitute the opening passage of the first volume of Charles de Gaulle's *War Memoirs*.

> All my life I have thought of France in a certain way. This is inspired by sentiment as much as by reason. The emotional side of me tends to imagine France, like the princess in the fairy stories or the Madonna in the frescoes, as dedicated to an exalted and exceptional destiny. Instinctively I have the feeling that Providence has created her either for complete successes or for exemplary misfortunes . . . ; that only vast enterprises are capable of counterbalancing the ferments of dispersal which are inherent in her people . . . In short, to my mind, France cannot be France without greatness.[8]

One might comment much on this passage, with its recognition of the deep emotions involved, its reference to common fantasies, or legends, and its sense of the anarchic instincts brewing deep within French minds; one might even note that in the *Memoirs* it is directly followed by the story of his childhood, and especially of the influence of his mother and father upon the development of his feelings towards his country. But the point—the importance of national emotions, conscious and unconscious—has been made at sufficient length, and our concern here is with those of Americans.

And it is in fact with a very limited facet of these American emotions that I propose to deal—their feelings of sympathy and antipathy towards the British. It is well that it should be so, for this problem of national emotions and their influence upon national actions is obviously of the utmost difficulty and complexity. It is an open field of research in which one might spend many lifetimes: I should like some time in the future to explore it for a few years at least, and in particular to make a fourfold study of Anglophobia and Anglophilia, and pro-Americanism and anti-Americanism. This paper simply embodies my first thoughts on entering the field and within such limited scope as this it will plainly not be possible to do more than touch very briefly upon a few aspects of even such a small facet of the whole subject of national emotions. But it may possibly suggest a few interesting lines of future investigation.

If full awareness of the unconscious motives of mankind had to await the genius of Freud, men have long understood how close sympathy and antipathy are. It is not, of course, merely that they often alternate, that there is as *Ecclesiastes* has it "A time to love, and a time to hate," but that they are manifestations which spring from the same well of feelings. As La Rochefoucauld characteristically put it, "Plus on aime une maîtresse, et plus on est prêt de la hair";[9] or, equally characteristically, Shakespeare,

> Sweet love, I see, changing his property,
> Turns to the sourest and most deadly hate.[10]

Thus it is right as well as convenient to consider Anglo-American loves and hates together, and they constitute in fact, like any emotional human relationship between two parties, a four-fold problem—Anglophobia and Anglophilia: pro-Americanism and anti-Americanism. In this brief space I must confine myself to American feelings, but it will, I trust, be borne in mind that four legs are needed before the structure is balanced or can make any pretence at even-handedness.

But can we, in passing, learn something from these very terms? Freud has shown how significant our unconscious choice of words (even sounds) can be. Do the British avoid the words "Americophilia" and "Americophobia," even in writing, only because they are clumsy, or also because the weaker ones, pro-Americanism and anti-Americanism, accord better with their feelings and with the way they tend to express them? Is it that there may be more here simply than real evidence of the important fact that Englishmen are as accustomed to understate things as Americans are to overstate them; and that the American choice of the stronger words expresses a much more potent emotion? It certainly does appear that British feelings towards America have seldom attained the bitterness, depth, or persistence, of the Anglophobia of some Americans in the nineteenth century. This was perhaps to be expected; anti-British emotions were in large measure inseparable from the birth-pangs of the infant republic, and the trauma left by the experience was accordingly deep and lasting. In the nature of things—the set character of the adult and the impressionability of the youth—the mark that we leave on our children is liable to be more pronounced than the effect they have on us.

And the familial simile in the history of the Anglo-American relationship is inescapable; so irresistibly does it spring to the lips that one feels it must describe a psychological reality. As sober a man as John Adams spoke in 1785, in his first interview with George III as American Minister, of "kindred blood";[11] the *Edinburgh Review* of November 1812 echoed a common British sentiment when it referred to this "unnatural . . . war";[12] the phrase "Mother Country" was long a commonplace in both lands; Senator Albert J. Beveridge actually referred at the end of the

nineteenth century to "our mother England";[13] even a
person so unsympathetic to the United States as George
Canning spoke of "mother and . . . daughter";[14] and
Alfred Thayer Mahan talked much later of "common
descent . . . , . . . the same blood. There is seen here the
working of kinship—a wholly normal result of a common
origin, the natural affection of children of the same
descent . . ."[15] Parent, father, son, brother, sister, cousin—
these living metaphors positively chase one another through
the pages of the story.

Furthermore, the circumstances of the relationship remained strongly reminiscent of family life after the breach
in which America established its adult freedom, for the
affairs of both countries remained closely related, indeed
physically entangled, thus reproducing exactly those conditions of independence yet enforced dependence or association which help to create the tensions within human
families. The son who breaks away entirely and seeks a
far country cuts the Gordian knot, although this solution
of the problem is in human terms (like that of Alexander)
a less than satisfactory one: it is the son who in his manhood
remains in—partly willing if mostly involuntary—prox-
imity to and close relations with his parents and siblings who
experiences the irritations, frustrations and passions of
family life.

The American Revolution could not cut the knot clean
through, and consequently the United States in the nineteenth century was in just this relationship to Britain, which
was in the plenitude of its power. As Lincoln said of North
and South, physically speaking the British Empire and the
United States could not separate. As America swept westward to accomplish its Manifest Destiny, British North
America, later coming of age itself in the Canadian Confederation, was always at its right elbow, raising a constant
succession of problems about the border, defence, trade,

the Indians, waterways, and the perennial intermingling of populations. To her left lay the Caribbean and the British West Indies; then, further west, Mexico, with which Britain had special connections as far apart as Texan independence and the downfall of Porfirio Diaz; and lastly, far off California, in which Britain seemed at one moment to dabble. Even though in the direct path of the westward movement, where Americans were much the most sensitive, British interests were limited to temporary phenomena (like the northwest posts after 1783, a possible Indian buffer state for some years thereafter, and the more important Oregon question which was settled in 1846). And when the frontier actually reached the Pacific coast the United States still found itself faced with the ubiquitous sea power of Britain. Such indeed is the nature of maritime ascendancy that Britain consolidated her Second Empire, under the protection of the Royal Navy, in areas of possible clash with American interests as remote from one another as the slave coast of West Africa, the Central American Isthmus, and Samoa.

Until 1814 in fact British sea power and American maritime commerce were hopelessly embroiled, and even when peace returned Americans remained persistently entangled in extra-political relations with Britain. Immigration to the United States from the British Empire between 1820 and 1945, even excluding all of that direct from Ireland, was by far the largest of any national group and constituted about one-fifth of the whole. The United States was almost as dependent on British manufactures and British capital as any colony, and in absolute terms took far more of both than any British colony in fact did, at least until the Civil War. There was the most intimate connection between British cultural, humanitarian, social and political movements and those of the American people, especially of New England, in the same period.[16] At every turn,

however much against its will, the United States found itself bumping into, or involved with, the British Empire.

Small wonder that for America Britain remained National Enemy No. 1. As Kipling put it in 1900, "And
indeed, when you come to think of it, there is no other
country for the American public speaker to trample upon.
France has Germany; we have Russia; for Italy, Austria is
provided; and the humblest Pathan possesses an ancestral
enemy. Only America stands out of the racket; and therefore, to be in fashion, makes a sand-bag of the mother
country, and bangs her when occasion requires." But historical and geographical circumstance is not enough to explain the passion or the action; as one of Kipling's Americans goes on to explain, we were "compelled to blow off
steam. Everybody expected it." Further, "whenever we
get on our hind legs we always express a desire to chaw up
England. It's a sort of family affair." An American audience
may have come to expect "sky-rockets" against Britain to
be "thrown in for effect,"[17] but why do they have this
effect and whence the irresistible impulse of the speaker to
let off steam? Obviously they struck a common series
of what Lincoln called the "mystic chords of memory,
stretching from every battle-field and patriot grave to every
living heart and hearthstone all over this broad land."[18]

The public speaker in the early years of American independence—which Tocqueville called years of "irritable
patriotism,"[19] when opinion in the United States was acutely
sensitive to criticism, especially from Britain—often had
excellent grounds for hating the English, whose super-
cilious criticism of all things American and belief in their
own ineffable superiority were at their height at this time,
but much of the emotional drive to do so came from
within. The contemplation of the iniquities of Britain, even
the mere mention of England, was enough to set the memories reverberating in his mind and heart; the verbal on-

slaught on the British which they evoked swiftly set up powerful sympathetic vibrations in his hearers. The occasion itself might be trivial but the host of repressed associations provoked a powerful emotional response, for it is the act of repression which creates the unconscious impulses and gives them their intense, pent-up force. Freud likened the mind to two rooms, and ideas to persons—a small antechamber capable of containing very few people which is the conscious mind, and a large chamber behind it, filled with people, which is the unconscious reservoir to which all the myriad memories of life must necessarily be sent for storage. Ideas in the conscious mind may summon associated memories forward from the unconscious, and often they jostle one another as they try to force their way through the narrow connecting door.

Obviously, as we know all too well, an orthodox Freudian psycho-analysis may take upwards of a thousand hours —this is a process of the utmost complexity even in a single individual, and individual experiences differ widely. An Irish immigrant in the nineteenth century to the United States might have bitter personal experiences at the hands of the British in Ireland; a newcomer from France might see England more distantly as a traditional national foe; a German-American might merely associate Britain in a general way with the tyrannies of the old world from which he had fled; and one man, for purely personal reasons of family background, might much more easily be touched on the raw by a political happening than might another with a different childhood history. But though the phenomena are infinitely complex, all men share, in greater or less degree and in different modes, the same passions, the same instincts of hatred and aggression, pride and fear.

Men of the same nationality, too, share many common experiences, not merely actual but vicarious. In the first generation of Americans after the Revolution there were no doubt many with striking actual memories of the British in the conflict; their children, too, must have imbibed these stories with their mothers' milk; and by the time of their children's children they might have passed into family lore. (How well I recall, born as I was in 1917, the persistent indictment in my family that the Germans were wont to commit that most dreadful of social errors, eating their peas with a knife.) But they also spread outwards, though often no doubt in an attenuated form, into local and even national legend, and, in due course, myth; in literature, however, can be found incidents almost as vivid, and hence as potent, as the original and real experiences. Finally, in the history books, facts, or sometimes supposed facts—real or occasionally exaggerated happenings—find a permanent record which is perhaps the most powerful influence of all, because it has the full authority of Clio, the majesty of supposedly objective truth. In whichever category they are, the effect of these on the mind of the child is liable to be much the same, and who can doubt that it is in some degree a common emotion which this shared vicarious experience prompts?

> Listen, my children, and you shall hear
> Of the midnight ride of Paul Revere,
> On the eighteenth of April, in Seventy-five;
> Hardly a man is now alive
> Who remembers that famous day and year.

Far more have remembered it since Longfellow wrote than had ever done so before. How many American children have not held their breath as they hear, "with secret dread,"

> The muster of men at the barrack door,
> The sound of arms, and the tramp of feet,
> And the measured tread of the grenadiers?

How many American girls and boys have not felt their hearts go out to the

... one who was safe and asleep in his bed
Who at the bridge would be first to fall,
Who that day would be lying dead,
Pierced by a British musket-ball.

You know the rest. In the books you have read
How the British Regulars fired and fled,
How the farmers gave them ball for ball,
From behind each fence and farmyard wall,
Chasing the redcoats down the lane . . . ?

Generations of Americans have indeed known deep in their
souls that they must echo that

... cry of defiance and not of fear,
A voice in the darkness, a knock at the door,
And a word that shall echo forevermore!
For, borne on the night wind of the Past,
Through all our history, to the last,
In the hour of darkness and peril and need,
The people will waken and listen to hear
The hurrying hoof-beats of that steed,
And the midnight message of Paul Revere.[20]

Small wonder that the redcoats, despite all our efforts—
both laughing and serious—to do so, seemingly cannot be
banished from the history books, for even an Englishman
versed in and reflecting on American history finds that the
American-type associations come pressing forward in his
mind, competing with those prompted by his own British
experience. He no sooner thinks, as is proper in a Briton, of
the "thin red line . . . tipped . . . with steel"[21] of Waterloo
and the Crimea (with overtones of the charge of the Light
Brigade) than these pictures are crowded out by very different, American ones. By the disciplined dumb stupidity
of Braddock's disaster on the Monongahela in 1755; the
equally costly if more successful operation at Bunker's Hill
twenty years later; two more years and it is, "There, my

boys, are your enemies, redcoats and Tories"[22]—even Hessian mercenaries; and the final and most calamitous but equally typical match of the series, at New Orleans in 1815.

The redcoats provide indeed a splendid example of exactly the sort of mental and emotional process which lies behind Anglophobia, as well as of the passions and hatreds of other nations. Here are experiences, exactly typified by the single symbol of the redcoat, which are so manifold and striking and well known that virtually no American can fail to respond, in a kindred fashion, to that symbol. Almost every American must have potent, sometimes violent, associations which the thought of the British Grenadiers and their fellow soldiers can evoke. Even the fact that it is the colour red is itself important. It is the colour of fire, of warning, of blood; in quite different connotations it is to be the colour of violent revolution, of the "bloody shirt," and of the red shirts of leaders as different as Wade Hampton and Garibaldi. But in the redcoat it is the colour of Britain and her soldiers, which was what Napoleon was thinking of when he said towards the end of his days on St. Helena, "Red is the colour of England; I cannot bear the sight of it."[23]

And with the direct associations come their related and swiftly ramifying successors; but even these, many of them, must be common to almost all Americans. How frequently it is "the redcoats and George III"!

> And what mortal ever heard
> Any good of George III?

as Walter Savage Landor put it.[24] "The history of the present King of Great Britain is a history of repeated injuries and usurpations, all having in direct object the establishment of an absolute Tyranny over these States . . . He has kept among us, in times of peace, Standing Armies without the

Consent of our legislature . . . quartering large bodies of armed troops among us . . . protecting them, by a mock Trial, from Punishment for any Murders which they should commit on the Inhabitants of these States . . . He has plundered our seas, ravaged our Coasts, burnt our towns, and destroyed the lives of our people. He is at the same time transporting large armies of foreign mercenaries to compleat the works of death, desolation and tyranny, already begun with circumstances of Cruelty and perfidy scarcely paralleled in the most barbarous ages, and totally unworthy the Head of a civilized nation."[25]

"The affairs of the British Empire 'had already begun' to fall into confusion"; Americans could not "basely entail hereditary bondage" upon their "innocent posterity";[26] therefore "these United Colonies are, and of Right ought to be Free and Independent States."[27] This is familiar enough, but it had, of course, formidable psychological implications for that posterity; even if the mind of the child is in truth as Locke declared a "tabula rasa"—and this seems much more doubtful than once it did—its family and its friends and, in a sense, all its society soon write much upon that virgin page. It acquires not merely the imprint of its own experience but that of much of the experience of its forerunners as well. This time-lag is a very real thing, which renders national emotions intensely conservative and slow to undergo permanent change; as Henry Adams, with his usual perception, noted on his first visit to England, in the heyday of what he called the "upper-class bourgeoisie," "Aristocracy was real. So was the England of Dickens. Oliver Twist and Little Nell lurked in every churchyard shadow . . . In November, 1858, . . . it was the London of the eighteenth century that an American felt and hated."[28]

And with this redcoated vision there come the spectres of arbitrary and despotic rule, social and political inequality,

a religious establishment; Americans cannot but see it as
Shelley (who said of America "That land is like an eagle . . .
An epitaph of glory for the tomb of murdered Europe")[29]
described it on the occasion of the Peterloo massacre:

I met Murder on the way—
He had a mask like Castlereagh—
Very smooth he looked, yet grim:
Seven blood-hounds followed him:

. . . .

Next came Fraud, and he had on,
Like Eldon, an ermined gown:

. . . .

Like Sidmouth, next, Hypocrisy
On a crocodile rode by.
And many more Destructions played
In this ghastly masquerade,
All disguised, even to the eyes,
Like bishops, lawyers, peers or spies.[30]

And even when these ghosts were largely laid by the coming of democracy in Britain in the late nineteenth century,
those of colonialism and imperialism come to the head of
the procession.

The fires of Anglophobia were thus fed by these common
feelings and sentiments, forming, because they were shared,
a sort of emotional cement binding together the American
people in a new national solidarity. We all participate in
greater or less degree in these group, mass, passions. But the
fires were also fed by the deepest individual feelings, operating empathetically. When a young American trooper,
fourteen years of age, was captured, along with his elder
brother, by a force of British Light Dragoons in South
Carolina in 1780, he was ordered by a British lieutenant to
clean the officer's boots. He refused. "The reply," in the
words of a historian, "was a saber-blow aimed at the head

of the young prisoner: it was warded by the arm of the recipient, but hand and head carried the mark of it to the grave. Robert was also ordered to do the same service and on refusing received a more serious wound than his younger brother."[31] As the young man himself recalled it in later life, "After that they kept me in jail at Camden about two months, starved me nearly to death and gave me the small-pox . . . Then Robert died of the small-pox and I barely escaped death."[32] This experience of Andrew Jackson could scarcely fail to become a vivid part of the experience of any young American, who read of it, indeed any young man anywhere, dreaming his dreams, "The quick Dreams, The passion-wingéd Ministers of thought."[33]

It has many of the classic features of the typical fantasy of brutality and power. Cleaning the dirty boots is almost the perfect symbol of degraded slave-like submission, getting as close as it easily could to "washing his feet" on the one hand or "licking his boots" on the other; and they are to be "blacked," from which sinister substance, by "spit and polish," the final touch will be given to the shining red-coated panoply of military power. The sabre-blow, the most vicious of all attacks, a wide-armed sweep which cuts deep, has for any imaginative reader all the force of every sudden brutal swipe or sudden onslaught he has ever undergone at the hands of enemy—or parent. The life-long scar is at once the dreaded physical disfigurement and the most fundamental and noblest badge of bravery and honour. It is David and Goliath: it is the incarnation of the bold defiance of the cowardly bully, for behind the lieutenant is all the dreadful apparatus of the dungeon, of bread and water and even of loathsome disease. Above all, it has the supreme merit of the myth—ultimate victory and exquisite personal revenge; victory not merely in the Revolutionary War but over the redcoats themselves, even including some Light Dragoons, at New Orleans. And beyond all that lay

the superb vindication of the boy hero, the White House—
worthy ambition of every youthful American.

Of such potent stuff was Anglophobia made. Yet we are
all conscious that it is far from being the whole story. At
least since the settlement of the principal Anglo-American
border disputes in the first half of the nineteenth century;
since the acceptance by Britain of full democracy in its
latter years (partly through American influence); and since
the rise of Anglo-American friendship, and ultimately alliance, in the twentieth century, the existence and importance
of Anglo-American ties have become so widely and persistently recognized as to seem often banal. Part of this
feeling arises from a cool American assessment of the
value of Britain as an ally; at this point the determination
and obstinacy of the British, so often a source of irri-
tation and fury to Americans in the past, becomes one of
Britain's principal assets in the eyes of the United States.
Emerson once wrote, "I find the Englishman to be him of
all men who stands firmest in his shoes,"[34] and this is a
comforting thought when he becomes your ally. Sometimes
the internal struggle between the two poles of American
feeling is apparent, as in Franklin D. Roosevelt's reputed
remark about Winston Churchill, that "no one could have
been a better ally than that old Tory." Indeed Churchill
embodies, more than any other Englishman living or dead,
the overt feeling of affection which Americans are capable
of feeling towards Britain; innumerable have been the times
on which I have heard admiration for him expressed in
America.

By no means all American feeling for Britain arises from
cold calculations of national interest, for there is a real
and spontaneous sense sometimes in Americans of the depths
of the common heritage of language, institutions and ideas
and of its fundamental value to them. And just as one

of the joys of the Briton in America is its vastness, so one of the notes struck by Britain in American feelings is its immemorial antiquity. This perhaps more than anything else is what has drawn a long succession of American expatriates to England; it is instinct, for instance, in Henry James, who shows it perhaps most vividly in that famous passage on those "items of high civilisation, as it exists in other countries, which are absent from the texture of American life . . . No . . . palaces, no castles, nor manors, nor old country-houses, nor parsonages, nor thatched cottages, nor ivied ruins; no cathedrals, nor abbeys, nor little Norman churches." By mid-twentieth century the English visitor to Salem, Massachusetts, or even Charlottesville, Virginia, may well feel that James for once overplayed his hand, and, in any event, as he himself reminds us, "The natural remark, in the almost lurid light of such an indictment, would be that if these things are left out, everything is left out. The American knows that a good deal remains."[35] So indeed does the sympathetic foreigner, but the American's need for self-identification, for "belonging," unquestionably finds an outlet in some feeling for the long English tradition.

American society is not only restlessly mobile, drawing its population from many lands, and putting down roots in general rather in the concept of being an American than in the soil of any particular locality; it is also dedicated to the creation of a new democratic order, it is pledged, almost, to novelty for its own sake. And this emotion carries its contrary with it. Americans have been remarkably sensitive to British opinion (Poe once wrote that "There is not a more disgusting spectacle under the sun than our subserviency to British criticism. It is disgusting, first, because it is truckling, servile, pusillanimous; secondly, because of its gross irrationality . . . ; we . . . day after day submit our necks to the degrading yoke of the crudest opinion that emanates from the fatherland."[36]) but have also often been fascinated by the largely tradition-engendered stability of British life and institutions.

This can find expression, for example, in an appreciation of the English countryside, bearing so clearly the imprint of the long habitation of men, with—if one can keep clear today of the urban agglomerations in which more than 80% of the population of Britain lives—its villages settled so securely in the landscape. Indeed to judge by the number of Americans (as well as Englishmen) who stream each year to visit the old country houses of Britain, one might suppose that some of them would go so far—and it is admittedly a long way—as to echo the verse of Felicia Dorothea Hymens (who had such a vogue in America),

> The stately homes of England!
> How beautiful they stand
> Amidst their tall ancestral trees
> O'er all the pleasant land![37]

But they would most of them prefer to substitute for the last two lines those written by Noel Coward in the 1930's,

> The stately homes of England!
> How beautiful they stand
> To prove the upper classes
> Have still the upper hand.

And in a curious way, because of the common literary tradition, much of England is familiar to Americans without their ever having been there. As Nathaniel Hawthorne wrote, "Almost always, in visiting such scenes as I have been attempting to describe, I had a singular sense of having been there before."[38]

But this is more than just familiarity, it is the very real fact that Americans rightly regard the English tradition prior to 1776 as being equally their own; as Hawthorne says in another place, "I never stood in an English crowd without being conscious of hereditary sympathies."[39] It is not mere historicism that Magna Carta hangs on the wall of the office of the Chairman of the Rochester University History Department, nor mere accident that in my years at Pembroke College, Oxford, the room which had been Samuel Johnson's was never occupied by any except Americans. As Whittier put it with real gusto:

> O Englishman!—in hope and creed,
> In blood and tongue our brothers!
> We too are heirs of Runnymede;
> And Shakespeare's fame and Cromwell's deed
> Are not alone our mother's.[40]

This common fund of vicarious Anglo-American experience has plainly been of incalculable importance: the Authorized Version and Shakespeare alone have obviously constituted an incomparable common source of thought and language, feeling and imagery. Nor did it in fact, of course, cease to be common after 1776, whether we think of impregnably native figures like Emerson on the one hand and Dickens on the other, or expatriates like T. S. Eliot and W. H. Auden in the twentieth century.

These feelings of Anglophilia naturally varied greatly in intensity from person to person and—since it was America, land of geographical diversity—from section to section: they also varied in kind. Thus the South, devoted to the more conservative arguments of Burke in politics and positively addicted to the historical romanticism of Scott in literature and life, always tended to be drawn to the aristocratic attitudes and notions of Britain. New England, on the other hand, was attracted to the very different England of the new commercial and industrial middle class; as Henry Adams observed, "the London of Robert Peel, Macaulay, and John Stuart Mill . . . felt instinctive cousinship with the Boston of Ticknor, Prescott and Motley."[41] In New

England, so closely bound to England after independence by maritime trade and a rising industry, by humanitarian endeavours and political sympathies, as well as by cultural ties, adoration for England could verge not only on the treasonable but the idolatrous.

To assess the strength of these feelings in the people as a whole is, however, a very much more difficult task. Plainly they are far more diluted when spread through the whole mass, and, even where they are intense, may exist side by side with strong elements of Anglophobia. They may of course, where mere indifference is not the predominant cast of mind, also exist side by side in the same person; it was just this mixture of emotions which produced, no doubt, the American remark heard by Dickens about England in 1843—that "unnat'ral old parent." There is even upon occasion a strain, albeit thin, of grudging respect and occasionally affection in the comprehensibly Anglophobe texture of Irish emotions, rather on the principle "Better the Devil you do know than the Devil you don't." But one argument for the broad existence of at least a substratum of pro-British feeling in the United States is the widespread British content of the American stock—and I use this word in no narrow genetic sense but with its most extensive cultural and social meaning.

Admittedly the calculations of national origins made at the time of the restriction of immigration by quota in 1924 were based on assumptions, some of which are questionable, and in a spirit which would not have led to an underestimate of the British racial strain; but the figures are striking none the less. The proportion of Americans in 1920 of British (i.e. United Kingdom of Great Britain and Northern Ireland) stock was put at well over 50%. And there are some grounds for thinking that this very large group did retain residual sentiments not unfavourable to the mother country, and that these constitute a force of considerable importance in American life. Paradoxically, it may perhaps be illustrated by the fact that there has never really been a cohesive, sought-after, let alone organized, "British vote," to compare with the German vote or the Italian vote. There certainly was an Anglophobe vote which was much cultivated, but it seems very doubtful whether there was no British vote because it was not respectable to favour the homeland of George III. It appears much more likely that it was because the "British" group was not a minority and had no such great need therefore to organize itself. There is certainly evidence, in World War I and even more World War II, of strong pro-British feeling in the United States.

It may perhaps be permissible to illustrate this by what can be regarded as extreme cases, in order to show the intensity of which some Americans were capable in their Anglophilia. Walter Hines Page, the Ambassador of the United States in London in World War I, admittedly had a very bad case of the disease, and he got into exceedingly hot water in certain American circles for a speech he made on 16 August 1913 when dedicating a monument in Southampton, England, in honour of the *Mayflower* Pilgrims. He declared, in a vein characteristic of the period, "Blood carries with it that particular trick of thought which makes us all English in the last resort. . . . And Puritan and Pilgrim and Cavalier, different yet, are yet one in that they are English still. And thus, despite the fusion of races and of the great contributions of other nations to her 100 millions of people and to her incalculable wealth, the United States is yet English-led and English-ruled."[42] Not that Page ever ceased to be very American, or to see the faults of the British— what he called "their dickering habits in trade and their 'unctuous rectitude' in stealing continents"—but his letters are filled with his admiration and affection for them; "You know," he wrote, "there's been much discussion of the decadence of the English people. I don't believe a word of it . . . The world never saw a finer lot of men than the best of their ruling class . . . —gently bred, high-minded, physically fit, intellectually cultivated, patriotic."[43]

Englishmen, indeed, reared since Thomas Arnold in the public-school tradition of the repression of emotion, of keeping a stiff upper-lip (an even more difficult feat physically than it is morally) can sometimes feel distinctly uneasy at the lengths to which expressions of American emotion on this subject can go. I well remember the slight sense of discomfort—shared no doubt it is true by many Americans—with which in 1946 in the United States, as a safe survivor of a war now comfortably won, I sat (with no Noel Coward to rescue me, as from the verse of the English Mrs. Hymens) through the popular recording of Alice Duer Miller's "The White Cliffs" of Dover:

> I am American bred,
> I have seen much to hate here—much to forgive,
> But in a world where England is finished and dead,
> I do not wish to live.[44]

But as so often, in literature as well as life, it is the simplest expression of emotion which is frequently deepest. There must still be many Americans to whom there is a peculiar poignancy in Robert E. Sherwood's description of Edward R. "Murrow's grim voice [in 1940] announcing, 'This— is London,' in a tone which seemed to suggest the thuds of the German bombs."[45]

Perhaps, too, this wide British content of the American stock is more important than we have supposed because our picture of the process of Americanization of the immigrant is so coloured by the vital public aspects of it; it was of course necessarily a process which took place principally outside the home, *coram publico*, if only because the parents, however much they desired Americanization, could scarcely know what it really was. Thus the psychological urge was to block out the memory of one's birthland when once one had entered the "golden door," and in a sense the more wretched the memories the easier it was to forget, because of the natural tendency of the conscious human mind to repress the bitter and recall the sweet. And whether or not it could be argued that the experiences of British emigrants were less hateful than those of many others (being after the earliest days seldom the result of direct human tyranny), it can scarcely be questioned that many immigrants must in their inner world have had memories and fantasies of sunny days in the land of their fathers. The Englishman long acquainted with America cannot fail to have been struck by the extreme frequency with which he is greeted with the words, "Oh, my mother, or father, or grandparents came from England," as if much more of the private, family lore—on which after all until relatively recent times all men depended for most of their knowledge—does get passed down from generation to generation, than may appear on the American surface. This is perhaps especially the case with those of British origin rather than others because, within the family itself, no language barrier exists to make communication between parent and child even more difficult than it often is in any event.

As with men's hates and fears, so with their loves and hopes, public matters may bring warm associations welling up from the inner recesses of the mind. As Disraeli said in the debate in the British Parliament on the assassination of Lincoln, with that insight into the thoughts and feelings of men which served him so well both as novelist and statesman: this was an instance "when the sympathy of a nation approaches those tenderer feelings that generally speaking, are supposed to be peculiar to the individual, and to form the happy privilege of private life; . . . it touches the heart of nations, and appeals to the domestic sentiment of mankind."[46] Observe, for example, the persistent tendency of men to think in terms of a golden age, sometimes in the future, sometimes in the past, and most often in both—that is to say, in terms of trying to recreate in Utopia the idyllic life of Eden:

> Time will run back and fetch the Age of Gold.[47]

And where in the past, "in ancient time,"[48] in what Dickens called the "good old times, the grand old times, the great old times"[49] were most Americans, with their cultural, if not genetic, heritage to find the golden age, except in English history, legend and myth?

> Or ever the knightly years were gone
> With the old world to the grave.[50]

The very usage by Americans of the phrase "old world" in an adjectival and also in a dual sense—geographical as well as chronological—is a fascinating illustration of this. (Actually it is doubtful whether the term appeared at all except in antithesis to the "New World," for its first recorded use is not till 1712 even in England.) Publicly many Americans might share the scepticism of the Irish poetess who wrote,

> Oh! those blessed times of old! with their chivalry and
>   state;
> I love to read their chronicles, which such brave deeds
>   relate;
> I love to sing their ancient rhymes, to hear their legends
>   told—
> But—Heaven be thanked! I live not in those blessed times
>   of old![51]

Some might go further and declare, with Emma Lazarus,

> Keep, ancient lands, your storied pomp![52]

But we may believe that this association of an inner imaginative world of legend and myth with warm feelings towards the old world, and especially Britain, was a real force in the American mind: it was no mere windmill—paper tiger perhaps is the contemporary metaphor—at which, as late as 1889, Mark Twain was tilting in *A Connecticut Yankee in King's Arthur's Court.*

And these are public aspects of the matter, which are at least partly conscious. What of the private and personal? I tried in discussing Anglophobia to suggest how the ordinary, and individual, suspicions, fears and hates of many Americans—like all human beings—could become, by the simple but extraordinarily powerful and subtle mechanism of the association of ideas, bountiful sources of energy for anti-British feeling. The sword slash across the face of Andrew Jackson becomes a focus in a multitude of American breasts for Anglophobe feelings, but in each case the force of the feeling derives from the deep and personal emotions of each individual, which by the sympathetic association of ideas becomes concentrated on this one symbol, along of course with many others. The trouble, for the historian attempting to analyze this highly intricate problem, is that this is not at the conscious level a rational process. The unconscious mind has its own logic—and a remorseless logic at that—but it is not the logic of pure reason. The pent-up forces of unconscious emotion which may impel certain individuals to a frenzy of anti-British feeling have often no apparent connection with Britain at all except an obscure mental association which is exceedingly difficult to unravel and reveal. What we are really saying is that all men in greater or less degree have instincts which if repressed in one sphere may force their way to the surface in quite another. A man who was bullied by his father as a child may be a much more fertile breeding ground for resentment of British nineteenth century braggadocio than one who had a happier youth.

And the phenomenon is in some respects much more

difficult to understand in Anglophilia than in Anglophobia, in love than in hate. This may partly be perhaps because in society at large our destructive instincts are more comprehensible and also more important to us than our constructive ones, that in the nature of things far more social problems arise from men's mistrust than their trust. Is not the tendency to love and protect only within the immediate family, or possibly tribe, deeply bred in us, whereas beyond these narrow confines we tend all too easily to give our dislikes and animosities a free rein? The sphere and strength of affection are much more limited than those of hate, and outside this magic circle these latter are much the stronger among those deep "instincts . . . inborn in us" to which, as Ernest Jones reminds us, the "unconscious . . . part of the mind . . . stands nearest . . . (B)ehind the veneer of civilization there remains throughout life a buried mass of crude primitive tendencies, always struggling for expression, and towards which the person tends to relapse whenever suitable opportunity is offered."[53] But these forces are far from all malign or sinister; indeed in Freud's own view they mostly arise from the fundamental sexual instinct, of which love is the supreme expression, and which may have great power.

There may thus be a deep well-spring of unconscious warmth of feeling which can sometimes provide for Anglophilia as ample supplies of emotion as its less pleasant counterpart does for Anglophobia. Who can gauge the effect of secret, withdrawn, individual fantasies which by association may be unconsciously linked to the idea of the mother country? Each man may in his own imagination and in a different way.

"Fleet the time carelessly, as they did in the golden world."[54] The old world, the "olden time," the old days, the golden days—even the very verbal, audible, similarity of phrases may have an associative effect which would have seemed totally absurd before the advent of psychoanalysis, and which will still seem so to many. As Freud put it with characteristic understatement, "Psycho-analysis finds little credence among laymen for assertions such as these . . ."[55] In how many minds may there not be an unconscious association between the "olden world" and "the golden world," with all the agreeable associations of that world—"all in the golden afternoon,"[56] "casting down their golden crowns around the glassy sea,"[57] "this majestical roof fretted with golden fire."[58] In some Americans it could possibly be that the idea of England may release "golden opinions,"[59] just as in others it may release dark thoughts of detestation.

The former was so, for example, in Washington Irving, in many ways a true Anglophiliac,

> a choice nature, not wholly deserving
> A name either English or Yankee,—just Irving[60]

as Lowell called him. Irving himself wrote, "The great charm, however, of English scenery is the moral feeling that seems to pervade it." All the "common features of English landscape evince a calm and settled security, and hereditary transmission of home-bred virtues and local attachments . . . It is this sweet home-feeling, this settled repose of affection in the domestic scene, that is, after all, the parent of the steadiest virtues and purest enjoyments . . ."[61] In other Anglophiliacs (themselves perhaps inheriting the affliction, maybe through the female line), like George Henry Boker, it obviously released deep feelings of kinship and affection; he was able to write in 1852, a rather unlikely year, in his poem *To England*, "thou great bulwark of liberty . . . and if your courage wane through force or fraud, look westward to your child." In the case of a not very notable figure like Boker, who knows what deep seated unconscious impulses may have moved him to

this love of the idea of England? And again, who can measure the adult influence of the childhood fantasy? Think of
Harry Hopkins' little daughter in the White House during
the visit of King George VI and Queen Elizabeth in 1939;
as Mrs. Roosevelt describes it, Diana "was very excited
because the only kind of a queen she knew anything about
was a fairy queen . . . The Queen . . . suggested that Diana
be in the hall as she and the king left for dinner . . . The
king was resplendent in his uniform, but Diana had eyes
only for the queen, who wore a white, spangled dress and a
jeweled crown. She looked like a fairy queen and the illusion was so perfect that . . . Diana . . . curtsied to the queen
and ignored the king . . . a starry-eyed little girl who will
never forget, I hope, what a fairy queen really looks like.
She said: 'Oh, Daddy I have seen the Fairy Queen.' "[62]
But we cannot well doubt that in many Anglophiles, the
depth of their feelings often owed as much to mysterious
and irrational motives as to overt and common-sense ones.

And in the last resort, most especially when we are seeking to cast doubt on the rationality of many human feelings
and actions, we have to submit our own motives to a ruthless scrutiny: we must continually ask ourselves how much
we, as historians, are seeing only what we want, or are
impelled, to see. For the mind of the historian is a very
fallible instrument, and has great need to mistrust itself. We
must subscribe to Carl Becker's "view of history," as described by George H. Sabine; it "was intellectually sophisticated in a high degree. . . . It implied in the historian an
extreme form of self-consciousness. The thing that the historian describes is a state of mind induced by a set of conditions which has itself supervined upon an older state of
mind. . . . It . . . is like a hall of mirrors in which image
reflects image until the reality vanishes in a never-ending
series of images."[63] The first mirror, the historian's mind,

must be as clear as possible: in other words, the first rule is, "Analyst—or historian—know thyself."

I certainly do not doubt that the reasons why I find myself, at this time and in this place, discussing this tangled and most perplexing subject of national emotions, in particular American feelings towards Britain, are not by any means solely rational. There were plenty of conscious reasons why I should have studied American history—the fascination of the subject, American friends in my youth, and the powerful stimulus which this great country provides to me. But why should the history of relations between the two countries have become my chief academic pursuit, important though it is? Why should I have developed this life-long interest in Anglo-American relations, as well as what my colleagues sometimes refer to (with their eyebrows perhaps a little raised) as my hands-across-the-sea hopes for their betterment?

I cannot but believe that it has curious, devious and at first sight seemingly quite unconnected roots in the fortuitous circumstances of my childhood. The Anglo-American story is the great international tale of separation and re-union—possibly even in the future, within a wider family, of institutional reunion. Would it be surprising if a child of early and permanently separated parents long and quite unconsciously identified these two nations of which he was fond with those parental figures, and sought, with more than normal fervour, to reconcile them? Such childhood influences have extraordinary ramification in the dim labyrinth of the unconscious mind.

And if thus formidable in the life—even if it be not especially cloistered—of the historian, who lives by study and by reflection, how much more so in the market place! How deeply in this fashion may not men and women be moved in the great arena of politics and international life!

To some no doubt this contention may still seem bizarre,

perhaps absurd. But the risk that it may seem so is well worth the running when the stakes are as high as they are here. If there be any truth in the thesis, then we must face the fact that in international affairs men are frequently moved—and with them whole nations—by emotions which are partly unconscious, and often atavistic and destructive. With these impulses their rational and conscious motives fight sometimes a losing battle. Unless we are aware of this, are any of us suitable custodians of the Hydrogen Bomb? So great are the hazards, that to try and explore even a little corner of the labyrinth is well worth the risk of folly.

1. *Pensées*, iv, 277.
2. William Cullen Bryant, *The Ages.*
3. *Richard the Second.*
4. William Crary Brownell, *French Traits* (quoted H. L. Mencken, ed., *A New Dictionary of Quotations* [New York, 1942]).
5. "Sir Walter Scott," *Westminster Review*, January 1838.
6. *Seminar on Children's Dreams*, 1938-9 (privately printed), (quoted in J. Jacobi, *The Psychology of Jung*, [New Haven, 1949]).
7. *Collected Papers*, Vol. IV, p. 303 (London, 1956).
8. *The Call to Honour, 1940-1942*, p. 3 (New York, 1955).
9. *Maximes.*
10. *Richard the Second.*
11. Quoted Beckles Willson, *America's Ambassadors to England (1785-1928)*, p. 9 (London, 1928).
12. p. 457.
13. Quoted M. E. Curti, *The Growth of American Thought*, p. 668 (New York, 1943).
14. Quoted R. W. Seton-Watson, *Britain in Europe, 1789-1914*, p. 85 (Cambridge, 1945).
15. A. T. Mahan, *The Interest of America in Sea Powers, Present and Future*, p. 108 (London, 1898).
16. See F. Thistlethwaite, *The Anglo-American Connection in the Early Nineteenth Century* (Philadelphia, 1959) *passim*, and H. C. Allen, *Great Britain and the United States: A History of Anglo-American Relations (1783-1952)* (New York, 1955) Part I.

17. Rudyard Kipling, *Writings*, Vol. XVI, *From Sea to Sea* Part II, p. 79 (New York, 1900).

18. First Inaugural Address.

19. Quoted A. Nevins, *American Social History as Recorded by British Travellers*, p. 3 (New York, 1923).

20. Henry Wadsworth Longfellow, *Tales of a Wayside Inn*.

21. W. H. Russell, *The British Expedition to the Crimea*, p. 156 (London, 1877).

22. John Stark at the Battle of Bennington, 16 August 1777, [John Bartlett, *Familiar Quotations*, (Boston, 1955)].

23. Napoleon I to Gaspard Gourgaud at St. Helena, 1815-1818. [H. L. Mencken, *A New Dictionary of Quotations*, p. 1011 (New York, 1942)].

24. *Epigram* (quoted Bartlett, *Familiar Quotations*).

25. *The Declaration of Independence*.

26. *Declaration of the Cause and Necessity of Taking up Arms, 6 July 1775*.

27. *The Declaration of Independence*.

28. *The Education of Henry Adams, An Autobiography*, pp. 33, 72-3 (London, 1919).

29. *The Revolt of Islam*.

30. *The Mask of Anarchy*.

31. John Spencer Bassett, *The Life of Andrew Jackson*, p. 10 (New York, 1911).

32. Quoted Augustus C. Buell, *History of Andrew Jackson: Pioneer, Patriot, Soldier, Politician, President*, pp. 51-2 (New York, 1904).

33. Shelley, *Adonais*.

34. *English Traits, Manners*. (Quoted John Bartlett, *Familiar Quotations*).

35. Henry James, *Hawthorne*, pp. 34-5 (New York, 1956).

36. Edgar Allan Poe, "Marginalia," *Works* Vol. IX, p. 310, (Akron, 1908).

37. *The Homes of England*.

38. Quoted R. B. Mowat, *The Diplomatic Relations of Great Britain and the United States*, pp. 159-60 (London, 1925).

39. Quoted *ibid.*, p. 161.

40. John Greenleaf Whittier, *To Englishmen*.

41. *op. cit.*, p. 38.

42. Burton J. Hendrick, *The Life and Letters of Walter H. Page*, Vol. I, p. 258 (New York, 1925).

43. *ibid.*, pp. 141, 139.

44. *The White Cliffs*, 1940.

45. Robert E. Sherwood, *Roosevelt and Hopkins: An Intimate History*, p. 236 (New York, 1948).

46. Quoted E. D. Adams, *Great Britain and the American Civil War*, Vol. II, pp. 260-4 (London, 1925).

47. Milton, *Hymn on the Morning of Christ's Nativity*.

48. William Blake, *Jerusalem*.

49. *The Chimes*.

50. *To W.A.*, 1888.

51. Frances Brown, *Oh! the Pleasant Days of Old*.

52. Inscription on the Statue of Liberty.

53. *Psycho-Analysis*, p. 123 (London, 1937).

54. *As You Like It*.

55. *Collected Papers*, Vol. IV, p. 314.

56. Lewis Carroll, *Alice's Adventures in Wonderland*, Introduction, Stanza 1.

57. John Bacchus Dykes, "Holy, Holy, Holy," *The American Hymnal*, p. 4 (New York, 1913).

58. *Hamlet*.

59. *Macbeth*.

60. James Russell Lowell, *A Fable for Critics*.

61. *Sketch-Book*, pp. 17-18 (Boston, 1907).

62. Eleanor Roosevelt, *This I Remember*, pp. 194-5 (New York, 1948).

63. Carl Becker, *Freedom and Responsibility in the American Way of Life*, p. XV (New York, 1947).

American Studies in Germany

HANS GALINSKY

HANS GALINSKY is Professor of English, Director of American Studies Division, Johannes Gutenberg University, Mainz, Germany. He was Fulbright Professor at Minnesota and Michigan in 1955. The ninth volume of the *Jahrbuch der Deutschen Gesellschaft für Amerikanstudien*, of which Professor Galinsky is co-editor, appeared in May, 1954. It was followed shortly thereafter by volume VI of *Mainz Contributions to American Studies.*

IN THE 1950'S PROSPECTS FOR AMERICAN STUDIES IN GERMANY looked auspicious. Area studies had entered German university life long before American Studies knocked at the door. Oriental studies reach back to imperial Berlin of Bismarck days. East European Studies and Ibero-American Studies, with Berlin and Hamburg institutes for centers, emerged in the early twentieth century. Southeast European Studies came to the fore in the 1930's. Nor did World War II stem the trend towards area studies, as the South Asian program at Heidelberg University demonstrates.

Moreover, cultural philosophy and cultural history had arisen, aiming at definition and evaluation of whole cultures. Arnold Bergstrasser and Ernst Robert Curtius had united to produce a brilliant analysis of French civilization prior to 1933. A chair and an Institute of Comparative Cultural Studies had been set up at Mainz in the late 1940's. Long before, Classical Philology had started conceiving of itself as "Klassische Altertumswissenschaft," with "Classical Antiquity" as a cultural whole for its proper subject of study.

The "gestalt" concept in both psychology and art theory, in the latter as well as in biology supported by the morphological ideas of Goethe and organicist notions of the Romantics, was another manifestation of the same trend toward a holistic view of the world of man and nature.

Scientific terminology, never to be despised in its trailblazing or at least groove-making services, would seem to have paved the way for American Studies by furnishing such namesakes and forerunners as "Études Germaniques" in France, "English Studies," a joint Swiss-Dutch-Scandinavian venture, "The Review of English Studies" in Britain, and "Englische Studien" in Germany. Characteristically, all of them are titles of scholarly periodicals, the former three still flourishing, while the latter became a war casualty.

Passing from the favorable conditions in the spheres of academic subjects, concepts and terms to the thing itself, or, more precisely, to one of its close relations or approximations, attempts at a theory of "Amerikakunde" had been made as early as the late 1920s by such pioneers as Schönemann, Fischer and Mutschmann. At the same time American visiting professors developing their ideas of "wissenschaftliche Amerikakunde" had been given a hearing before and, increasingly, after World War II.[1]

Thus it is not surprising that at the 1959 convention of the German Association for American Studies a distinguished American guest speaker and Founding Father of American Studies in their country of origin, Robert E. Spiller, in his Cologne address on "Value and Method in American Studies," should have envisioned a complementary cooperation:

The pragmatic approach of the Americans may help to bring the more nearly *a priori* approach of the Germans into closer bearing with the facts of the given situation in time and place, but the German approach should continue to offer, as it has in the past, much of the theory and system for the movement.[2]

On looking back at the four years that have elapsed since these words were spoken, it may be timely to ask, "Has this complementary cooperation come about in the meantime? Or are there signs of its coming about in the near future?"

II

The "America Institutes" and the "American" or "Americanist" Divisions of "Departments of English" which had come into being between 1945 and 1959,[3] are still operating; another "American Division" has been established since at Freiburg University; and the old "America Institute" at the Free University of Berlin is about to expand to an institution of identical name but of revised structure and extended scope. Universities such as Bonn and Göttingen, which in the 1950's did not set up chairs of "American Literature" or "English Philology with special emphasis on American Literature," have done so or have made provisions for 1964. The University of Erlangen-Nuremberg and the Free University of Berlin recently added to their chairs of American Literature chairs of American social and intellectual history. A similar dual organization is planned for Freiburg and Cologne.

In the field of serial publication of research, including dissertations, two series, *Beihefte zum Jahrbuch für Amerikastudien*[4] and *Mainzer Amerikanistische Beiträge*,[5] are devoted entirely to things American. Two others, *Britannica et Americana*[6] and *Frankfurter Arbeiten aus dem Gebiete der Anglistik und der Amerika-Studien,*[7] welcome both British and American contributions.

The personal side of organized activity, the union of scholars, teachers, administrators *et al.*, interested in American Studies, was effected as early as 1953, the year witnessing the foundation of the "German Association for American Studies." Its *Yearbook, Newsletter,* and annual conventions have become permanent features.

Enumerating these facts is neither identical with proudly showing one's medals nor with counting one's blessings. A few other facts remain, however. Without them there would be no genuine balance sheet.

III

"American Studies" understood as research in, and teaching of, "the nature" of a specific "total culture," "the culture of the people of the United States," American Studies defined as "a single discipline to which scholars may devote their researches and students their work toward higher degrees"[8]—American Studies of this description have not been practised by Germans at German universities after 1945.

What has been done on a steadily increasing scale is the teaching of, and research into, American literature, economics, history, law, political science and sociology, linguistics, geography, philosophy and religion. The non-literary arts would seem to march at the end of the procession. In each of these fields regular course work has proceeded separately: the "procession" has moved forward "single file."[9] Admittedly, there have been exceptions. Coordination of at least two aspects of American civilization has been most frequent with linguistics ("American English") and literature. Jointly they have been added by several universities to their catalogue of majors in which a Ph.D.

candidate may write his dissertation, and of minors which a candidate not majoring in "American English and American literature" may elect for doctor's orals. After all, British English is no patent key to the language of American literature. Whitman's question, "Have you studied out the land, *its idioms* and men?" touches upon a spot whose soreness the non-native reader of American literature is likely to feel much more intensely than the "insider." This fact is sometimes forgotten by Americans (including American Fulbright professors). When familiarizing myself with "American Studies" programs at various American universities in 1955, I could only regret the then very modest role assigned to American speech and its literary uses in those programs. Naturally, American pursuers of American Studies can take a good many things for granted which the outsider simply cannot. Whether the study of one's native tongue ought to belong among these "many things" is debatable. American linguistics and stylistics have made rapid and incisive advances. The relative neglect of one of their areas of concentration, i.e., American English, within American Studies programs in the United States will strike a German observer as being unfortunate. The very trilogy which for its theme and setting has taken the whole of the United States, John Dos Passos' *U.S.A.*, ends its introductory part on the affirmative note "But mostly U.S.A. is the speech of the people." Thus the coordination of American linguistics and literature study as attempted at many German universities may have something to be said for it.

Correlation of three fields (linguistics, literature and geography) was tried out twice at Mainz University. It focused on the study of California, a region my colleague from the department of Geography and myself happened to know fairly well. The regional approach was experimented on for the third time, but varied so as to concentrate on the "Deep South" and include the collaboration of sociology.

Around sixty junior and senior students enrolled each time, the majority of them English majors, around fifteen combining an English with a geography major, only two coming from the department of sociology. Student response was uneven. In the coordinated California seminar a good many English majors were dissatisfied, believing as they did that the geographical and sociological approaches did not appreciably improve the understanding and evaluation of the literary texts chosen. In the "Deep South" course, however, the contributions made by the geographers, and particularly those of the sociologists, were found to be much more helpful. Correlation between the literature and the visual arts of America was tentative only, with nineteenth century symbolism serving for example. Professor Marshall Fishwick, then of Washington and Lee University, was invited to help illuminate literary symbolism by pictorial symbolism. Results of this venture in collaboration were thoroughly encouraging. Partly this may have been due to the caution applied not to *prematurely* relate symbolism in two of the arts to other spheres of contemporaneous American civilization.

Cooperative courses like these have been the exception, not the rule at my university. With the assistance of American guest-professors willing not to multiply literature courses but to co-pilot such cooperative ventures much could be done along inter-disciplinary lines, given sufficient time to get to know one another, and to program a course. Improvisation, however, would be disastrous.

Without drawing rash conclusions from limited experience, I might be permitted a general statement. While offerings in individual fields of American civilization studies have increased considerably in German universities, coordination in the classroom and/or in special research seminars has, to put it mildly, not kept pace. The sum total of these efforts and achievements of individual disciplines has not resulted, and cannot result, in "American Studies" unless the term is defined merely from the listener's viewpoint, as "the integration of lectures on various fields of American culture in the mind of that 'ideal student' who did attend all of these separate classes." I trust I shall not be the only one to doubt the existence and synthesizing capacity of such a prodigy.

Outside of regular classrooms and seminars, the *German Association for American Studies* has, for ten years running, been fighting to show American Studies at work. On two successive days of Pentecost Week such comprehensive problems as "The So-Called Americanization of Germany," "America's Self-Interpretation in the Twentieth Century," "The Contemporary American Analysis of the 'American Way of Life,'" "The German Image of America," "The Development of Racial Integration in the American Educational System," "The Importance and Efficiency of Religion in American Life," "Britain and America: Cultural Unity or Duality?" were treated along interdisciplinary lines. Each of the three speakers, often including an American guest, will tackle the common subject to the best of his disciplinary possibilities, but remain open to problems, if not to methods, of neighboring fields. Here "American Studies" are defined from the questioners' and answerers' viewpoints. The questioner is assuming the existence of problems bearing on "total" American "culture," and not only on one or several of its parts. The answerers share this basic assumption, use the tools of their individual disciplines for formulating their answers and are present at their partners' efforts at answer. Integration is effected in the mind of each speaker, successively turned listener and discussant. Thus, unlike the procedure outlined in the previous paragraph, the task of synthesis is not left to the audience alone. The "unity" of American Studies would seem to rest in the Americanness of the initial problem posed, and in the cooperative effort to solve it, but not in the method applied to solving it.

"American Speech and Literature," "American Social and Intellectual History" (or "American Cultural History"), a two-days' "American Studies" lecture and discussion program every year—it is practically in these three main shapes only[10] that German scholarly interest in America has become institutionalized in explicit terms, in labels including the term "American."

So far, so good. But is it far enough, and is it good enough?

IV

It would seem to be far enough, in view of the length of the road traveled, and of the obstacles on it patiently removed. Finding room for "American literature" within the manor house of "English," adding "American English" to "Modern English" *and* its history, emphasizing "American History" within "History" more strongly than before—all these kinds of annex-building are usually frowned upon by architects of "ideal" programs and "ideal" universities, but they were no easy matter. Laying the foundation of interdisciplinary cooperation and moving on by trial and error were even less so. A simultaneous effort to establish American Studies as a new discipline would have been so difficult as to border on the hopeless. Wherever "America Institutes" as embodiments of the more ambitious and genuine "American Studies" plans were set up at German universities, collaboration with already existing "seminars" (departments) and, through it, influence on exam regulations and teacher training were apparently found to be not less but more hard than at universities at which scholarly occupation with things American started from within, and was institutionalized as a new division of, an old department. Naturally, a time-span of around fifteen years is too short to allow for a final estimate. The chance of *two* ways toward institutionalization has assuredly been a stimulant. Robert Spiller may have had in mind this very duality when he, in the final part of his above-quoted statement, declared: "The pragmatic approach of the Americans may help to bring the more nearly *a priori* approach of the Germans into *closer bearing with the facts of the given situation in time and place.*" Substantially, if not literally, it implied the same advice as another dean of American Studies, Tremaine McDowell, had given me during my Minnesota months in 1955. It was a lesson to be learned to one's advantage.

Fundamentally, however, it was not adjustment to existing conditions in German Humanities Schools that recommended the policy of "American extensions" of traditional departments. As outlined in section I, "American Studies" interpreted as a variation upon the already domesticated type of "area studies" or as a national species of the genus "Kulturwissenschaft" or "Kulturgeschichte" might have found academic allies inside the German Humanities Schools, yet this alliance would have been of little help for three reasons: (1) These allies were, for better or worse, subjects rather for researchers than for large groups of students, most of them planning on a high school teaching career. (2) These subjects did not include a language closely linking them to another, already "traditional" discipline. The special relationship existing, on linguistic grounds, between American Studies and such an important research *and* teaching subject as English had no parallel among the regular subjects of the "area studies" type. One might point to Latin-American Studies as a potential counterpart to American Studies with the comity of area studies. The parallel is valid inasmuch as a language, Spanish for that matter, connects Latin-American Studies with the tra-

ditional German discipline of Romance Philology. The parallel lacks validity insofar as Spanish is but one of the two
languages, Portuguese being the other, linking Latin-
American Studies to Romance Philology, and Spanish occupies a considerably less important place than English in
the German Humanities School. Besides, unlike American
Studies, their Latin-American neighbor has been confined to
one institute each in Berlin and Hamburg. (3) Area studies
had been discredited by the special favor they had received
from the National Socialist regime. It had encouraged their
organization first in a separate Berlin institution of higher
learning and later incorporated it in the University of Berlin as a new "school" ("Fakultät"). Humanities Schools,
already at that date, began to sense a competitor and an
encroachment of politics upon scholarship. Their legitimate
apprehensions survived the fall of the regime and, with it,
the fall of the rival.[11]

Metaphorically speaking, it was not such practical obstacles on the road but theoretical obstacles, convictions
in the hearts of the travelers which governed the policy of
"American extensions" of traditional departments. The triad
binding together the German "Faculty of Philosophy" as
reshaped by Wilhelm von Humboldt's Neo-Humanism consists of Philosophy, Language and History, three basic
facets of Man—Man thinking, Man establishing communication, Man acting, working out his salvation in time and
change. Man as such, and not men as members of national
groups, still seems to be "the proper study of (academic)
mankind." Accordingly, culture as such and not "national
cultures" is felt to be the fundamental objective. The equa-
tion of *a* language with *a* nation, of *a* culture with *a* nation
is sidetracked by thinking in terms of "language communities" or "culture communities" cutting across national
boundaries. The German member of the "Faculty of Philosophy" is not alone in thinking that way. For a similar

view held by a prominent Dutch philologist, I would like
to refer to R. W. Zandvoort. His remarks are the more to
the point as they stem from a scholar with long and profound interest in American English and American literature.
Moreover, they were published as part of his review of
*American Studies in Europe, their History and Present
Organization*, the deservedly well-known two-volume survey by Sigmund Skard. Says R. W. Zandvoort:

> . . . though "American Studies" cannot dispense with the
> study of American literature, the latter would be acting
> against its own interests by regarding itself merely or
> mainly as a department of the former. On the contrary, it
> will have to beware of any encroachment on its autonomy,
> and to maintain its primary connections with the study of
> literature as such, and with English literature in particular.[12]

The recognition of concrete national varieties—"English
literature in particular"—*and* the predominant desire for
basic unity *in abstracto*—"literature as such"—are obvious
and will be shared by German colleagues. The same wish
for linking the specific to the general appears to have motivated the establishment in Germany of chairs for General
and Comparative Linguistics and, though much later and
more rarely, for Comparative Literature and, rarer still, for
Comparative Culture Study ("Vergleichende Kulturwissenschaft").

The roots of this attitude reach far back into the past.
The international diffusion of Greek and Latin languages
and cultures, the supra-national character of the Roman
Catholic Church and the Holy Roman Empire, the split
of central Europe's German language area into several
national divisions, the far from happy experience of the
Germans with nineteenth century nationalism in a belated,
virulent twentieth century form have all helped cultivate
in the German scholar a preference for supra-national phe-

nomena, and a tacit dislike of a nationally limited or even nationalistically distorted view of "culture." Patiently looking upon *one* (supposedly) "total culture," e.g. the American one, as a type or even prototype[13]—such a typological view of a concrete national culture has not yet taken root. Not even German "Departments of German" have provided for anything similar to "American Studies." "German Studies" understood as the study of the "total culture" of the German people simply does not exist as an inter-disciplinary activity, let alone a separate discipline, within the German Humanities School.[14]

Nor should the influential example of German "Romance Philology," elder sister of "English Philology," be overlooked in this context. But a few months ago, *Romanische Forschungen,* a leading quarterly in the field, with understandable pride in its 75 year long tradition, saw fit to remind readers of its editorial policy by stating:

> Die romanische Philologie erscheint hier in ihrer Einheit und Vielfalt als Wissenschaft von den *Sprachen und Literaturen* aller europäischen Völker, die eine Tochtersprache des Lateinischen sprechen . . . Zu ihnen gesellen sich Sprache und Schrifttum der aussereuropäischen Länder, z.B. Mittelund Südamerikas.[15]

In this statement the above-mentioned principle of a history-founded language community embracing European as well as transatlantic countries is operating again. Surely, it is not from this quarter that American Studies, with their orientation toward one total national culture, could expect any support. There seems to be something basically universalist in the traditional German view of scholarship which does not believe in the genuine value of such specifics as "American" or even "German" Studies for a profound intellectual training. Calling it mere prejudice would mean deceiving oneself as to the issues involved.

V

Ironically to say, this German traditional view of scholarship *has lately found voluntary or involuntary supporters among American* guests at German universities and not infrequently among those who came to replete the then thin ranks of teachers of American literature and linguistics, core subjects in any curriculum designed for *foreign* students of American life. Linguistic systems as almost self-sufficient organisms, individual works of art as similarly coherent wholes, "history of literature primarily as an art"[16]—such battle cries[17] have gone up so often that by now they have been domesticated as "household words." To Germans, in particular to literary scholars, they have had a familiar ring. "Let's find out the goodness of American literature as literature, and not the Americanness of American literature" can be recalled by the present writer as a simplified version of the tale coming from the mouth of an American colleague. So is it to be wondered at that to a good many scholars over here there is no point in trying to find out the "Americanness" of American literature and American English by "relating" them "to their culture"[18] or in conceiving of American literary scholarship and linguistics as "contributions" to American Studies?

Taking into account all of the practical and theoretical obstacles mentioned previously and adding to them this American support given them occasionally, one is driven to the conclusion that what has been achieved has gone far enough. But to resume our complementary question, "Is it good enough?"

VI

The answer, an answer from four different quarters, would appear to be "No."

(1) There are the thoughtful planners inside the Free University of Berlin. They are bent on converting the present "America Institute" into an academic structure of the same name but, in addition to its present two sections, of American Literature and Civilization, comprising another four, viz. Government, History, Economics and Geography. Each of these sections will be headed by a professor whose chair is in one of the traditional departments of the university.[19] It is to be expected that coordination will be established not only in the minds of students listening to six professors but earlier than that, i.e. in the mind and lecture of each professor, or at least in seminar courses to be conducted jointly. It remains to be seen whether correlation will stay at its old stage of a confederation of specialists or advance to the federal union of a unified study program which sees "an organic unity in the subject itself."[20] At this point it is appropriate to heed Roy Harvey Pearce's warning that a unification like this presupposes "a shared concept of the study of civilization."[21] One should also be aware of such requirements for genuine American Studies as were emphasized by a critical British observer of their German brand:

> The truth is, the inter-disciplinary approach, to which so much lip-service is paid, needs more than a common theme. It needs a common and mutual understanding, or common will to co-operate and a common conviction that such an approach is worthwhile. All the pressures in the contemporary university world in America and elsewhere are against it, except one. That is the existence of a common meeting place, a "common-room" in fact. This a university can—must—provide for its members.[22]

(2) Will the new University of the Ruhr District now being established in Bochum provide for American Studies as one of its "common-rooms"? News of far-reaching plans

to abolish the traditional "faculties" (schools) and regroup disciplines have been circulating for quite a while. Indeed, two types of institutions of higher learning that, as a rule,[23] have been kept separate in the German academic world, i.e. the university and the institute of technology, will be fused. But excellent as the recipes may be,[24] the proof of the pudding will be in the eating. The final test of the "goodness" of the new university will be the type of man leaving it after five or six years.

(3) The academic desire for new patterns of grouping "disciplines," which manifests itself in Berlin and Bochum organizing committees is not restricted to Germany. A "School of English *and American* Studies" (italics are mine), with such an experienced and energetic person as David Daiches for Dean, has recently been set up within the new "University of Sussex" at Brighton, England. A key man in British American Studies, the historian Frank Thistlethwaite, has been appointed Vice-Chancellor of the equally new "University of East Anglia" at Norwich. British developments are bound to have repercussions in German universities, especially in departments of English. In brief, shared outside Germany, this desire for new patterns of grouping may give a chance to American Studies as *one* of these new patterns. In German universities, however, this chance is likely to be confined to research, i.e. to individual research carried out by professors and other staff members as well as by small groups of graduate students working toward their Ph.D. If regulations for the M.A. degree lately revived at some German universities can be kept elastic enough to permit focusing work in the major *and* the two minors on American (or, for that matter, any other) civilization, slightly larger groups of students might be induced to choose American Studies as a unifying principle.

(4) Any appreciable number of German students will not be tempted to do so as long as the *university training* of

the high school teacher of English (or any other modern language, including the mother tongue) and the *high school teaching* as such stick to the present-day rule of two majors and, on the university training level, two compulsory minors (philosophy and pedagogy). It is from the senior students and the high school teachers alike that in the long run the most emphatic "no" to our question of "Is it good enough?" might be expected, and this for the following reasons: The terrifically increased quantity of knowledge in any high school subject has made selectivity imperative. "The exemplary" as one of the meaningful principles of selection is being advocated by educators continuously but practised less continuously. It is here that American Studies have to offer at least three exemplary phenomena. Ranging from economics and government to the arts and religious life, they permeate every sphere of culture. They might be defined as (1) the process of decolonization extending from political independence to racial desegregation; (2) the attempt to reconcile the demand for liberty with the demand for equality in a "nation of nations," and in a space comprising a half-continent; (3) the founding of modern civilization on thoroughly rationalized industry so that American civilization can be considered as "prototype" of modern civilization all the world over. A few months ago Ralph Gabriel quoted Gertrude Stein to the effect that "Americans are the oldest people on earth—they were the first to enter the twentieth century."[25] What at first sight appears to be a mere witticism, does it not imply an "exemplary" lesson twentieth century America has to teach?

By selection of the exemplary and by experimenting on inter-disciplinary correlation the German high school has come to challenge academic teaching conventions. The recent and as yet tentative introduction into the senior high school curriculum of *Gemeinschaftskunde* ("social studies"), a hoped-for integration of history, geography, economics, sociology and political science, has been much debated. A conference of university teachers that in June 1963 met in the Otto Suhr Institute of the Free University of Berlin thought it "indispensable" that in all of the states of the Federal Republic the discipline *Sozialkunde* be recognized as a special exam subject for the teacher's diploma, and be taught not only on the senior but on all the three levels of the German high school system.[26] It remains to be seen whether *Gemeinschaftskunde* (or *Sozialkunde*) understood either as an inter-disciplinary activity or, more ambitiously, as a new, unified subject will really condition an atmosphere favorable to American Studies in school and university. The term "Kunde" may serve as an unfortunate reminder of *Amerikakunde* and of the dichotomy of "Kunde" vs. "Wissenschaft," the former *allegedly* restricting itself to assembling facts and presenting them pre-scientifically. But "Volks*kunde*" (folklore) seems to have overcome this terminological sound barrier, and required full academic status.

Another challenge to the traditional kind of the high school teacher's university training is older than the one furnished by *Gemeinschaftskunde* or *Sozialkunde*, and it has been less fiercely debated. In the long run, however, it might prove to be more powerful. Regulations for the teaching of modern languages in German high schools usually, and rightfully, demand of the teacher that he be able to introduce children and adolescents into the "culture" of other peoples. In practice this mostly means two ancient (Roman and Greek) and one modern (English or French) or two modern (English and French) cultures and one ancient (Latin). The crucial question to what extent foreign languages and "texts," i.e. literary monuments and non-literary documents, are adequate to serving as a kind of patent-key to foreign cultures, and the related problem of how the non-language-based spheres of cultures should be taught, has not been threshed out yet. Can American Studies, not only as a research but also as a teaching subject, put at the disposal of the foreign language, say English, teacher a workable method of introducing young people into the "total culture," both its language-based and its non-language-based spheres, of a foreign nation, into its non-literary arts, its customs, its tacit assumptions and taboos, the silent decisions of its statesmen and martyrs, the manual work silently done by its pioneers? If it can, American Studies, a problem child in the present-day German academic family, will have the merit of not only *posing* but also of *solving* at least one of them. It is only then that American Studies as practised in Germany will be felt to be "good enough."

For the time being many German practitioners in such parts of American culture as American literature, American English or history, and many colleagues in other disciplines will contribute to American Studies the function of the experimental thorn in the academic flesh, a usefulness indispensable but limited to offering a second, inter-disciplinary, approach beside the older, as yet more practicable intra-disciplinary one. Some of them might even go so far as to vary a well-known statement of an Anglo-American, T. S. Eliot, on "German thought"[27] to the following individual effect:

> I believe that I have myself found American and non-American thought on American Studies of inestimable value, simply because I tend to disagree with it violently; and it therefore forces me to think violently in order to discover the grounds of my disagreement.

It is only fair to add that some such voyages of intellectual "discovery" have, in the past, led to "new-found lands." For sceptics, provided they be open-minded sailors, sense the intellectual and educational winds of the future, and not yearn for rapid promotion, studies in the total cultures of the peoples we are living together with in an ever-shrinking world may be one of these "lands." Will American Studies ever develop to be the systematic proto-type of studies like these or will they just remain that ex-perimental thorn in the academic flesh?

VII

Winding up on this note of questioning hesitancy, I would like to return to Robert Spiller's statement quoted at the end of the introductory remarks. Worth repeating once more, its first part, the wish that "the pragmatic ap-proach of the Americans may help to bring the more nearly *a priori* approach of the Germans into closer bearing with the facts of the given situation in time and place," has met with fulfillment. The second part, the request that "the German approach should continue to offer, as it has in the past, much of the theory and system for the movement," has so far served as a challenge rather than produced a co-herent response. For the present writer and, he hopes, a good many colleagues of his as well, at least one thing has re-emerged from all of these family squabbles about the problem child called "American Studies," and this more clearly than ever: his own specialty, the study of Ameri-can English and American literature, has as it were a double linkage, one as natural as the other, one with the study of language and literature as such, especially of English as spoken and written, the other with American Studies un-derstood as the study of American culture. The one links the specific to the general, the other the part to the whole. Trivial as this grain of truth may appear, it would not be amiss to cling to it at times of "family disputes" tending to blur distinctions and call for monomaniacs when a com-posed Janus head is needed. Surely, Janus is always shown as having two faces but he is not reported to have been given to squinting.

1. For a more detailed description cf. Sigmund Skard, *American Studies in Europe, Their History and Present Organization*, vol. I (Philadelphia, 1958), 209-357, and, by the same author, *The American Myth and the European Mind: American Studies in Europe 1776-1960*, (Philadelphia, 1961), esp. 100-103.

2. "Value and Method in American Studies: The Literary Versus the Social Approach," *Jahrbuch für Amerikastudien*, IV (1959), 12-13.

3. Berlin's "America Institute," also functioning until 1945 as "American Division of the English Seminar," was set up around 1936.

4. Carl Winter Publishers, Heidelberg.

5. Max Hueber, München.

6. Cram, de Gruyter and Co., Hamburg.

7. Carl Winter, Heidelberg.

8. Spiller, *loc. cit.*, 11.

9. Of the 111 lecture and seminar courses offered on American subjects at German universities and Institutes of Technology during the winter semester of 1962-63 only two were interdisciplinary, the one of them, however, serving not intra-American, but American-German comparative purposes.

10. American-sponsored programs such as the "American Studies Seminar" held at Falkenstein from mid-July through early August and staffed by American professors are not included in this report. It limits itself to *German* initiative.

11. For Arnold Bergsträsser's view cf. his "Amerikastudien als Problem der Forschung und Lehre," *Jahrbuch für Amerikastudien* I (1956), 8. Cf. Skard, *op. cit.*, vol. I, 286-287.

12. *English Studies* 39, no. 4 (August, 1958).

13. Cf. Marshall W. Fishwick, "New Frontiers in American Studies," *American Studies* VI, no. 1, (April, 1963), 3, reporting Ralph Gabriel: "He recalled the remark of Gertrude Stein that Americans are the oldest people on earth—they were the first to enter the twentieth century. What many Europeans mean when they say they don't like *American* civilization is that they don't like modern civilization."

14. As for their non-existence in the United States as well and for a critical view of this state of things cf. Bergsträsser, *loc. cit.*, 10.

15. Vittorio Klostermann, Frankfurt am Main, 1963.

16. René Wellek, "Literary History" in René Wellek and Austin Warren, *Theory of Literature*, New York, 1949, 282.

17. For a British echo cf. David Daiches' "General Preface" to Clifford Leech, *Webster: The Duchess of Malfi*, (London, 1963), 5: "Without taking up the anti-historical position of some of the American 'New Critics,' we can nevertheless recognise the need for critical studies that concentrate on the work of literary art rather than on its historical background or cultural environment."

18. Cf. Spiller, *loc. cit.*, 14.

19. Cf. "American Institute in Berlin," *American Studies News*, vol. I, no. 2 (April, 1963), 1-3.

20. Spiller, *loc. cit.*, 20.

21. Cf. "American Studies as a Discipline," *College English* 18 (1956-57), 179-186.

22. D. C. Watt, "A German View of American Studies," *British Association for American Studies Bulletin*, no. 2, new series, (March, 1961), 80.

23. Exceptions are Berlin's Technical University and in pre-World War II days, Danzig's Institute of Technology.

24. World War II days, Danzig's Institute of Technology. As to the attitude of Herr Lenz, Federal Minister for Scientific Research, cf. *Frankfurter Allgemeine Zeitung*, June 22, 1963: "Lenz von Amerika beeindruckt." He is reported as pleading, on the strength of his American impressions, "for a promotion of teamwork in German academic life" and for "the reduction of the rigid faculty boundaries."

25. Cf. footnote 14.

26. *Frankfurter Allgemeine Zeitung*, June 27, 1963, "Kulturelle Nachrichten."

27. *The New English Weekly*, 26 (1945), 192.

The American Scholar and the World

LUDWIG BORINSKI

LUDWIG BORINSKI is Professor of English Language and Civilization at the University of Hamburg. He has published widely on both British and American fiction, especially that of the twentieth century.

THE MOST ELEMENTARY FACT IN OUR PRESENT WORLD IS American political and economic leadership. Is there any parallel in the cultural sphere? Yes. American literature has reached maturity in the twentieth century; its influence and popularity probably exceeds today that of any other national literature. Two Americans, Henry James and T. S. Eliot, have dominated twentieth century English literature to an extent which we are only beginning to realize. America's contribution to twentieth century science and technology is equally impressive. Nevertheless there is one field of intellectual culture where American leadership is even more undisputed—historical and literary scholarship.

This is little realized because this field has no publicity value; and because it contradicts all *a priori* assumptions about the older and stronger cultural traditions of Europe. But the fact remains that European scholarship in the humanities has progressively declined in the last forty years. The decline has been accompanied by a parallel rise of American scholarship, which has definitely taken the lead since the 1930's. Not only the two world wars, with their enormous losses of talent and tradition, are to blame. European countries hardly affected by these catastrophies have also declined, as have Germany and France. The ultimate cause may lie in a deep-seated cultural differentiation of Europe and America. American literature remained realistic and naturalistic while European literature and art became abstractionist and manneristic. The decay of European scholarship runs parallel with the rise of "modernism" in art and literature. Scholarship is necessarily concerned with reality—a truism sometimes forgotten in present-day Europe.

American scholarship in the humanities has more than "ornamental" value. It contains enormous political possibilities, and could enable America to benefit the whole world. The function of academic scholarship in society is an interesting theme which hitherto has been given insufficient attention. Scholarship is not a mere "ornament" of society with perhaps some snob value and nothing else, but an indispensable function without which society cannot flourish.

Americans may find this difficult to understand because it applies more to Europe than to America. In America the scholar may become politically important as an expert adviser of the rulers. But historical facts, historical awareness, hardly affect the feelings and reactions of the masses. Even religious prejudices are mainly connected with elementary social facts, social differences, recent immigration, social stratification. But in Europe tendentious falsification of history and related cultural influences have always been a major political force which may even endanger the existence of society. On the continent state officials, clergy, and liberal professions have always been the rulers of society. Universities were and are professional schools where this numerically small class receives its training. The rest of the population takes its ideas and standards from this minority. The minority thinking is shaped by "cultural" influences, mainly by diluted scholarship absorbed in the university

years. All Europe can thus be turned upside down and even
destroyed by historical myths and stupid philosophies. Adolf
Hitler is only the spectacular climax in a long series of similar figures and "movements."

What is more: Europe is a hotbed of religious and
national prejudices. They and not social and economic
problems create many of the cleavages and enmities which
obstruct a reasonable long-term settlement in Europe, thus
endangering world peace. These prejudices are produced
and kept going by historical myths, which could be dis-
pelled by honest and intelligent scholarship. The entire
intellectual atmosphere of a whole continent could thus be
purified. By such a positive program by an intellectual minority, society could be influenced to the good. What the
future official, clergyman, schoolmaster and lawyer hears in
his university years determines the intellectual climate as a
whole. Through scholarship society can be changed for the
better.

What is first needed for such improvement is a clear
understanding of the shortcomings of traditional European
scholarship. I spoke of historical myths and tendentious
falsification of history. The existence of these evils has long
been known. But their real extent has never been realized.
They reach much farther than has ever been suspected. For
example, much of our historical thinking is colored by a
hidden bias against the Christian religion as such; seldom
articulated, it is consequently hardly realized by most people. Many regard pre-Christian antiquity, especially "the
Greeks" as the climax of the world's culture. Destroyed by
Christianity the classical spirit was revived in the Renaissance. Such a happy revival meant the "real" end of Christianity. That it survives to the present day is considered an
irregularity which has no legitimate right of existence. The
sufferers from such delusions are not the practicing Christians (who are vital), but the intellectuals who hold them.

People who live in a world of their own will never gain any actual power.

Around 1900, when this "neopagan" view of history was at its height, much of Europe was ruled by clerical parties. This anti-Christian myth, fully developed in the early eighteenth century, later produced a romantic and clerical counter-myth. The world, in good shape only in the middle ages, has been hopelessly out of joint since the Renaissance. The climax of history was in the thirteenth century. Such a view is more absurd than the other one; but the worst thing is that the historical thinking of most educated people is a confused mixture of both. Few men, even professional scholars, ever reflect on the first principles of history. Therefore such self-contradictory inheritances from the ages of reason and romanticism can exist side by side in the same brain.

It would be wrong to assume that these two views correct each other, or that truth might result from a compromise between them. They are both so far from reality that reality is not in between them, but somewhere else. Then there is the Teutonic myth, the third ingredient of that jumble in our brains called "our usual view of history." All that is good in our world was produced by the Teutonic races. The Latins are hopelessly degenerate. Their main occupation in life is adultery. They may have produced some good art. But all art is really immoral, though one must not say so. Curiously enough this view has been largely adopted even in the Latin countries, because the nineteenth century Prussians and English were so frightfully efficient in self-advertisement. Besides they had coal, scarce in the Latin countries. This gave them a temporary advantage in the early age of industry.

These myths have a political background, but they are not due only to political forces. They could gain their mastery only because of certain shortcomings in formal thinking and method which exist quite independent of political manipulation. These shortcomings are particularly manifest in the German mind, and Germany dominated European scholarship before 1914. Again I can only touch the fringe of a great subject. German scholarship excelled in the aesthetic and philosophic interpretation of history and culture and improved factual exactitude in research; but it lacked common sense and realism in the interpretation of these facts. It neglected the realities of life behind concepts and rules. Our social history was too much orientated on legal history. But laws in former ages had little to do with the realities of social life. Similarly it is useless to know "the British Constitution" (which even legally does not exist) unless one knows the political and social forces which are working in it. Every author was credited with a fixed "Weltanschauung." It was forgotten that men's opinions change constantly, that a man may have two or more contradictory opinions at the same time, and that the most valuable knowledge is not conceptual. All ideas of an age were derived from literary "influences" and "sources," overlooking that ideas can spring up spontaneously as a response to the necessities of life in a given period.

Thus it was with the ideal of chivalry in the middle ages. Some professors thought that the ideal of chivalry came into being because people in that age had read Cicero. This lack of awareness of the realities of life resulted in the rule of rigid historical patterns. In reality in the middle ages all Eastern and Northern Europe imported textiles from Flanders and exchanged them for cereals, timber, furs and flax. This was ignored because of the notion that medieval commerce dealt in spices and nothing else. The rule of historical myths (about which we heard before) became possible only through this predominance of conceptual thinking and inadequate awareness of real life. Political wishful thinking played its part. History was explained by one agent, economic, religious, race, or "Volksgeist." They are the result of intellectual laziness, for history is an interplay of all sorts of forces—intellectual, spiritual, economic, social, political. Only long experience can show which force or group of forces is paramount in a given instance. These same historical ideologies are also inevitably politically inspired. They are the ideal means to create prejudices. Where there is only one agent in history mankind necessarily is divided into angels and devils, the members of one religion against those of the other, dolichocephalics against brachycephalics, the Teutons against the Latins, etc. Intellectual shortcomings and political manipulation work together.

American scholarship has not only the task but also the ability to overcome these traditional shortcomings of European historical thinking. From the beginning it has been more impartial and objective, owing to distance and detachment from European feuds. But it has also common sense and awareness of the realities of life in the interpretation of historical facts; this is a heritage of Anglo-Saxon culture. All this is combined with political awareness. We saw that European myths have also a political background. The American scholar who is also the citizen of a free country with a tradition of political life sees such political "inspiration"—at least he is aware that it exists. Only in America has historical scholarship become something like an exact science with incontrovertible results.

Rigid specialization and a new thoroughness in the collection of material have made this possible. All older scholarship looks amateurish compared with it. This is extremely important. Most of our knowledge of the past consists of assumptions copied from textbook to textbook, often originating some centuries back in a tendentious lie about which we now know nothing. Everybody repeats the epigram that the Prussian schoolmaster won the battle of Koniggraetz. It would be easy to prove that Austria actually had the better schools. We read in textbooks that social changes in sixteenth century England weakened the rich nobility and strengthened the gentry. In reality they doubled the number of magnates and reduced the gentry. The Reformation in the German cities has been ascribed to the rapacity of merchants greedy for Church funds. But in truth it was everywhere opposed by the merchant class who benefited most from those same funds. The majority of the facts in Sombart's well-known work *Der moderne Kapitalismus* are wrong. But this work was long regarded as an unassailable textbook. The most disconcerting phenomenon is the persistence of these myths. That France before the Revolution was a country of peasant-owners has been rediscovered every thirty years since Tocqueville. Yet we still read that "in the Revolution the peasants of France took the land." All this is the fault of the glib textbook, bane of academic education. Only the American standard of exactitude and completeness can rid us of such flaws. That present American scholarship has greater impartiality and more common sense than Europe's can be seen in numerous scholarly periodicals. Yet even in America much remains to be done. The first prerequisite is to investigate the historical background of prevailing historical distortions. It is not enough to rectify them and give an authenticated objective picture of the past. Even then the correct version of history will not be believed unless we show how the tenacious myths originated; how and why they were fabricated. This would be a fascinating task for dedicated scholars.

Little has so far been done in this line. In the last resort most myths can be traced to political forces, management, and manipulation. Not only scholarship, but all cultural life in the last 250 years has been so manipulated. Everybody knows about governments cultivating national myths of history and their own brand of national culture. But this is not all. More important is manipulation by international forces, often directed from one point, and serving certain very specific interests. One goal has always been the control of intellectual life, a control effected by indirect means without direct compulsion, often unnoticed by its agents, because it worked with a superb technique of insinuation.

We need also new *aspects* of history. Because historical teaching has mainly served political forces, history is seen too frequently under religious and national aspects. (By religion I mean here religious sectarianism.) Because history was misused to teach religious hatred, the influence of different forms of religion on civilization has been grossly exaggerated. Even economic misery and prosperity and the general standard of cleanliness was directly derived from prevailing forms of religion.

History should first of all be seen under neutral aspects, removed from sectarian and national jealousies. It should be taught to illustrate the gradual growth of the foundations of our present-day civilization: the growth of the exact sciences (including their philosophical foundation) and technological invention; the growth of industrial civilization which is really much older than the industrial revolution of the eighteenth century; the growth of free political institutions *and* of the modern state. Both are indispensable in an industrial civilization. Industrial civilization is (in the long run) incompatible with despotism. It depends on an efficient administration and the rule of law. The contribution of continental absolutism to this element of our civilization should not be ignored, though absolutism as such is a thing of the past; it made the peoples politically immature and cannot exist in an industrial society. The growth of moral standards and of moral and intellectual forces is vital in an industrial civilization. Religion, literature, art, philosophy, and the humanities should be seen under this light. They are not "ornaments" of civilization, but essential elements in it.

Literature and the arts suggest moral forces and intellectual insight in a preconceptual fashion. Literature also makes us understand human nature and human society better than most psychology and sociology; true understanding of human nature is essential in a complex industrial society. Religion should be seen as the strongest of those moral and intellectual forces without which society and even the individual cannot exist. This would make it possible to view all higher religions and more especially Christianity in a positive light. "Real" doctrinal differences between the Christian Churches should not be ignored; but the historian has also the right to investigate and point out the large element of artificial verbalism in the pretended differences of religious creeds which are in fact more important than the real ones.

History should be seen under the aspect of humanitarian progress in law, social structure, social services and international order. Forms of federalism and of supernational structure in the past should receive the special attention of historians; here is a case where the political tradition of Germany can make a contribution to the solution of present political problems. The wars of the past could also be seen under this aspect. Many wars were purely destructive (e.g. the wars of religion). Others helped—but no longer help —to extend areas of peace and order or to restore the balance of power. One of the most pernicious of the prevailing historical fallacies is the attempt to construe a conflict between religion and humanitarian progress, or between morality and humanity. This has been persistently attempted since the eighteenth century. The role of the Church in humanitarian and educational progress should be recognized. On the other hand it should not be overlooked that religion has often produced hatred and intolerance. This is a latent temptation inherent in all organized forms of belief, including nonreligious creeds. Nowhere is the awareness of the realities of life more important than in the evaluation of the symptoms of religious intolerance in the past. Much has been exaggerated and more has been falsified by isolating facts from the social realities of the age.

All these aspects of a new view of history could be comprehended in the notion of social function. All historical phenomena should be judged by the criterion whether they were in the well-understood interests of society as a whole in a given age. This would provide an impartial standpoint. Absolutism was socially useful in the seventeenth century, but no longer in the age of industrial society after 1750. Feudalism had its value in the early stages of civilization, but its remnants are evil in an industrial society. Much of this sounds like a truism. Most European history is written not from the standpoint of social usefulness, but from national or sectarian standpoints, to prove the superiority and impeccability of a nation, race, class, or religion.

The artificial opposition of the middle and modern age has often been criticized, yet is as potent as ever, serving the interest of certain political forces. The middle ages and the modern age are two stages in the one process of the growth of Western civilization. The former are the immature stage, and can never be extolled as a model. They were an age of experimentation and semianarchy, not one of "order," as we are told. They were nevertheless the forerunner of the modern period. Modern science started then. Technical inventions were made then; industrial civilization, the modern state and free institutions have their roots there.

Europe's view of history is often vitiated by a one-sided glorification of everything revolutionary, unorthodox and nonconformist. If a writer was an honest adherent of the established order this is either excused as a deplorable weakness, or explained away. Here is another very potent reason for our current falsification of history. Many great minds in history were on the side of order in a well-understood sense of the word. Owing to our prejudice in favor of all that looks "revolutionary" the greatest names are little mentioned outside the college textbook (Dryden, Corneille and George Eliot are examples); or else they are misrepresented as heretics or nihilists, which again distorts history. Dante, Milton and Dostojewski are cases in point. Many of the most valuable products of the human mind are simply ignored for this reason. Orthodox Christian theology is a masterpiece of human intelligence, and should therefore be known also by the nonbeliever. Close to the realities of life, this literature—especially postmedieval theology—is not only unknown by the educated public; it almost has the status of forbidden books. Indirect manipulation and insinuation have achieved more in our world than all the censorship and inquisitions of the past.

Again it is largely American scholars who have defied this taboo and even utilized orthodox theological thought. The discovery of the sixteenth century Spanish jurists is an example. New England theology has been investigated. The theology of English Puritanism—much more valuable and a major achievement of the English mind—has never been adequately studied. Theology has a place of honor in contemporary American thought.

We live in an irrational age. Consequently the temptation is strong to fight prejudices by the same irrational means by which they have been created and disseminated—by "subliminal" propaganda which appeals to the subrational, semiconscious layers of the mind. This may have some limited success, but a real solution will only be effected by rational methods. Silence is the mother of prejudices which are either insinuated or inherited in silence. Consequently prejudices can be overcome by outspokenness and an open discussion of relevant questions. The present situation in Europe where most elements of the real situation are unmentionable is the ideal breeding ground for prejudice and evil propaganda.

But more is needed than open discussion. Prejudice is also the result of ignorance. Therefore knowledge is the most potent weapon against it. Intimate personal contacts between members of different groups help to dispel prejudices. Knowledge must be combined with intelligence, i.e. judgment and common sense, which draws the right practical conclusions from knowledge.

All this has an important practical application in present-day Europe. The very existence of a continent is endangered by prejudice. The way out can never be in a lowering of the general intellectual level, but only in an improvement of the standards of knowledge and intelligence.

I have mentioned the possible political value of American scholarship in the present European situation. The explosion of historical myths by honest intelligent scholarship is in fact an indispensable contribution in an attempt to overcome the feuds and cleavages of our tradition-ridden continent. But this would be only a first step in the right direction. Hatreds and cleavages are not only produced by historical prejudices, but also by "philosophies" and ideologies. Ideological thinking is the second great evil of traditional continental culture. Academic teaching should not be aimed against one or several ideologies (e.g. Communism or racialism). It should be skeptical about *all* ideologies as such, because any ideology perverts reality. Even systems of philosophy should not be taken too seriously. Not all well-known philosophers were especially intelligent people. Real intellectual progress is often outside these systems. Philosophies are reflections of the mind and conditions of their age. Sometimes they contain a practical element. This also applies to systems of economics. Many economic questions have long been solved, but these solutions have often been ignored, and things have been deliberately obscured and complicated in order to prove a political case.

Today all these inherited "systems" are artificially kept

alive, mostly by mere repetition. Often all the traditional arguments for a given system are refuted by what everybody sees in daily life. They are kept alive to disturb the peace, to produce political schisms and cleavages and to prevent an openminded and clearheaded approach to the problems of the day. Ideologies and theories cloud the mind. As in the case of prejudice we see that unity is produced by raising the standard of intelligence. But there is also a strong moral element in this tower of Babylon of conflicting ideologies. They mask greed and the lust for power. We found the same moral element in prejudice. Intellectual and moral decay have produced the schisms of our world; only intellectual culture combined with religion can overcome them.

What sort of intellectual culture should that be? The ultimate aim of all culture must be knowledge of reality to enable us to find a sane and undistorted view of life and the world. This is by no means a truism. Existing traditions of culture are mainly political and aesthetic. Cultural values, literature, philosophies, art, religion, are misused to teach loyalty to a nation, a political "system," a party; or cultural values are a means of aesthetic escapism from real life and its problems.

I said that "ideas" and "systems" are nowadays propagated to create strife and to disturb the peace. But they are also promoted and even fabricated to subvert morality and thus to destroy society itself. As there is only one reality, so there are fixed standards of morality which derive from this reality, namely the very nature of human life which is in its essentials unalterable. It is symptomatic that our current ideologies deny traditional morality. This is only a further consequence of the fact that the low intelligence of our age is no longer able to grasp reality. Pseudo-science and pseudo-scholarship, unfortunately widespread in our world, serve the same aims of disruption and dissolution in the more specialized fields of knowledge. They too can be resisted only by a critical mind and the appeal to reality. We also need some reflection on the reasons for the present widespread appeal of pseudo-science. An important protection against pseudo-science is a wide and solid knowledge of facts. Well written popularized pseudo-history and pseudo-science, politically inspired, thus becomes a screen between the educated public and reality.

I already mentioned the dangers of the glib textbook. Textbook reform is one of the urgent needs of our world. Learning of exact facts is also an indispensable means to cultivate formal intelligence and judgment. I have noted the sinister power of political manipulation in our world. Schools and universities must create an awareness of the methods of political sophistry and insinuation. They must also give a true overall picture of the powers influencing our world and of the working of political life.

American leadership in the long run will be possible only if there is an intellectually and morally homogeneous political class in all major industrial nations of the Western world. Such a political class does not exist on the continent, least of all in Germany. The German is deficient in political judgment because his mind is not habitually turned to reality, especially in politics. Absorbing his knowledge and ideas from books, he lacks the habit of observation. This habit is also a vital weapon against prejudice. What one sees refutes preconceived notions. The culture of a political class is necessarily a culture of mutual understanding and discussion. But in traditional German life there was little need of both because common obedience to a ruler made both unnecessary. This is a further reason for the power of prejudice in the German mind: it is the result of this nonpolitical isolation which could do without compromise and tolerance. The romantic lure of power is also a result of detachment from reality and sociability. Who lives in the world knows the limits of power. The type of culture which I have tried to outline would help to create such a political class. The essential function of American scholarship will by now have become clear. A large amount of personal contact and assimilation, and of collaboration in common political institutions would be further indispensable conditions. The result would be a class of political leaders and high officials spread over the entire free world who speak the same intellectual language, have a similar moral character, and share a common loyalty. Here is a goal worthy of our best efforts.

American Literature in the World Today

RICHARD BEALE DAVIS

RICHARD BEALE DAVIS, Alumni Distinguished Service Professor of American Literature at the University of Tennessee, has served four times abroad since 1947 in lecturing and research. His most recent book is *Intellectual Life in Jefferson's Virginia, 1790–1830* (1964), which received the first Annual Manuscript Award of the American Association for State and Local History.

YOU MAY BE, OR ARE ABOUT TO BECOME, ONE OF THOSE TENS of thousands of Americans who are annually now pounding the airlanes of the world into beaten paths. If you are already, you probably acquired the habit long ago of taking a quick appraising glance, just after you fastened your seat belt, at the person who was to be your closest companion during the hours of your flight. You may have wondered half idly what was impelling this casually dressed man sitting beside you to visit Cape Town, New Delhi, Buenos Aires, or Bangkok. He may have been a business man or an engineer representing American capital. But he was almost as likely to have been a college professor carrying a somewhat different stock of American goods to some remote portion of the globe.

For more than a decade now, the United States as a nation has invested a modest sum in the professor's commodity. Already the dividends appear to be great, in some ways enormous, though not entirely or exactly in dollars and cents.

For since 1947 the American college or university teacher has become a familiar sight in almost any part of the world outside the Iron Curtain. And recently he has even been visiting in the Soviet Union. You may meet him, as you would any other tourist, on an elephant in Jaipur or in a gondola on the Grand Canal, but ninety-nine times out of a hundred this situation will be for him only incidental. He is on his way to or from an experience more strenuous and serious, a real labor of learning and of love. The labor is varied, even more varied than it is for him at home. Possibly he may be bringing technical assistance to some far-off land, setting up an atomic reactor, instituting a health program, or explaining soil conservation. But he wouldn't have to be a professor to do these things. Most of our college instructors now roaming the world are doing so in order that they may demonstrate, in a number of different ways, to our friends, would-be friends, and critics among many people and nations, what we actually are and why we are what we are. By their demonstration they hope that they may clear away misunderstandings and ancient prejudices, develop respect for America's moral and intellectual as well as her technical achievement, and win friends when and where we need friends.

The Department of State and its representatives abroad, along with the related personnel of the United States Information Service, are to be sure also trying to demonstrate these things along with others. And they do a good job within limits imposed by the nature of their larger program. But the professional diplomat always has been and inevitably always will be suspect: to the non-American, he, like all diplomats, is a paid propagandist. The university professor, on the other hand, traditionally and almost universally respected around the rest of the earth (at least a *little* more so than at home) for his eagerness to learn and to teach truth —and I am not exaggerating his reputation—carries more weight. The Spanish-American, the Indian, or the Norwegian feels that almost every professor is really informed, he is relatively unhampered in what he may say, and he is by nature and vocation candid. For this reason, and a combination of others, the burden, or the privilege, of explaining to the rest of mankind what America is and from whence it comes has to a remarkable extent fallen upon our university teacher.

The privilege fell upon him somewhat fortuitously, when in 1946 and 1948 the Congress enacted two basic pieces of legislation making effective the strong feeling of a group of lawmakers that in the new age of air and nuclear power the world had become very small and that mutual understanding was urgent as it had never been before. Public Law 584, the Fulbright Act, literally turned swords into plowshares by authorizing the use of foreign currencies, accumulated by the United States through sale of surplus property materials, for educational exchange. Public Law 402, the Smith-Mundt Act, made further *dollar* funds available for exchange purposes. Even earlier, in 1938, the government had begun a cultural exchange program. Since 1938 sixty thousand exchanges with more than eighty countries have been arranged.

From the American side, by far the largest segment of those sent abroad have gone in the capacity of lecturers, and of these the overwhelmingly greatest group are teachers of American literature. American history, politics, and art are widely represented too. But the fact is, with the exception of the United Kingdom and certain other members of the British Commonwealth, the foreign intellectual world seems far more interested in our creative literature than in our history, our technology, or the nature of our government. Highly conscious of this fact, our agencies have sent abroad a growing number of men and women who can explain, analyze, trace the tradition of our writing. For the 1962-

1963 session, to Europe, Africa, the Near and Far East, Australia, New Zealand, and Latin America, through Smith-Mundt and Fulbright, we shall send abroad, usually for a year's stay, some seventy-five persons who will talk about American literature. As American Specialists under the State Department, probably ten or twelve more will be added to present the subject. *You well may ask why.* My answer must be a fairly complex one, including some consideration of world knowledge of American literature and America in the remoter past, what it has been in more recent years, and why we must continue to explain our writing. The answer involves values, values for American prestige and influence abroad, and values for ourselves. It involves the significance of what we have come to call THE AMERICAN IMAGE in a rapidly shrinking world.

Though some foreign nations, especially in Europe, took some slight notice of the intellectual character of the new nation across the Atlantic from as early as 1779, the first and greatest attention, and the last, has in this regard been paid by the educated peoples of the world to one phase of it, our literature, beginning with Irving and Cooper and continuing through Faulkner and Frost and Salinger. Their reasons have been varied, but usually and largely out of their curiosity to see one or both the faces of America that this writing represents. For it is a double image we have shown, though perhaps inadvertently, from Irving's and Cooper's time to our own.

In one way, it is a matter of what may be called tradition and anti-tradition, or what one American critic has labelled Paleface and Redskin. That is, some have sought to see in us a continuation of a European tradition in letters, well represented by Irving, or Longfellow, or T. S. Eliot, the Palefaces. Others, wanting to see whether we have distinctive traits, have focused their attention on Cooper or Twain or Faulkner or Dos Passos, the Redskins, whose strongest features derive from our new and different way of living. In another way, the outside world has looked either for the artistic fulfillment of the American Dream, *or* for the Disenchantment of those who fail to find that Dream, or finding it, declare it Nightmare. Thus some like to read and know our idealists and optimists, from Jefferson and Emerson and Thoreau and Whitman to Sandburg. Others, and they have been greatly in the majority in the immediate past, are pleased to find that all that glitters is not gold, that this is not entirely a land flowing with milk and honey, that man's depravity in exploitation and blind avarice have produced tragedies such as those described by Dreiser and Steinbeck or bitter satires such as those of Sinclair Lewis and the later Mark Twain. In other words, men of the outside world have found what they wanted to find in our literature. That they were interested in looking is the first important fact that we must recognize.

To nineteenth century Europe especially, America was the land where democracy worked, where there were broad opportunity and inexhaustible resources, where there was freedom of mind and body. Emerson and Whitman as much or more than Jefferson and Lincoln represented this idea and ideal. Emerson came slowly to be read and pondered in the rest of the world, including India and Latin America. But Whitman was fairly early in his career an inspiration to idealists, a model for poets longing for national independence, an embodiment of the long-suppressed voices he claimed to represent. They took him at his own evaluation. If there were dissenting and cynical voices, and there were, these represented in most instances a then declining and traditional conservatism.

To twentieth century Europe and the rest of the world, America presents a very different image. Now she is the bulwark of capitalism, a champion of holding the line, a monument of materialism. As one British commentator who saw this observed, it is Europe and the rest of the world which has changed, not America. For old imperialisms have become new, hopeful, somewhat naïvely optimistic nations believing that some form of collectivism will be their salvation. These last see our writers attesting our smugness, our mercenary acquisitiveness, our insensitivity to the finer things of the mind and spirit.

This is by no means the only twentieth century image. For, thanks to thoughtful critics in these nations abroad and to the purveyors of American literature we are sending to the four corners of the earth, a new image is forming, one which is giving us new stature and, perhaps more important, respect and sympathy from the minds which are guiding and *will guide* the destinies of many nations.

A glance at some names of American authors and the titles of their books, and a few statistics and other details accompanying them as to their reception abroad, will afford some indication of what I mean by past and present image.

The Scandinavian reader, thanks largely to the strongly anti-American writings of the Norwegian novelist Knut Hamsun, was well into the twentieth century convinced that America was but another name for Mammon. In Sweden, for example, little good could be found in anything American. Jack London and Sinclair Lewis, widely read in that country, entered through the back door. They *proved* for the Swedes all that they needed to know about smugness, narrow provinciality, violence, and *barbarism* (in the rest of the world this last word was used with both favorable and unfavorable connotations). But by 1930 Sweden had accepted the fact that there was an American literature, and awarded to Sinclair Lewis the Nobel Prize as a symbol of this acceptance.[1] In the 1920's this acceptance was primarily as social documentation, though in Lewis' case there was something more: he had demonstrated that there was at least "one little doubter" of the values of American society, and therefore there was some hope for future American writing. By the 1930's and 1940's, once these people began to read more of America by Americans, some of them discovered that amid the dark there was light, amid the weakness strength. To the average Swedish novel reader, one must admit, American fiction is still largely sociological documentation or thrilling detective story or melodramatic violence. There as elsewhere in Scandinavia in the 1950's favorite American novels, seen in every bookshop in paperbacks with lurid designs, were Richard Wright's *Nigger* (our title is *Native Son*), Lewis' *Kingsblood Royal* (his discussion of the Negro question), Faulkner's violent *The Wild Palms*, and Steinbeck's *The Grapes of Wrath*. But they also liked Hemingway ("for we are tired of introspection"), Steinbeck's idyllic *Tortilla Flat*, Maxwell Anderson's plays as well as O'Neill's, and *Huckleberry Finn*, in the last case usually for qualities other than its dark determinism.[2]

With variations, this Swedish pattern holds for the rest of Scandinavia, and indeed for much of free and Soviet Europe. In Norway, Finland, and Denmark, all more sympathetic to American aims and achievements than Sweden is for a number of historical reasons, the reading of our earlier classics is more widely prevalent. *The Scarlet Letter*, Poe's *Tales* and *Poems*, Whitman, even *Moby Dick*, appear on school reading lists. In Norway the secondary school Anglo-American Reader includes about one-third American materials. Conditions in Finland and Denmark are comparable.

In Germany reading of American literature began in much the same way as in Scandinavia, but it was accepted more rapidly and imitated more freely. Poe and Whitman, and to some extent Emerson, were known in nineteenth century Germany.[3] But even then they knew best our novels. Between 1871 and 1914, 997 American novels were published in Germany. Jack London and Upton Sinclair were overwhelming favorites, partly because they depicted the evils of capitalistic society, but more generally because of the freshness, the lust for life, the elementary forces of the New World they represented. German socialists liked *The Iron Heel*. Sinclair Lewis was admired for the usual two reasons: he demonstrated that there were soulless creatures in America for those who wished to say "I told you so"; on the other hand, certain thoughtful critics realized that he dealt in satire, and that his raucous laughter came from a genuine love for his country, a desire to improve it. This double appeal of Lewis continues. Dreiser has met with the same reactions.

Sharing the *Kultur pessimismus* of American writers after World War I, German artists and intellectuals generally had great sympathy for the post-War American fictionists Hemingway, Faulkner, and especially Wolfe. One German observed that every young novelist of his era had gone through "his Hemingway gate" as the only path leading to modern and new techniques in fiction. Klaus Mann (son of Thomas) sympathized with Hemingway in paraphrasing him: " 'Do you love life?' " " 'Yes, I do, because it's all we've got.' "

Conscious of the American South's contribution to the new literature, the German has viewed Faulkner's "puritan theology" and haunting studies of dissolution and decadence with real sympathy. But Wolfe has been the great favorite, partly because of the German's mistaken assumption that he was of German ancestry, but more largely because of Wolfe's genuine love of the old Germany and the conviction of the German that here at last was a writer who matched in the immensity of his grasp, in the gusto, the emotion, and the violence of his work, the qualities of the continent and nation he represented. Dorothy Thompson tells a moving story of 1945-1946, of sitting with a distinguished German writer among the ruins of Berlin, of finding him concerned only with the tragedy of the life of Thomas Wolfe cut off before its time.

Our theater too has been most successful in Germany, especially since World War II. O'Neill, Tennessee Williams, and above all Thornton Wilder have been acclaimed in Germany and Austria. Wilder's novels had already met a favorable reception between the wars. In 1945-1946 *Our Town* and *The Skin of Our Teeth* were performed scores of times in German theaters, and have been repeated often since. *The Matchmaker* (Guthrie's production) was the most popular play of the 1954-1955 season. Wilder has been awarded the *Ordre pour le Merite* of the West German Republic, an honorary degree from a Frankfurt university, the Goethe Prize, the annual Peace Prize of the German Book Trade, and the Austrian Medal for Science and Art.[4] Part of this recognition has personal origins, for Wilder made frequent appearances in the two countries, translated a tragedy by Austria's greatest dramatist, and of course spoke German. With one of these awards came a citation, however, which indicates that there were more significant reasons for his reputation:

> [This is awarded] to the great artist and dramatist who in a chaotic age helped to preserve the faith in intellectual powers and who affirmed affinity for spiritual forces, who knew how to interpret fate and responsibility, who depicted life seriously and serenely, and strove to create the ideal of true, noble humanity.

In this country in which 365,000 copies of *Gone with the Wind* were sold in four years of the 1930's, in which seven hundred volumes of America literature were translated between 1945 and 1950, we need not fear that American writing is not read. We want to be sure it is understood.

It is in France that American literature has been received with most enthusiasm, critical and uncritical, where it has been paid the sincere homage of imitation, where men have seen things in it Americans themselves have never seen.[5] The story goes back to the beginnings of our national history, but it is best dramatized, as far as our earlier literature is concerned, by the French reception of Edgar Allan Poe. Patrick F. Quinn's recent *The French Face of Edgar Poe*[6] advances the thesis that from Baudelaire's first study of his idol during Poe's own lifetime to Valéry in the twentieth century, the French have found in the American a quality and peculiarity of genius we have failed to recognize and that, if we wish fully to understand the creation of our compatriot, we would do well to consider the bases of the French image. Quinn points out the qualities of logic, of explicit guidance in technique, of sustained eighteenth century critical virtues, the deep sense of one aspect of nature—the horrible and grotesque—never hitherto stressed by a great artist, as some of the reasons for this constant and profound attention to Poe. He concludes with the French that "Poe's unique quality as a writer consists in this: . . . his stories offer us [the opportunity] of participating in the life of a great ontological imagination . . . a voyage of the mind."

Poe's case but anticipates others more recent. One of the significant events of French literature between the two World Wars, says Simone de Beauvoir, was the discovery of American literature.[7] She means the discovery of twentieth century American fiction, particularly of the work of those the French refer to as the five great Americans— Faulkner, Hemingway, Dos Passos, Steinbeck, and Caldwell. Introduced to all these men in the felicitous translations of Maurice Coindreau, a professor of French at Princeton, usually followed by a thorough reading in English, the French critics and novelists found much to admire and to ponder. That sincerest of flatteries, imitation, may be observed in the Dos Passos-like techniques of the earlier

Jean-Paul Sartre novels, of the Faulknerian in Simone and Sartre and others, of the Hemingwayan and Faulknerian in Camus. Time shift, interior monologue, association of ideas, dialogue within dialogue, dual or treble points of view, are Faulknerian techniques evident everywhere in the French novel. Perhaps the most striking example of the enthusiasm for American fiction is the enormous sale of one novel, purportedly translated from English and allegedly written by an American, but recently discovered actually to have been written in France by a Frenchman!

Reaching its height of popularity in the earlier 1950's, the American novel almost drove the French product off the market, as the instance just cited may suggest. The French still saw in it *barbarisme*—for them a word thus used in a favorable connotation—of elemental forces, of violence and basic morality. Camus in his early career certainly thought American novelists were crude realists with a degraded view of man, but such is not always the view of other major French novelists and critics. One (Maurice Nadeau) declares, in half-agreement with the early Camus, that American literature today is no more talented than French, but its attraction is that "it expresses more forcefully, more sincerely, and more brutally the despair of our time."[8] Simone de Beauvoir stresses the American novelist's depiction of "life in its dramatic aspect." Sartre, who attests the profoundly significant effect of the "Big Five" on French literary development between the Wars, declares flatly that "There is one American literature for Americans and another for the French," pointing out what the French see in our novelists. Sartre noted the puritanism of Faulkner long before it was noticed in America, time as theme and technique, and the Greek-tragedy-in-the-detective-story quality of the work of the whole group. How many Americans look at our novel as he did?

What fascinated us really ... was the constant flow of men across a whole continent, the exodus of an entire village to the orchards of California, the hopeless wanderings of the hero in *Light in August*, and of the uprooted peoples who drifted at the mercy of storms in *The 42nd Parallel*, the dark murderous fury which sometimes swept through an entire city, the blind and criminal love of James Cain.[9]

Since 1950 we as well as the French have come to see Faulkner as the greatest novelist writing in English, perhaps, in any language, in the world today, though as my colleague Professor Percy Adams has shown, we have not yet come to agree as to many of the details of his literary portrait. We are just beginning to consider his concept of time, a quality the French examined early. Our kind of analyses of his techniques and language, as those of Mrs. Vickery and Beck, the French have not paralleled. We find primitivism; the French little or none. We thoroughly enjoy and see significances in his humor and satire; the French almost ignore them. So we might go on.

Erskine Caldwell is another American writer whose French portrait is quite different from his American. His reputation has held steadily and perhaps increased in France as it has declined in the United States. To the French he is a major figure, to the Americans generally a pot-boiler exploiter of sex and sadism. To the French, he seems in the major tradition of Poe, Hawthorne, and Melville. They compare Hemingway unfavorably with Caldwell, for the latter does not possess the former's tendency to pose. They see Caldwell as a sociologist (again part of his appeal is the dark face of America he presents), a real humorist, a major technician.

One is tempted to go on with what Steinbeck, Dos Passos, and Hemingway have meant to the French, and why they have almost ignored Thomas Wolfe. But perhaps I have given already sufficient evidence that contemporary American literature is read and esteemed in France, where Faulkner, at least until recently, enjoyed that rare privilege of having a greater reputation in another country than in his own. Any survey of American literature in France inevitably brings us to self-searching questions (this group is suggested by recent American teachers in France): Did we underestimate Faulkner, at least until he won the Nobel Prize? Is he a puritan? Is Caldwell also undervalued? Is the Steinbeck of *Of Mice and Men* and *Tortilla Flat* a classicist in his formal unities? In more general terms, we may ask ourselves the questions the French ask about us: Does our alleged immaturity result in an epic period in American literature? Is the determinism of American novels similar to that of Greek tragedies? And so on.

We would by no means demand that we gauge our literature as France does, nor that she accept our assessments of our writing. But critically each country may profit greatly by a long look at the attitudes, and especially the reasons for them, of the other. Among other things, for *us* it is the one way to begin to comprehend what our image is abroad.

Because of obvious kinships in language and tradition, the British have in 150 years consumed more American books than all the rest of the world put together. Yet the old superciliousness of 1820 which caused a critic to ask in print, "Who in the four corners of the globe reads an American book?" still lingers in academic circles, even among those who do read American books. For culturally, as a Norwegian suggests, though we may be to the French the favorite adopted child, to the British we have remained in some ways the unrepentant prodigal who never returned. Politically compelled to recognize the new nation, the British have for a century and a half studied our history rather carefully; at Oxford and Cambridge are endowed professorships of American history, and the subject is taught at almost if not all British universities. But at Oxford and Cambridge American literature is ignored officially almost as if it didn't exist. At London and Nottingham and one or two other red-brick universities, to some extent at Glasgow, American writers are studied fairly intensively. But one may safely say that even behind the Iron Curtain American literature receives more academic attention than it does in Great Britain. This incidentally, carries over to Ireland, where a recent Fulbright lecturer at Dublin was asked why American literature should be studied any more than Brazilian or Yugoslavian.

Yet this attitude by no means holds among ordinary people nor indeed among journalists and men of letters. A recent study has indicated that middle-brow and low-brow English readers devour an enormous number of American sentimental escape novels, detective stories, and adventure fiction, as well as better things like *The Great Gatsby*.[10] One commentator hazards the guess that this popularity is because our fiction is less class-conscious than the novels of, say, the Waughs or Graham Greene.

The British novelist, like the French, has paid us the flattery of imitation. There is, for example, the influence of Hemingway slang on English writers like V. S. Pritchett and Christopher Isherwood. But far more startling is the sudden explosion of the British press, especially the literary press, on American literature since 1954. Actually from the early 1950's issue after issue of critical journals have carried essays on American authors or literary trends. But that major British magazines should devote whole issues to American literature would have been unthinkable even ten years ago.

Yet there was a special number of the *London Times Literary Supplement* in September 1954 entitled "American Writing Today: Its Independence & Vigour." Five years later, in November 1959, the same journal returned to the subject, broadening it somewhat to include also some other phases of our civilization, in a special issue called "The American Imagination." Between these two, *The New Statesman* in September 1958 published an "American Literary Number," in some ways the most astonishing phenomenon of the three, for it came in a journal frequently highly critical of America.

The 1954 *Times Literary Supplement* contains comprehensive and sympathetically critical grouped essays on "Poetry and Drama," "Critical Appreciation," "Intellectual Opinion," "The Craft of Fiction," "Modes of Feeling," "Literary Methods," and several other topics.

The key to the recent British attitude lies, however, in the editorial accompanying the essays, beginning

> Nothing, in the history of twentieth century opinion, is more striking than the change of front which has taken place in respect to American writing. Even thirty years ago voices could be heard to declare that there was no such thing . . . , it is now generally recognized that nowhere in the modern world is there a more rewarding literature than that which America has to offer.[11]

The 1959 issue of this journal includes a still more radical statement, for it comes to particularities at the expense of Britain's own individual writers. After noting that "Of all that the American imagination has created, American literature is perhaps the most impressive," the writer declares that "It might well be argued that Robert Frost is now the greatest poet writing in English [and the] greatest novelist . . . is possibly William Faulkner."

The story of American literature in Italy is much like that in France, though in neither reputation nor influence has it ever gone quite so high or wide. The Summer 1960 number of *The Sewanee Review*, made up entirely of translations of "Italian Criticism of American Literature" selected from writing of the last thirty years, afforded us striking proof that for at least a full generation the Italians have been aware of our major authors, nineteenth as well as twentieth century. First Whitman and Poe, then Longfellow and Hawthorne, Cooper, Irving, Twain, Dickinson, engaged their critical attention, and several imitated them. In a second period between the Wars the Italians concentrated largely on Eliot, Pound, and Melville but also studied Dickinson further, Dos Passos, Lewis, Anderson, Hemingway, and Dreiser. Mario Praz, who has done more to introduce American literature to his countrymen, still considered it as barbaric, in both the good and bad sense. Cecchi, Vittorini, and Pavese, among others, then and more recently have translated and analyzed earlier and recent contemporary literature. Since World War II a third period of Italian interest in American literature shows a new realization of an older American maturity (as opposed to Praz's *barbarism*) and tradition, a realization that Faulkner and Frost and Hemingway are not first blossomings, but late fruit of a now old and developed culture.

Though I should like to point out the extent and nature of the reading of American books in Syria, Greece, Spain, The Netherlands, and Belgium, in which it varies in quantity and quality, time at my disposal demands that I go on for a glance at one other European nation—Soviet Russia itself. Before I do so, I think we should glance at one little episode of American literature in Holland as related by Professor Perry Miller of Harvard, then a visiting professor at the University of Leyden. Miller tells of his invitation to Leeuwarden, ancient capital of Friesland, in the autumn of 1949, on the one hundredth anniversary of Poe's death. He describes the bankers, lawyers, government officials, and ordinary citizens who gathered for four hours (closing all their business establishments during this time)

to hear orations on or readings from Poe. Naturally he
was embarrassed by the inevitable question: What are the
Americans doing on October 7?[12]

Though Poe was most influential in the Czarist regime,
since 1917 the Russian interest has been in somewhat different directions.[13] Jack London was read by liberals before
and after the Revolution for some of the same reasons he
was read elsewhere in Europe. And Upton Sinclair, Dreiser,
Richard Wright, Caldwell, and others were and continue
to be read, though apparently in lessening degree, for their
"depiction of social progress" or attack upon the lack of it.
In other words, the Russians like the ugly side of American
life, for obvious reasons. Yet this only slightly explains the
tremendous popularity of O. Henry, whose books sold
three-quarters of a million copies in Russia in the twenties.
O. Henry depicted in some detail American life, or so they
thought; they admired his slick short story technique, and
he diverted and amused them. There is a story of a Russian
officer who read O. Henry calmly as mortar shells whizzed
by him during the seige of Stalingrad. One may also note
that Lenin had his wife read him Jack London's stories as
he was dying, and we may be fairly sure that this reading
was not for their social implications.

By 1946 forty million copies of books by 201 American
writers had been sold in Soviet Russia. In that year the
journalist Ilya Ehrenburg commented that "Between the
two world wars, the only really great literature was produced in the United States" (he referred primarily to the
group the French call the Five Great Americans).[14] But
the widening rift since then has naturally had its effect.
Although American books are still read, the range has
become narrow, and they are published with Communist
doctrinaire introductions. Recent observers testify that
Russian officialdom has not been content with presenting

one of the two faces of America—the dark one; it has determinedly twisted and distorted that face into a monstrous caricature. Upton Sinclair's shocking 1905 stock-yard exposé *The Jungle* and Harriet Beecher Stowe's 1852 *Uncle Tom's Cabin* are presented today, we are informed, as reflecting typical existing American conditions!

The only ray of light in eastern Europe is in Poland, where the national predilection for the West rather than the East has resulted in some letting down of the bars, an importation of many sorts of American books, and a relatively objective study of them in the universities. Very recent information on this subject indicates some hope for the future.

In Asia the Iron and Bamboo Curtains veil from us the great bulk of the land mass, but even in Asia, or I should say especially in certain parts of Asia, the discovery of American literature is apparently one of the pleasant and stimulating experiences of life. In Ceylon, Iran, Formosa, Thailand, and other smaller countries we are in various ways introducing it along with other elements of our civilization. In Japan, Pakistan, and India the study of American writing has become a major academic activity, sponsored alike by the universities and our own representatives abroad.

In Japan today our authors are so much written about that the bibliographer of the American Literature Group of our Modern Language Association complained not long ago that, if he included every Japanese essay on Poe, Dickinson, Hemingway, Faulkner, Twain, etc., in his annual published lists (and he would like to do so), he would leave no room for what we ourselves are writing about our literature. It is a fact that there are today in Japan dozens of periodicals devoted exclusively to American in combination with English literature, some printed in English and some in Japanese, and that American books are on sale everywhere. And all this is despite a strong protest and occasional boycott from leftist elements among students and certain other groups in the country.

Perhaps Poe is our most popular writer in Japan, as a Japanese critic asserted recently. At any rate, Poe has been read, translated, recited, and analyzed by the Japanese, in and out of the university, for two generations. Exactly what qualities attract them I have not yet been able to ascertain, but I gather they are very much these which have made Poe a model and a favorite author in Latin Europe and Latin America.

Today the Japanese seem to like Twain and Melville too, though one American observer describes that they fail to see *Huckleberry Finn* as anything but a "happy book," and that he never saw a Japanese student who really liked *Moby Dick*. Like the people of other countries, the Japanese in our time have come to prefer what they have found most distinctive in our literature. They choose, then, the work of our Redskins to that of our Palefaces, of Twain, Whitman, Faulkner, Hemingway, and Frost to Longfellow, James, Wharton, or even T. S. Eliot, though naturally they write a great deal about the last.

Knowledge of American literature seems to have come to Pakistan and India since World War II, and indeed much more recently than 1946. One white-haired Indian author, also a Member of Parliament and early follower of Gandhi, told me how he had known and read Thoreau and Emerson years before World War II, as we know Gandhi did. But I suspect he did not read Thoreau until the man of Walden was brought to his attention in Gandhi's writings.

Until 1947 India was a dependent part of the British Empire, and in its reading in the English language and in the teaching of literature in general followed pretty closely what the British were doing. The Indian university and its curriculum were avowedly modeled on the English. According to the records recently sent me by our Fulbright Office in Washington, no formal course in American literature had ever been taught in the universities of the great sub-continent until an American Graduate Dean (who was also a Professor of American Literature), on a three-months leave from his home institution, inaugurated such a course at Osmania University, at Hyderbad on the southern Indian plateau. Herman E. Spivey not only gave the inaugural course, as the Fulbright Office informs me, but also was largely responsible for outlining and putting into practice what has happened in India since that time. For it was he who suggested that the State Department send at least two teams of specialists in American literature to India for three-month periods, their duty being to lecture on the subject for a week at a time in the stronger Indian universities. The hope was, of course, that the appropriate authorities of these institutions would be thus impelled, or stimulated, to introduce American literature, as at least a single course, into the English curriculum. The results have been almost phenomenal, if the official figures recently sent to me are not at fault.

Today (as of January 1962) twenty-nine Indian universities offer courses in American literature, all on the graduate level, to small groups ranging from a half dozen to forty or fifty. The first full-time native Indian American Literature professor, K. R. Chandhrascharan, is now in charge at Osmania after training in this country. Five other professors of English have been sent to the United States for further training in America. At Andhra University, three of the Ph.D. dissertations now being written are on American authors. Three Fulbright professors now in India are now preparing a two-volume anthology of American literature just for the Indians.

At a conference held at Srinagar last June thirty-two

Indian universities participated in an extended discussion of the possible place of American literature in the Indian University Curriculum. The agreement was general that it should be there, and steps were taken to introduce it where it was not already.

One of the heartening things today is to read what the Indians write about us. In the *Hindustan Weekly Times* (the *Sunday New York Times* of India) there is likely to be a full-page article on some phase of American writing or American writers. In *The Literary Criterion*, originally devoted to English literature, the last two volumes have contained thirteen essays on American literature, from Edward Taylor to Faulkner and Eliot (as an American author). Sri Aurobindo is quoted in one essay as saying that "Whitman [is] the most Homeric voice since Homer." In another Wallace Stevens, still too little known in this country, is declared "the greatest of modern American poets" on sound critical bases. Cambridge-educated C. D. Narasimhaiah, after a lengthy commentary on the American literary scene as it appeared to him on a recent visit to this country, summed up: "It is these writers—poets, novelists and critics, with their abiding concern for human values [,] that can redeem and give meaning to acquisitive American society."[15]

India's foremost literary critic, K. R. Srinivasa Iyengar (some will recall his essay in a recent number of *Tennessee Studies in Literature*), has edited Thoreau's *Walden* as a college text for Indian students. In his preface he comments on Thoreau's influence on Mahatma Gandhi, and then puts his finger on what Thoreau and the writers of the great American tradition since have been trying to do:

> Thoreau was one of the few descendants of Adam to have known the meaning of happiness and to have cherished his fate . . . [to have] wrested the secret of happiness from life and nature. . . . [His] influence is not confined to one country or people.[16]

In the Philippines, Africa, Australia, and New Zealand the story of American literature parallels closely that in one or more of the countries just mentioned. In the former British colonies it made its way rather slowly and even the Fulbright lecturers on the subject in Australia and New Zealand, for example, found indifference or even a vague hostility. One who will read the Fulbright reports over the last fourteen years will note a gradual thawing and changing of attitude, until today we have unusually sympathetic response.

In Latin America Poe especially and to some extent Emerson supplied critical and philosophical and even technical modes. A recent visitor to Brazil notes that Poe is the greatest single influence on contemporary verse in that country. Our current writers are read and read about with interest, so much interest that Latin America has become one of the areas of concentration in presenting American literature. Perhaps in the end Faulkner's Yoknapatawphians and Steinbeck's Joads will aid the Good Neighbor Policy.

Thus the image of America has already been formed, or vitally affected, by a reading of our literature throughout the habitable globe. In the nineteenth century it offered the best picture and proof of a working democracy. In the twentieth it gave Gandhi Thoreau and the idea of passive resistance with which to create a revolution and a nation. To Italians under Fascism it was the "first breathing hole of liberty."

To every reader it offered a picture of American life, good and bad, which he might wish to acquire out of sheer curiosity, in a natural desire to be reassured that his own way of life was still to be preferred, or to prove to him that it wasn't. It has afforded the French new techniques and new themes. It was an antidote for despair in post-War

Germany and at the same time the "best expression of the despair of our time" in France and Scandinavia.

The status and stature of American books abroad have also taught Americans a great deal. We have found, in the light of what the French and Japanese and Brazilians see in Poe, in what the Germans see in Wolfe and the French in Caldwell and Faulkner, that we must look at them anew, revise our estimates, reassess our literature. And, in so doing, get another view of ourselves.

What else remains to be done? Is it worth while to spend even the modest sums we have allocated for sending professors abroad, translating our books into seventy languages, and making cheap paperbacks available? One must answer immediately that there *is* much yet to be done, that the whole thing is most worth our while.

Rightly or wrongly, as I have already suggested, our technical achievements have been accepted for a long time now in the rest of the world as a matter of course. Even Russian rivalry and ascendancy in some phases of technology worries us more than it does the rest of the free world. I was in India when Sputnik I was announced. It did not create nearly the furor there it did in America. The Indian intellectual usually shrugged his shoulders and said the equivalent of—"So what? There are more important things in a civilization."

Sometimes rather bluntly we are told by citizens of other countries that what they want to know is not what new gadget or cyclotron America has invented, but whether it has a mind, an imaginative mind, a soul if you will, with which to lead the rest of the world's free people. They have looked at our writing for an answer. And because they have not always understood that writing, or knew it only out of context in isolated instances, they mistook it for something other than it was.

The oldest and most persistent mistaken conception is

that our literature shows us to be exactly the soul-less, acquisitive, materialistic people our enemies have made us out to be. Though a few French and Italian critics have seen beyond this in the writings of Faulkner, Caldwell, Sinclair Lewis, Dreiser, and Steinbeck, most of the world still wants to know whether America is "as bad as that." *Time* and *Life* and Van Wyck Brooks, among others, disturbed profoundly by this fact, have pled for a *"positive"* American Literature.

Robert Penn Warren a few years ago (in a front-page essay in the *New York Times Book Review*) pretty well gave the answer our representatives abroad are trying to give. He began

> Once upon a time there was a nation, which we shall call X. At the time of which we write this nation stood at a moment of great power and great promise. A few generations earlier it had concluded a long and bloody civil war to achieve unity. More recently, in that unity, it had won a crashing victory over foreign foes. It had undergone and was undergoing a social revolution; there was unparalleled prosperity, a relaxing of old sanctions and prejudices, a widening of opportunity for all classes, great rewards for energy and intelligence. Its flag was on strange seas; its power was felt in the world. It was, even, producing a famous literature.
>
> But—and here is the strange thing in that moment of energy and optimism—a large part, the most famous part of that literature exhibited violence, degradation and despair as part of the human condition: tales of the old time of the civil war, tales of lust and horror, brother pimping for sister, father lusting for daughter, a head of the state doting on a fair youth, an old man's eyes plucked out, another man killed in his sleep, friendship betrayed, obligations foregone, good men cursing the gods, and the whole scene drenched in blood. Foreigners encountering this literature might well conclude that the

Land of X was peopled by degenerates sadly lacking in taste, manners and principle.

This is England, Elizabethan England, that we are talking about, and not the United States in this year of Our Lord and the Great Prosperity. . . .

Insofar as literature struggles to engage the deep, inner issues of life, the more will that literature be critical— the more, that is, will it engender impatience with the compromises, the ennui, the naturalism, the self-deception, the complacency, and the secret unnameable despairs that mark so much ordinary life.[17]

Or the American literature teacher abroad may want to put the matter more as has Henri Peyre, professor at Yale:

But America need not blush at this literature of despair. Its pessimism is not the sterile mockery of cynics nor the decadent obsession to soil the beauty of the world. It is the expression of sincere idealism, of lucid faith. It asserts with eloquence that all is not well with the world, but that, by facing realities boldly, we could make life more worthy of being lived. If American literature has scaled epic heights more courageously than any other, it has also plumbed the depths of tragedy.[18]

We must show, as does the French critic Malraux, that what our literature is really obsessed with is *fundamental man:* "[the] wheel has come full circle, through the American novel and play, [America can] communicate with free men everywhere. Because there is a literature of critcism in the name of fundamental man, it is the literature of freedom."[19]

This is but a portion of the context in which our literature must be presented if it is to be understood. Since it is already read, it has become incumbent upon us to see that its parts are explained, placed in their proper places in its full body, related to the long tradition, and above all presented as a coherent body (which involves introducing to foreigners more works with which they have not been acquainted). Here is where the Fulbright and Smith-Mundt visiting professor, and the foreign nationalist trained in our universities and returned home, comes in.

So we send these men and women around the world. Trained in depth in American literature, they aid foreign university students in understanding what our artists have said. And by pointing out to these students American writing they may never have seen before, they enlarge the picture and the understanding. These teachers set Faulkner, say, in a long tradition dating back to C. B. Brown and coming down through Poe and Hawthorne and Bierce; Hemingway in a tradition of which Mark Twain is a famous but not first example; Frost in relation to Emerson and Dickinson; Sandburg's progenitors in Jefferson and Whitman. They show that modern American literature springs from an older body matured in experiment and experience.

The American lecturer may explain the purpose of American writing along the lines suggested by Warren above. Sometimes he spends a term on a poem, an author, or a novel like *The Sound and the Fury*, often explicating every line. Above all he is candid. He is expressly directed to discuss American life in relation to literature as he sees both. This honesty, as quickly discerned among foreign students as the opposite would be, is perhaps his greatest asset in gaining a sympathetic understanding. He must demonstrate that at the same time we are both Palefaces and Redskins, both optimists and pessimists, both idealists and realists, that when our books are most American they are also most universal—that they deal with fundamental man.[20]

This is a big order, and in every instance it is not accomplished. Even when he is most successful, the visitor reaches *directly* only an infinitesimal portion of the voting mind of any country. Indirectly, through succeeding dispersements of the understanding he has given, he may reach a large portion of the population of a small but advanced country like Norway, where literacy is almost universal. In India, on the other hand, he is addressing himself to a tiny portion of the two percent of the population who attend institutions of higher learning, and a not much larger percent who can read in English or some language into which our literature has been translated.

But the mind of all the literate fortunately does not have to be filled to saturation to affect the destiny of a people or the world. One recalls that only a few leaders in America knew Locke's great essays on government, a few men like Jefferson, Adams, and Madison. Yet the ideas from these essays went into the shaping of our nation, as one man's chance reading of Thoreau when he was a young lawyer in Africa was instrumental in the genesis of modern India. The American literary lecturer *can* do a great deal.

For example, though fewer American novels are sold today in France than were sold a decade ago, the French are now much nearer, though relatively they were always near, an understanding of our writing in context than they were in 1950. New professorships of American literature held by Frenchmen have been created in the universities, seventeen great universities offer courses in American literature, and half a dozen American professors divide their time among a dozen universities in explaining and explicating. The new understanding is borne out by the tenor and depth of recent French writing on our literature, and again it is a new understanding of America as well as of American literature.

Yes, the professors have for a decade been doing their share in exporting America. Man for man, they are among the most valuable agents of our foreign service, as many permanent and professional diplomats will attest. Man for man, they may be causing as many Pakistani or Japanese or Turks to respect if not admire America as any construction engineer or business man who demonstrates our technical know-how.

So, when you take your seat and fasten the safety belt on that not too distant journey, cut your eye toward the fellow sitting next to you. He may be that new kind of exporter, who sells a part of the United States of which for various reasons we have too long failed to explain the virtues. And you might do well yourself to take a new and long look at his product.

1. Carl L. Anderson, *The Swedish Acceptance of American Literature* (Philadelphia: Univ. of Penn., 1957), *passim*. See also Stephen E. Whicher, "Swedish Knowledge of American Literature," *JEGP*, LVIII (1959), 666-671.

2. R. B. Davis, "Some Observations on American Literature and Other Arts in Northern Europe since 1945," *Bulletin of Randolph-Macon College*, XXVII (September 1955), 26-29, 38-39.

3. For some appraisals of American Literature in Germany, see Anne M. Springer, *The American Novel in Germany* (Hamburg, 1960); John R. Frey, "Postwar Germany: Enter American Literature," *American-German Review*, XXI (1954), 9-12; "Postwar German Reactions to American Literature," *JEGP*, LIV (1955), 173-194; Mary Gaither and Horst Frenz, "German Criticism of American Drama [since World War II]," *American Quarterly*, VII (1955), 111-122; William W. Pusey, "*Gone with the Wind in Germany:* Translation and Criticism [to 1940]," *Kentucky Foreign Language Quarterly*, II (1955), 178-188; "The German Vogue of Thomas Wolfe," *Germanic Review*, XXIII (1948), 131-148; "William Faulkner's Works in Germany to 1940: Translation and Criticism," *Germanic Review*, XXX (1955), 211-226.

4. "Austrian Honor for Thornton Wilder," *American-German Review*, XXVI (1959-1960), 35; Horst Frenz, "The Reception of Thornton Wilder's Plays in Germany," *Modern Drama*, III (1960), 123-137.

5. Among the many studies of American Literature in France, most useful for the present purpose were Thelma M. Smith and Ward Miner, *Translantic Migration: the Contemporary American Novel in France* (Durham: Duke Univ., 1955); Percy G. Adams, "American Literature in the Universities of France," *Studies in*

Honor of John C. Hodges and Alwin Thaler (Knoxville: Univ. of Tenn., 1961), pp. 175-184, and his "The Franco-American Faulkner," *Tennessee Studies in Literature*, V (1960), 1-11; Stewart H. Benedict, "Gallic Light on Erskine Caldwell," *South Atlantic Quarterly*, LX (1961), 390-397; Neil D. Isaacs, "Faulkner with a Vengeance: 'The Grass is Greener,' " *South Atlantic Quarterly*, LX (1961), 427-433; Richard Lehan, "Camus' American Affinities," *Symposium*, XIII (1959), 255-270; Harry R. Garvin, "Camus and the American Novel," *Comparative Literature*, VIII (1956), 194-204; Henri Peyre, "American Literature through French Eyes," *Virginia Quarterly Review*, XXIII (1947), 421-438; Jean-Paul Sartre, "American Novelists in French Eyes," *Atlantic*, CXLVI (August 1946), 114-118.

6. (Carbondale: Univ. of So. Ill., 1957), p. 274.

7. "An American Renaissance in France," *New York Times Book Review* (June 22, 1947), p. 7.

8. *La revue internationale*, III (1947), 115. See also Harry Levin, "Some European Views of Contemporary American Literature," *American Quarterly*, I (1949), 264-279.

9. "American Novelists in French Eyes," p. 114.

10. Richard Hoggart, "The Unsuspected Audience," *New Statesman*, LVI, no. 1434 (September 6, 1958), 303-305.

11. P. 591.

12. "Europe's Faith in American Fiction," *Atlantic*, CLXXXVIII (December 1951), 52-56; "What Drove Me Crazy in Europe," *Atlantic*, CLXXXVII (March 1951), 41-45.

13. For American Literature in Russia, see especially several studies by Deming Brown: "O. Henry in Russia," *Russian Review*, XII (1953), 253-258; "Sinclair Lewis: the Russian View," *American Literature*, XXV (1953), 1-12; "American Best-Sellers in Soviet Bookstores," *Reporter*, XV (November 29, 1956), 36-38; "Soviet Criticism of American Proletarian Literature of the 1930's," *American Contributions to the Fourteenth International Congress of Slavicists* (1958), 1-16. Also Maurice Hindus, "What They Read of Ours in the U.S.S.R.," *New York Herald-Tribune Books* (September 2, 1945), 1-2; Robert Magidoff, "American Literature in Russia," *Saturday Review of Literature*, XXIX (November 2, 1946), 9-11, 45-46.

14. K. S. Loucheim, "Ilya Ehrenburg on American Writers," *New Republic*, CXIV (July 1, 1946), 931-932.

15. *The Literary Criterion*, edited by C. D. Narasimhaiah, is published at Mysore.

16. This edition was published at Andhra in 1953.

17. "A Lesson Read in American Books," December 11, 1955, pp. 1, 33.

18. "American Literature through French Eyes," p. 436.

19. Perry Miller, "Europe's Faith in American Fiction," p. 56.

20. Most of the material in this essay came from the author's personal experience as Fulbright and State Department Lecturer, and as Guggenheim Fellow, in Scandinavia, India, and England; his own observations elsewhere in Europe and Asia; and the oral and written reports of his Fulbright colleagues, received during the years while he was a member of the Advisory Committee in American Studies to the national Fulbright Board.

Cosmotopian Possibilities

LAWRENCE W. CHISOLM

LAWRENCE W. CHISOLM is Assistant Professor of History and American Studies at Yale University and Director of the Honors Program in American Studies. He is the author of *Fenollosa: The Far East and American Culture* (1963), and editor of *The Life and Letters of J. Alden Weir* (1960); "An American Style of Cultural Change" is in progress.

PESSIMISTS SCOFF AT THE IDEA AND OLD MEN DENY IT BUT what marks our era is a sense of the expanding variety of human possibilities, a sense quickened by the reality of the people of other cultures. Alternative styles of life are no longer merely acknowledged rationally as parts of some description of the world; they are felt to be relevant, to be possible, in some respects, here, for me, and soon. This feeling of new possibilities is part of a revolutionary sense of change, part of an awareness that change is widening the range of human alternatives and that while this is not necessarily a meliorative process it is potentially so, and, in any case, unavoidable. The rising generation in the "emerging" nations dramatizes this sense, but citizens of established nations share it, often in more cosmopolitan forms. The stimulus which brings life to a dream of world civilization is, quite simply, experience, a cumulative experience now well past the "synaptic threshold" of immediacy. More and more people from different cultures are confronting one another directly. They are continually assessing various styles of life, challenged and charmed, often frustrated and perplexed, variously attracted and repelled.

The conditions of world interdependence which have brought this about challenge education and scholarship fundamentally. American Studies has an opportunity to initiate new strategies. The emphasis of attention which underlies American Studies can make a difference in the kind of world culture that is developing.

The question which stirs imagination is "What does it mean to be a human being?" Our answers to this perennial question involve a substantial consideration of all the various styles of life which men have created in different times and places so far as these can be known and—more important—felt in the sense of implied as part of the context of any human situation. Put in another way, the process of understanding a human act or attitude is now felt to involve a worldwide range of perspectives. The web of implications around a single act extends across cultures in a series of comparative cultural assessments. The inadequacy of ethnocentric perspectives has been made evident by experience, especially by crisis on personal and collective levels. And this widely shared sense of the inadequacies of parochial viewpoints is turning attention to those possibilities of world culture which might summon human energies toward more appropriate forms of order.

The sense of world life at issue here is not so much a matter of the forms of world federation or of economic development (although such economic and political trends are instrumental for the idea of world civilization in the speculations which follow). If the economic and political forms of the future do not stir men's imaginations very widely, it may be because they appear to many men as mere extensions of the present order, all too similar to the arrangements which exist within certain societies of the technologized northern hemisphere. North Americans, for example, are often puzzled by the lukewarm response of Latin Americans to northern models. Part of the explanation may lie in the quality of the future held up for emulation. Men in "underdeveloped" areas are not likely to risk and sacrifice in transforming their societies in order simply to catch up, perhaps, to "advanced" countries. If learning new ways means only a slow approach to superior models, learning can seem one more proof of inadequacy, a reminder of the superiority of other people. As Eric Hoffer has pointed out, "They need the illusion that, in trying to catch up tomorrow with other people's yesterdays, they are actually running ahead and showing the way to the rest of mankind."

Prospects of more business as usual and of politics partially bureaucratized are important prospects, but their appeal is limited further by prospective standardization. What world order presumes at economic and governmental levels is a universally accepted framework of expectations, legitimized and rationalized in the interest of efficiency and cooperation, a uniform code of rules and procedures. Even if this ideal uniformity provides essential securities, an ideal variety is properly complementary. And it might be more appealing since the vision of a future world civilization keyed to variety avoids the invidious scale of "advanced" and "backward" cultures. The forces which are producing a revolutionary rise in aspirations may as easily lead to a revolution of resentments unless the aspirations include some sense of a future whose beauties and civilities connect with the present in ways to which all cultures contribute. At issue may be the question whether the future is to be shaped by exclusions, envies, resentments, or, somehow, by an inclusive respect for the variety of cultural attainments and human styles. The sense of possibilities here postulated assumes change to be continuous and based ideally on awareness of alternatives and on "free" selection.

To make this contention clearer, consider Cosmotopia and one of its citizens. By education and experience he feels himself heir to worldwide styles of life whose mingled and mingling traces have shaped his chances. His present style reflects the cultural emphasis set by birth and early training; it also suggests his awareness of other styles available to him and present by implication as alternatives variously adapted, rejected, imitated, or renewed. This sense of several cultural styles adapted "instinctively" and, at other times, playfully is clear when he moves: walking, resting, dancing. Those who know him are alert to the nuances of a gesture, a pause, a satirical sequence; strangers are accustomed to cultural variations. The language of his thoughts and speech—he is multi-lingual—suits his own sense of mood, utility, fitness: each has its special qualities. He seems free in the sense that his elected styles seem his own, suited to his temperament and talents. He balances in his life traditions and experiment the relaxations of the customary with a tonic play among novelties. If he seems to have invited cultural anarchy by exploring many of the world's cultures it is clear that he has also accepted the limits imposed by common standards of civility, standards which vary somewhat in different parts of Cosmotopia but which assume as axiomatic mutual respect and humane relations. And, of course he is free to move around without official restriction or penalty. Cultural emphases in different parts of the world vary enough to suit the range of human temperaments; no one need stay if stifled.

What makes this Cosmotopian a citizen is his assurance that in concert with others he continues to shape the direction of affairs. The balance in his own life of traditional civility and knowledgeable experiment sustains his insistence that those who administer political and economic affairs appraise all proposals for their likely effects upon human relations. To decisive groups of Cosmotopians this is the leading requirement for political and economic administrators. Some years past a cumulative impatience with the ethnocentric cant of militarism and conspiracy obliged ambitious men who sought positions of public trust to demonstrate their competence as cultural analysts and their respect for human dignity. Demagogues were revealed progressively by their own simplistic views to be deceivers or, if self-deceived, too uncivilized to hold responsible positions in a complex world society. For some time, now, all candidates for upper-level administration have been required to be fluent in several cultures and to have demonstrated their support of humane principles.

This view of Cosmotopia raises problems. Putting aside the question of the likelihood of such developments, is Cosmotopia not rather mandarin, providing an elaborate stage for a cultivated elite amid a generally homogenized mass culture? And, furthermore, why wouldn't cross-cultural perspectives induce a cultural relativism which would destroy the roots of moral authority with no assurance that any comparable standards of behavior and judgment would function universally, much less that such universal standards would uphold mutual respect and humane relations?

In reply to these formidable questions suffice it for the moment to postpone the problem of relativism and to emphasize the conservative, centripetal forces at work in existing cultures. The homogenization predicted, for example, in the case of Japanese "westernization" may turn out to be superficial; new combinations of elements may be developing out of an assimilative tradition. More generally, the "Americanization" of the world, even when redefined as "modernization," involves gross simplifications which scant the stubborn resilience of diverse cultures. On the score of elitism this multi-lingual dancing Cosmotopian may seem something of an aesthete. But the most cosmopolitan adaptations of diverse cultural behaviors, techniques, and tastes have occurred already at the most elementary biological and social levels: eating, love-making, killing, healing. The artistic analogy is proposed because it contains an idea of style which may have extensive application. Human capacity for complex associations in individual development remains largely untested. And it is among the arts that the shapes of an emerging world culture can be seen most clearly.

In painting, for example, what we call "modern" art might as easily be called international or world art. Japanese prints, African sculpture, Chinese calligraphy have opened Western eyes to new ways of seeing. Archaeology, travel, and photography have extended artistic frames of reference well beyond regional, national, or cultural limits. The process has been part of civilization from the very beginning; a dramatic acceleration has taken place during the last hundred years. The effect has been not only to liberate the artist from parochial conventions but to present him with a greatly increased variety of achieved solutions to artistic problems. World art is felt as relevant, and familiarity with its various forms is assumed to be properly preparatory to individual work. The security of traditional approaches and training has been replaced by a variety both bewildering and stimulating, but in either case unavoidable; the confidence born of ignorance or parochial standards is no longer really possible. The true primitive is disappearing, in art and in life. Something new is in the making. The problem for the individual artist is how to locate himself in world art while preserving the fruitful roots of his own place, time, and temperament. If there is a new danger it lies in aimless eclecticism.

Picasso's artistic development suggests an answer to the problem, and his painting style implies a model for a Cosmotopian life style. Picasso's protean style is really several styles at once. Each of his mature works contains within it by implication alternative ways of painting developed in the past and still interesting. A woman's profile, for example, may suggest an African mask, a cubist guitarist, an archaic statue, a surrealist fear, a loving mother, and more; the art includes playful comparisons. The analogy with world art and with cultural styles has been drawn by A. L. Kroeber who sees a world art of multiple styles prefigured in the best contemporary work. Where weaker artists may blend, fudge, eclecticize, "the stronger ones will not only be able to manage multiple manners, but the essence of their creativity is likely to lie in the contrast they feel and can achieve between these manners. We shall have in that event something new in the world: a style that is comparative instead of exclusive, and conscious instead of ignorant of universal art history."[1]

The development of world art, of international styles, reflects the extraordinary stimuli of diverse examples now felt as relevant. The exotic has been transformed into the real; a sense of separation and distance has shifted toward a sense of common delights. The feeling is one of liberation and experiment. Consider architecture, an art especially relevant for Cosmotopian conjectures because along with its sense of novel possibilities runs a strong concern for traditions, a regard for the appropriateness of a particular structure for the place and for the people. The public nature of architecture, especially in civic forms, forces consideration of the relation of new forms to what has gone before. When the site and the human occasion are given, the range of possibilities is thereby limited. Architecture exemplifies the simultaneously liberating and limiting forces of materials and technology, of expenditure, of function. All the more significant, then, that contemporary architecture is thoroughly international, its spirit quickened by a lively sense of expanding possibilities. Yet the social nature of architecture, its necessarily cooperative and often compromising career, reminds us properly of the limits which confront a man's sense of virtually limitless possibilities.

It may be argued that Cosmotopia reflects a naive zest for possibilities and that the idea of Cosmotopia is itself ethnocentric. The patterns are notoriously western in their emphasis on individual assertion, on man's ability to direct and shape the flow of possibilities and to select from among them. Moreover, this western dream is perhaps exaggeratedly American in its insistence that an individual by trained choice can create that style of life which is not only most suitable for his particular temperament but which contains by implication all possible alternatives, rejected or not. The dream seems to deny that there are limits to man's capacity to grasp implications and associations, to play with them, and to integrate new patterns with old. To many, this citizen of Cosmotopia is unimaginable, presumptuous, and in his implied empiricism, absurd, since one cannot try out in experience very many possibilities. Better, many would say, to take what is given.

But that is precisely the point: what is given, in the sense of traditions, is no longer given. The familiar has been robbed of its reassuring strength. A crucial element, confidence, is gone. Neither those who convey traditions nor those who receive them are convinced any longer that they are wholly adequate—that customary ways and views make sense out of things. When experience finally breaks into perception and it can no longer be pretended that customary interpretations fit, the situation is called a crisis.

The way out of crisis leads toward interpretations which come closer to realities, usually by considering broader ranges of evidence. Reducing the cultural lag which becomes apparent in crisis is difficult; one way might be to reduce observer error or, at least, the ethnocentric elements in observer error. All human observations and interpretations of social phenomena involve errors induced by cultural bias. Cultural predilections severely reduce objectivity (at best approximate)—the more unacknowledged the biases and the more culturally inadmissible the alternative interpretations. American Studies might be able to reduce ethnocentric errors made by citizens generally and more particularly by scholars and those who shape opinion and policy.

One of the tasks of American Studies, then, is to carry on cultural analysis, not only in the well-established area of investigating patterns within American experience but with a special emphasis on developing an awareness of the extent to which Americans' perceptions tend to be skewed by American experience. The inquiry is, of course, related closely to efforts to become aware of larger and smaller contexts as well. Cultural analysis in a national focus involves assessment of one's predilections as a western man and of regional, class, local, familial screens of interpretation. National experience as an area of study is simply one field in a spectrum ranging from human predilections at the most generalized to the infinitely various gestalts of unique individuals. Once these qualifications have been made, however, national bias remains a convenient and historically important focus.

But why are comparative studies of other cultures an integral part of this conception of American Studies? And if so, is it not a matter of supplementing the usual American Studies training by some foreign area program? More is involved, I would contend, than that. Consider again the question of ethnocentric error. The need for training which would reduce this element in observer error is most dramatic in the area of United States foreign aid. It is generally agreed that in order to appraise the possible consequences of a program carried out in another culture extensive study of that culture is essential. However, even after such study the consequences may be appraised with ethnocentric bias. And the categories of analysis will be almost certainly ethnocentric in the case of a non-western culture since the language of cultural analysis was created by westerners, since the concepts of even the most sophisticated social psychologies bear the imprint of their western matrices— a matter to be considered later. For the moment the point to stress is not simply that the recipient culture must be analyzed, nor even that American analysts should know their own culture so well that they will be alert to detect their own ethnocentric errors; the point is that an analysis after intensive study of, let us say, Vietnam by an American, even by an American knowledgeable about his own cultural biases, will tend to be skewed by salients of cultural comparison. His analysis may be distorted because he attends unduly to differences and similarities; he notices the things an American would notice. What he sees is affected by the way he sees, a way inevitably comparative, and if his frame of reference includes only the United States and Vietnam it is inadequate. It is inadequate because first, the two cases involved are too few; and second, because the process of thinking about two cultures simultaneously is probably novel. Problems of "translation" are unfamiliar. The analyst has not made a habit of taking ethnocentric error into account always, at all stages.

How, then, might ethnocentric error be reduced by training? On the first count, if two cases, the United States and Vietnam, are too few and tend to induce false salients in analysis, how many would be enough and which ones? I don't think we know yet. Perhaps some kind of wise Human Relations Area File would be a model for the ideally informed analyst familiar with all human cultural arrangements and behaviors and especially with cultural dynamics and complex social systems.[2] As for the second likely source of ethnocentric error, the novelty of "translation," there is a more plausible remedy. The habit of cross-cultural thinking could be acquired young. One could learn to think habitually in comparative cultural terms, possibly even learn to think "instinctively" as a participant in world life. To this end a man's training should include systematic study of and experience in several cultures: his own, always, and, let us say, two others—one comparable and one contrasting. Such a man might have developed his ability to think habitually about cultural context by training, for example, in United States, French, and Chinese cultures. This man would be an incipient Cosmotopian by virtue of his habitual world perspectives. He would tend to assess other men's competence by their capacity for understanding the complex implications of the most varied cultural contexts, and he would esteem world leaders for their ability to create culturally appropriate forms of order which respect individual dignity and humane relations.

The comparative study of cultures, then, is proposed as one important way to reduce ethnocentric error or, put more positively, to help modern men see the world as it is within a larger framework of human experience than most ethnocentric educations provide. Such studies are historical, unavoidably so when cultural change is assumed as the normal state of affairs. These studies are historical not only in the familiar western sense that answers to most cultural questions are expected to include some account of how a given custom or situation came to be the way it is; they are historical in their special concern with how customary ways of living affect responses to changing conditions, how ways of interpreting and responding are affected by the conditions in the past which engendered them.

Illustrations of these legacies abound. Take, for example,

in the American field the history of the discussion and study of poverty or, even more dramatic, the development of the discussion and study of race relations. The clarity of Myrdal's *An American Dilemma* owed much, clearly, to comparative cultural perspective. It is likely that every culture has many slanted perspectives which literally blind the eye to what exists. The forms of interpretation, the stock of concepts available to make sense out of experience will probably always lag behind the emerging patterns they are focused on, distorted by past and present conditions cultural and personal, but this distortion might be reduced by systematic training in cultural self-observation through comparative cultural history.

In this view history, itself, is most significantly comparative cultural history. Any account of how certain people acted there and then involves, unavoidably, comparisons with how the same or other people were acting and do act in circumstances similar in some respects and different in others. The trained effort to reconstruct past events is analogous to assessing the implications of participation in another culture. The observer's error across time is not so unlike the observer's error across space that training in "translation" might not help both enterprises. Furthermore, for any history but the most local, elements from outside cultures must be taken into account. If I labor the point unnecessarily it is because nationalistic preoccupation and bias are not only myopic in their distortion of experience but increasingly dangerous. I may be killed by misinterpretation of the actions and responses of members of other cultures—no novelty, historically, but if avoidable, inane.

Whatever one's historical method it could only be helped and clarified by comparative cultural studies. Not long ago American historians were urged to regard psychoanalysis as an essential part of their training; cultural analysis is equally necessary for the perception of realities. Just as psychoanalysis aims to increase awareness of previously unacknowledged psychological determinants and to replace compulsion by judgment, so cultural analysis aims to develop awareness of unacknowledged cultural determinants and to thereby reduce bias. And liberation from cultural biases is probably less painful. In fact, in many areas of comparative cultural studies explorations would be marvelously playful and exhilarating. Experience of another culture is tonic at the outset, and the complexity of comparisons is intrinsically attractive to men of speculative bent. As a Cosmotopian poet has already declared, "To be a man is to have the power to make associations; and that's that."

A reorientation of American Studies toward comparative cultural history should develop new kinds of questions and some new areas of study as part of a collaborative international enterprise. A useful social psychology, for example, might be developed out of Japanese experience in "westernization," its concepts derived from Japanese views of personality and social order. Its hypotheses might then be used to analyze patterns of change elsewhere. The conceptual categories and procedures of western psychology may well reflect their cultural matrices and the tendencies of western linguistic categories, much as theories of laissez-faire economics or Marxian cultural analysis reflect the limited perspectives of the conditions under which they were developed. Or take the concept of feudalism: the difficulties encountered when applying the concept to non-western experiences have already proved stimulating to western scholars. Now, if a Japanese historian, for example, were to create a terminology of social analysis better suited to Japanese experience than such western notions as feudalism, his terms might then be applied to western feudal experiences in stimulating fashion; Japanese artistic and architectural concepts have pointed the way.

Other interesting avenues might open from compilation of

a world "dictionary" of gesture, a systematic filmed record of man as gesturing and grimacing animal. Such a project may even now be under way; it is common sensical. Every traveler should know as a matter of courtesy, or even protection, what hand gestures and facial expressions mean from culture to culture. Researches would add immediately to knowledge of cultural diffusion, to theories of role playing, to studies of symbolic forms, sexuality, communication. Phenomenologists could then theorize about the "lived body" with an extensive empirical base connected to the emerging field of kinesthetics. Ignorance of the varieties of bodily expression is itself, of course, interesting to a cultural analyst. In comparative cultural studies of what it means to be human, American Studies might well begin with the "lived body."

Along more familiar academic lines new groupings of traditional studies would likely proliferate. A good indication of prospects is on record in a notable journal, *Comparative Studies in Society and History*, which began publication in 1958, and in an extensive literature on economic development which indicates a growing concern with "noneconomic" factors.[3] The excellent bibliographical work being carried on by the American Studies Association might well include a section on comparative cultural materials.

There remains the question of cultural relativism, raised earlier and laid aside; the objection that cross-cultural perspectives erode morality and eventually blur all standards. Certainly before universal standards can be set, more should be known about what it means to be a human being, but the cultural relativist's assertion that judgments cannot be made is a premaure view which prejudges the case. Comparative studies of cultural history cannot avoid dealing with values, with judgments of human justice and with decisions as to the human appropriateness of certain customs and forms. Inquiries should face the difficulties directly and try to clarify discussion. In analyzing a culture are there any criteria agree-able to members of diverse cultures on the basis of which cultural forms can be judged? Can it be said, for example, that certain kinds of civility and humane relations have been achieved most beautifully in a particular culture while other aspects of the same culture are less estimable? What are the requirements for meaningful statements in these areas? Are universal standards possible, perhaps, along the lines stated in the United Nations Universal Declaration of Human Rights? Can cultural arrangements be compared and evaluated in terms of their effects on human development? Is a "good" culture one which enables all members in their wide variety to discover their abilities and to train and exercise them? Are there self-corrective channels within the particular culture?

This is an area of inquiry which might be part of a uni-versal education in which American Studies would par-ticipate as one emphasis in a worldwide pattern of cultural studies. To develop a proposal made earlier, the education of all citizens, especially scholars, teachers, and those who shape opinion and policy, should include systematic study of at least three cultures: one's own national culture, another national culture within a common larger cultural group, and a culture outside one's common cultural area. For a United States citizen, for example, such study might include in addition to United States culture, study of and experience in French and Chinese cultures. A Brazilian might study Spain, Japan, and Brazil. The study of each culture would take place most extensively in that cultural area, but each in-stitutional arrangement for cultural studies would normally include members of other cultures participating as teacher-researchers and as students. Studies from a distance would supplement at preparatory and continuing levels. The prin-ciples of resident study abroad and of international faculties are basic for the strategy of research and for the education of citizens. Centers of American Studies in the United States would be models for centers in an international network.

United States educational enterprises should take the lead in such a program because of their relative affluence and independence, their strong traditions of free discussion, and their eclectic tendencies. Most important, an extensive program of international free inquiry along these lines would reassert the crucial role of critical thought at a time when hard-won but fragile protections against censorship and police force are threatened all over the world by ignorance, resentment, and organized expediency.

Some such reorientation of education and research on a large scale is necessary if the dream of a civilized world is to survive. American Studies as a comparative historical study of American forms of world culture might help Americans see the world as it is and themselves as they are, or at least help avoid the worst ethnocentric errors. In the long run American Studies should point toward a future world civilization whose citizens may justify the sense of expanded human possibilities which is abroad in the world today.

1. A. L. Kroeber, *Style and Civilizations* (Ithaca, N. Y.: Cornell University Press, 1957), p. 51. In his application of "style" to culture Kroeber insists on the presence of alternatives, even if they are never elected; "where compulsion or physical or physiological necessity reign, there is no room for style." *Ibid* p. 150.

2. Directions are suggested in the works of Robert Jay Lifton, Karl Deutsch, and Seymour Martin Lipset.

3. *Economic Development and Cultural Change*, a journal published since 1952, is most relevant; also a special number of the *Journal of Social Issues*, XIX (January 1963) on "Psycho-Cultural Factors in Asian Economic Growth."

Why So Much Pessimism?

ROY F. NICHOLS

ROY F. NICHOLS has been Dean of the Graduate School of Arts and Sciences at the University of Pennsylvania since 1952, and Provost since 1953. His more recent books include *Advanced Agents of American Destiny* (1956), *Religion and American Democracy* (1959) and *Stakes of Power, 1845-1877* (1961).

COMMENTATORS ON THE STATE OF THE WORLD USUALLY MORE or less balance each other out on the basis of what might be called a mean average temperament distribution among men. Those of one temperament paraphrasing Dickens proclaim, "It is the best of times" while those of contrary glandular orientation contradict with the melancholy dictum "It is the worst of times." Such ambivalence is to be expected and upon most occasions need arouse no particular concern. However in these times of ours there appears a decided tendency to pessimism and it is the prevalence of this attitude that has induced these remarks.

There are many indications that the world most familiar to us is clouded by a sense of doubt and discouragement which has not been characteristic at least in the American past. A few examples may be cited.

Recently the organ of the American Studies Association featured a discussion entitled "Are American Historians Losing Ground?"[1] and the answer was "yes." A distinguished historian in a widely read book asks "What has become of the American Dream?" and clearly implies that it has become a nightmare.[2] A year ago the President of the American Historical Association warned us that history might be losing its social usefulness.[3] Then as we look around us in today's world, we see so many disturbing phenomena. So much seems to indicate a loss of surplus, status, security and even sanity.

In such discouraging circumstances historians are unfortunately likely to be susceptible to the virus of pessimism because of certain limitations which they impose upon themselves even by their training and which invite frustration and discouragement. A listing of such limitations indicates the nature of these handicaps.

The first is an overcommitment to specialization. The tendency to think in terms of small segments of behavior in narrow areas and in constricted periods of time has shut us up within restricted physical and temporal boundaries and shut us off from any broad vista or wide horizon. Within such narrow limits we can be source bound, timid, fearing to generalize beyond the very confined limits of our complete mastery of the evidence available. In consequence some have succumbed to an occupational agoraphobia which invites seclusion and pessimism when we should be impelled by a claustrophobia which drives us into the market place, there to mingle with the throngs and influence their thinking.

Secondly we fail to generalize sufficiently or effectively. We read too little in the general literature even of history, let alone that of cognate fields. The press of specialized writing and teaching together with the complexities of life outside the profession often lead us to think we have but little time for study in other fields of history or in the behavioral sciences. But this is what is so much needed, knowledge and thinking in cognate disciplines and the assimilation of the fruits of that study with our accumulations in the realms of our specializations.

Would that there were more scholars of courage and vision who might be willing to project the knowledge they gain in a specialized field into other areas and eras and to develop meaningful syntheses. More are needed who will depart from their particular stances and move either forward or backward in time. Anyone who does this will soon learn that the specialist in a sense perverts history. Ancient wisdom proclaims that there is nothing new under the intellectual sun and any historian can if he wishes prove this. Only those who have searched for the origin of behavior patterns can know how old most of them are. It is of course asking too much of even mature scholars that they explore the sources of all fields as they do those of their areas of specialization, but the last seventy-five years of monograph writing have produced an extensive corpus of secondary literature which yields insight if approached with the techniques of cultural comparison such as are common among anthropologists and which are used to advantage among those in departments of American and other regional studies. So to the limitation of specialization we add a weakness in generalization, in synthesis.

A third self-imposed limitation which has cramped the comprehension of historians and likewise invites frustration has been their concentration on the unique. They have done this because of a sincere belief that they thereby provide the key to true understanding. By concentrating on changes that are spectacular and cataclysmic and by using them as punctuation points, historians create an explanatory framework or theory of causation and provide analogies which highlight these unique events as determinants, as great points of remembrance and enlightenment. But there are those who maintain that cataclysms, trauma, are not worth the undue attention devoted to them. They admit that this method often provides a good story but ask does it promote knowledge of process and the nature of the constant change? Their contention is that continuity is probably more significant than interruption, the constant more important than the unique, the non-recurrent.

A fourth factor in our problem is the tendency we display to encourage some of our limitations by the traditional and current Ph.D. training. This degree work too often encourages overspecialization, discourages generalization, enforces preoccupation with the miniscule. Besides it is frequently dragged out in duration and ends in frustration. There has been too little reconsideration of our methods of graduate training in the twentieth century. It is now overdue because some of its fruits seem so bitter.

Finally a fifth factor impelling historians and analysts to gloomy outlook is the loss of a sense of direction. In the beginning of historical effort, perhaps the historian's chief concern was to collect facts and traditions and make them into a story. At a much later time he undertook to recount man's struggle for salvation. He thought almost as the theologians tracing the works of God. Later he followed the thought patterns of the astronomers and the physicists applying the laws of nature. Next he was impressed by possible application of human experiences, by the biological rhythms of birth, growth, maturing, declining and death and the crowning concept of Darwinian evolution as illustrated by the rise and fall of societies and civilizations. This organic determinism invited him to embrace a concept of progress. In a "progressive" age it seemed so obvious that the pathway of mankind was an upward one. Mankind would be ever climbing to new heights.

Scholars therefore became conditioned to the concept that theirs was the responsibility to trace the course of this progress, implying or declaring that it would continue indefinitely in the future. But as the twentieth century has advanced it has become harder to believe this in the face of cumulative evidence to the contrary. The growing fear, even knowledge, that progress is not a constant, has been a shock at least to the older generation. In the meantime relativism had entered the picture and seemed to deny the possibility of knowing anything with any absolute certainty. Science, progress and democracy were undercut by irrationalism and agnosticism and progress became merely change. Men were wandering aimlessly creating ephemeral works. As they had lost their sense of direction, history had lost its goal. So pessimism succeeded the optimism which had prevailed.

II

But despite all these inducements to become pessimists we have no business to yield to such temptation. We who are historians and students of American culture in general despite today's unfortunate climate can by our own acts and decisions create a different atmosphere in which to work and think. By a not unreasonable effort on our part we can abandon certain of the self-imposed limitations which both narrow the scope of our intellectual activities and influence, and invite frustration and discouragement.

First we should carefully reexamine the Ph.D. program which seems to have an unfortunate tendency to perpetuate our handicaps. Several of its features are unsatisfactory. Our practice of admitting so many students to Graduate Schools without adequate subject matter training because they are generally intelligent means that they have to make up deficiencies in knowledge by using too much of their residence in taking what amount to cram courses. This practice postpones examinations for admission to candidacy and tends to make them factual rather than tests of the students' capacity to reason and interpret historically. It also postpones what they are really in the graduate school for, namely research training. This type of "education" puts too great an emphasis upon memory, postpones the thesis and in sum it takes too long.

The real object of Ph.D. training should be recovered. From the first weeks the emphasis should be on the intellectual challenge of the requirements of research and discovery. Experience in generalization should be emphasized. The insistence often exclusively on courses in history can limit the opportunity for students to learn, to understand and to generalize in the manner which today's problems require. There should be as much training in generalization as there is in specialization. We emphasize and rightly so work in original sources but do we as much as we might in requiring independent reading in the subject classics and in other general works for the purpose of writing experimental generalizations as well as research reports?

Nor do we do enough to make the students aware of the contribution which a developing insight may make to understanding. I have seen graduate students so immersed in source material that they had no real knowledge of the literature of the subject, no real comprehension of the generalizations in the framework of which they should be interpreting their findings. In our insistence that the student learn to discover do we not on occasion deprive him of the capacity to understand what he is discovering or its meaning?

Graduate training in sum should be designed to introduce the student to a series of experiences which he will recognize as significant and some phases of which he will wish to continue. These should be experiences in discovery, in understanding and in communication undertaken under men who can do these things, in the company of men and women seeking similar experiences which will be so stimulating that he or she will never be content to cease searching, finding, interpreting and transmitting. But too often the long shadow of the graduate school means a series of limitations, a multiplication of monographs or nothing, an ironical life history for doctors of philosophy. We owe it to ourselves and our students to offer them as rich an experience as we can devise, one which will protect them from the imposition of such limitations as we have just been listing, encourage generalization and the development of insight and, rather than to drive them to pessimism, to open a vista of opportunity which will do quite the opposite.

Besides reconsidering our training programs we should seek a second and more immediately possible antidote for pessimism. This should be a redefinition of our functions so that we may thereby remedy our failure to sense our own importance and to realize our own potential. The labor and thought of an historian and of a cultural analyst are really invitations to optimism. The experience of these scholars is unique because they live on two planes of time. They most certainly dwell in the present but by definition they must also live in a world of the imagination which is past time reconstructed. They are confronted with the opportunity for constant comparison. They constantly have to deal with two sets of phenomena, each of which gives meaning to the other. The harmonization of these two sets of phenomena gives them a unique experience which we should invite and feature.

The possibly inspiring nature of the scholar's experience in history and analysis further encourages a redefinition of function which in turn can show how much more reason there is for encouragement. The weakening of the seemingly determining factor of *progress* has been in reality a great boon, for it has been succeeded by emphasis upon the much more significant factor, change. The constancy of change insures the absence of monotony and, more important, provides a more realistic sense of self-determination and the liberty to exercise it. Though there may be uncertainty as to destination, the realization of the inevitability of change gives the individuals and groups who make up society the responsibility of choosing a direction and defining a goal.

The historian therefore has as significant or even a more significant objective than when he blithely thought that all he had to do was to trace progress, indefinitely, even in spite of certain long past "declines and falls." He should now know that he must record, recover and explain something less easy to find. As science and philosophy may be losing prestige and the confidence of historians, Aron reminds up, history can become "the principle of the movement which spans and carries along all man's works," and which can aid man "to penetrate that mysterious power, God, or the demiurge of those who have lost all faith in science and reason."[4] Free to make a commitment to search for knowledge and find truth, the historian is free to triumph over nihilism by seeking objective knowledge and by engaging in thought. He must travel a path which is not necessarily an upward one but more probably a generally horizontal road with only occasional hills and hollows which by the law of averages level it so that it neither dips into depths nor scales heights.

In travelling this horizontal road, the historian, better than anyone else, knows how old it is and how ancient and firmly established are the behavior patterns of those travelling thereon and therefore how unlikely they are to be obliterated. Also because the road is a level one not only without great heights but also without overwhelming depths, the lack of upward climbing may not be so desolating. Under these circumstances the historian does well to factor out his emotions, his hopes and fears, to continue his search, his analysis, his growth in understanding and to communicate them in the light of his wisdom in a manner which shall show their depth and their inclusive character and convey the contagion of the confidence of understanding. He alone can do this, therefore he cannot afford to succumb to the comfort and seduction of pessimism, so tempting and so satisfying. Nor can he enter the fearful and frightening falsity of optimism which is such a snare and so ruinous a guide. He must walk, explore and mark out the horizontal path of constant, continuous and eternal change.

Furthermore he has a special role to play which requires he live under a discipline, he must develop an historical yoga or detachment from the present, which will enable him to exclude to a degree at least, the confusion of current experience, to rise above it and to relive the past in its *own terms*. To accomplish this he must develop a metaphysics that transcends most of his own immediate experience and adjust his emotions so that he can correct his understanding by factoring out extraneous circumstances of the moment which only hinder his comprehension of the past. His knowledge of history should no longer be influenced by his hopes and fears for today and tomorrow. He can by discipline live on a plane of existence in which past and present are blended and in which he is dominated not by the unique or the immediate but by a concept of the continuity of process which enables him to rise above contemporary terrors or ecstatic hopes and to reduce the variety of happenings to a line of direction which is horizontal.

These possibilities display to the historian the value of cultivating a new asceticism. He can well develop an emotional discipline based upon the absence of both hope and fear which comes from the expectancy of an infinity of continuity. Such an asceticism will provide the historian with a new liberty and a new confidence in the validity of his labors. This intellectual and emotional readjustment to a realization of the richness of experience which is possible for the historian, should dispel the shades of pessimism. If the historian revises his methods of intellectual activity and the training which he imparts, he can acquire greater insight and understanding, he can view human behavior with a broader perspective, he can make more valid generalizations and can more convincingly report to society the findings which will guide thought and action in a fashion which may be described by the adjective "wiser."

Under such circumstances the historian need never lack for responsible employment. They provide a challenge for the greatest use of hard work and wisdom and therefore offer the most satisfying of human careers which has no room in it for pessimism, nor any time for it either. This can be his experience, an experience which requires him likewise to excel in all the arts of communication so that he may share it with society.

The success of the scholar in the long run depends upon the richness of his experience, and no one with a rich experience can be pessimistic. If he leads a full intellectual life this experience will be rich because it will be filled with understanding. If he is skilled in communication, the life of society will likewise be enriched. The German historian Dilthey believed that the historian according to the measure of his own spiritual life and in proportion to the intrinsic richness of that life could infuse life into the dead materials with which he was confronted.

III

Having dealt thus far with the general, I would bring this discussion into nearer focus by turning to the particular and considering the challenge of the moment which despite some of its discouraging characteristics may provide the historian and the cultural analyst with the greatest of stimuli to optimism.

History which is so inevitable and inescapable can be immediately useful because of the peculiar nature of the times in which we live. We are in an era of unusually accelerated change, so swift is it that we may be in the midst of another age of revolution still largely unperceived and undefined, certainly unnamed. We stand on the verge of space, conscious of the masses in Eastern Europe, Asia and Africa, and of a population explosion to which we have been contributing. Race relations are altering. Our own political system administratively has become the play-thing of bureaucracy, legislatively or solons seem to be playing politics rather than exhibiting concern for the na-tional welfare. Our ethics, political and private, have been strained. This is a day of increased automation, unemploy-ment, and variously determined leisure, all of which stimu-late social change. Our enterprise is altered by subsidies of various types. Our emotional reserves are depleted. Too many look back to a past which is certainly gone and may never have existed.

If these factors and others add up to an unnamed revolu-tion they are creating a new image which too many either ignore or fail to understand. We who were the product of a rational revolution may be now living in an age of visceral revolution in which emotion rather than reason prevails, or we may be in the midst of supranational transformation. Nations are giving way to mass conglomerations based on different conceptualizations of cultural patterns, different ideologies and power aggregates. Within our own democ-racy our fears are so obvious. The fear of the radical left stimulates a strengthening of the conservative right which has grown to such proportions that it has produced a mili-tarism incompatible with our traditional concepts of free institutions. If one believes he sees signs of a communist conspiracy others can also become aware of fascistic utterance. One feeds the other. Nor can we ignore some of the implications of the calamity of November 22.

There is discernible a tendency to flee from the new realities, to take refuge in ideologies and to insist on conformity to them, to resort not to fortune tellers but to model builders who create monoliths. As former Ambassador Galbraith has reminded us[5] we tend to revolt against new things which are successful and go back to something old and familiar even though it may no longer be useful. Publicists and lesser fry have seized upon the techniques of the egghead and are now building models but they insist that we ride around in intellectual "model T" Fords. They wish to freeze Democracy when the age demands adjustment. In 1860-1861 we were swayed by an attack of conscience over the sin of slavery. Now a century later we are confused and worried by our violations of the Declaration of Independence and the Bill of Rights. This age which features nihilism and existentialism is an age so different from the polite rationalism of the age of reason. It is an era in which forces and winds from the East find the Western mind bending before "a new climate of opinion."

In the face of such a possible revolution historians and cultural analysts are indispensable. They are the ones upon whom society must depend to keep it posted on why things are happening insofar as this information can be obtained from studying the past in the points of time variously denominated the present.

But for what should these observers, recorders and searchers be on the alert? As we have already noted historians have a tendency to be overspecialized, to live intellectually in compartments. This impairs their capacity to understand and to interpret which should be their principal objective. Historians have developed an adjectival proclivity designed to make them more perceptive in depth but which causes them to lose much of their capacity for understanding in breadth.

If we are in the midst of a revolution the historian should be boning up on all that he knows or can find out about revolutions. And as revolutions are usually designed to change government and are operated through politics we need to know as much as we can about politics. And ours is such a complex politics. We have fifty-one systems in this republic and I have no hesitation in saying that we do not really have adequate knowledge of any one of them. We students of American culture, we American historians must grasp the implications of our revolution and its cultural ramifications. The call goes out to historians and cultural analysts of all sorts whether political, economic, social, intellectual, whatever the adjective so tightly embraced, to take on a new responsibility to meet a new challenge to find and present a new pattern.

The meaning of this suggestion may be clearer if enlarged a little. One speaks of political history sometimes as though it were an interest which restricts research and understanding, almost as if the adjective were a dirty word. And undoubtedly in certain contexts it can and does serve as such an agent. But now in the frame of reference of the present experience of the United States it should and can have just the opposite influence.

We hear much today of images. Each society has over the years created one, some of them are much too simply conceived and too glibly described. But these images are instruments of folk definition and in their shadow and under their domination, societies, groups and individuals behave. The image which is most common in our western world is that of a democracy and democracy is undoubtedly a concept of political origin. The American people by and large conceive of themselves as a democracy. The most significant of their mass thinking and their mass acting is done in a quasi political frame of reference and it has become the unifying force in American thought and action.

A basic understanding of our pattern of behavior therefore can only come from knowledge of its evolution. Scholars should not continue in any narrow definition; rather the historian should recognize the variety of the facets of this image and attempt to consolidate them in one which is comprehensive. Most adjectival designations are by definition too narrow. Economic interpretations leave out too much. Social history is too diffuse and generally lacks meaning. In the understanding of American society an image is needed with an all embracing cultural comprehension which in the terms of self-conscious, self-direction and adjustment to external determinants, combines internal and external dynamics. Such an image is the comprehensive cultural image of democracy which demands a history which should not be damned as political history in the phrase of a bygone day. The use of political, economic, social, intellectual as fruitful descriptive rubrics should be abandoned and a new one put in their place. To find such is a real challenge; we could use one which is really new but so far to my knowledge, none has appeared. For my purposes I find it useful to think of what may be termed the history of democratic culture.

The sum total of the behavior of any society can be described as its culture. This culture is like a complex textile pattern made up of colored threads. Despite the many colors in all such patterns usually one predominates. To use but two examples, Russia is a communistic society, the United States is a democratic community. The history of such societies is how they came to assume these images. To be sure you can pick out minor threads and small patterns in any cultural aggregate and spend much time in tracing them and accounting for them—but in so doing there is a temptation to neglect the main design. Presumably no threads in the pattern should be ignored but if minor elements obscure the main scheme or if the overall pattern is misunderstood, the analysis will be inconclusive or deceptive. The various threads must be traced in reference to the whole design.

Democracy is not an absolute which someone or some group invented, it is a mode of behavior which has been evolved to meet certain needs which arose at various times and places. It is a pattern long in weaving created in a definable area—it has yet to be shown that it is of universal application.

It was not created in the period between 1776 and 1800 in the United States—in fact most of its basic concepts came from elsewhere. They emerged during the transplanting of folkways over a millennium in a variety of regions and their adjustment to meet the needs of migrants. The history of the American democratic image can have no meaning if it is held to begin in 1763 because the greater part of its conditioning factors were in anterior operation.

Democracy was never prescribed by law or even by a constitution, national or otherwise. In was a slowly evolved pattern of behavior which was conditioned by the dynamics of migration and community creation. It has certain characteristics which were never legislated into existence; they became accepted habits of behavior which are now instinctive.

If our democratic culture is in the throes of an unnamed revolution, it is surely so because of many influences with a long history, a history of which we are still painfully ignorant. The dispelling of this ignorance is our responsibility and surely no one can conceive of a greater challenge. This challenge should inspire us all with a greater imperative which exhilarates in a most optimism-provoking and compelling fashion. Society needs something and we alone can provide a major element in it.

This something is a comprehensive synthesis of past behavior which illumines the present and the future. Thus synthesis should vie with specialization for our attention. This synthesis will concentrate on a cultural conceptualization to make possible the recording of the evolution of the image of our society or any civilization in question which is the joint responsibility of the historian and the cultural analyst. For this task we need a new training.

So we have a new challenge and we should have a new sense of purpose. Relativism takes on a new importance. The historian should have a new sense of discipline, a new metaphysics. He must have a new sense of the inevitability of history and the indispensability of the historian. For as Lincoln once said we cannot escape history—any more than the normal individual can escape his memory. Let us take heart. We are faced with the mighty challenge of living up to our intellectual responsibility and if we strive to meet this challenge there can be no pessimism. With a new sense of our own intellectual significance we shall feel the glow of optimism returning to us as we realize we are standing on the threshold of discoveries much more meaningful than those of the past, discoveries which may reveal to mankind a new sense of capacity.

Historians and cultural analysts of America unite, take a new look around you, you have nothing to lose but your limitations.

1. American Studies Association, *American Studies* V (December 1962), 1-4.

2. Daniel J. Boorstin, *The Image or What Happened to the American Dream?* (New York: Antheneum Publishers, 1962), *passim.*

3. Carl Breidenbaugh, "The Great Mutation," *American Historical Review*, LXVIII (January 1963), 315-331.

4. George J. Irwin (trans.), Raymond Aron's *Introduction to the Philosophy of History; an Essay on the Limits of Historical Objectivity* (Boston: Beacon Press, 1961), p. 298.

5. John Kenneth Galbraith, "Our Quarrel with Success," *Department of State Bulletin*, July 8, 1963, 52-56.

American Studies: Bird in Hand?*

MARSHALL W. FISHWICK

MARSHALL W. FISHWICK, who holds a doctorate from Yale, was professor of American Studies at Washington and Lee University from 1956 to 1961. He is currently director of the American Studies Institute sponsored jointly by the Wemyss Foundation and Lincoln University. He has served as visiting lecturer at a number of universities including assignments under the Fulbright Program in Denmark, Germany, Poland, and India.

As American Studies began with a flirtation between literary and historical studies, it would seem now in danger of ending in a divorce because it asks that union become total unity.—ROBERT E. SPILLER in *Studies in American Culture.*

THE FOUNDING FATHERS ARE QUIETLY DISAPPEARING. DEATH has claimed A. Whitney Griswold, Tremaine McDowell, F. O. Matthiessen, and Stanley Williams. Ralph Gabriel, Kenneth Murdock, Willard Thorp, Roy Nichols, and Robert Spiller have retired from their academic posts. A new generation must take command of the American Studies (or Civilization, or Culture) movement. Will it, like the hardy English sparrow, adapt to the American environment; pass quietly away, as did the passenger pigeon; or, like the phoenix, rise from its own ashes, to soar off into new skies?

The question is critical not only at home, where scores

* This chapter appeared originally in the Winter 1968 issue of *International Educational* and *Cultural Exchange.*

of colleges and universities ask it, but also abroad, where American Studies Associations and programs represent the high water mark of academic interchange and penetration since World War II.

So great are the ambiguities and imponderables that no simple answer is possible. It is neither a unified nor a cohesive movement but six (or more) disciplines in search of interdisciplinary harmony; a loose confederation dependent more on personalities than principles. Men as different in temperament and method as Parrington, Van Wyck Brooks, Mumford, Lovejoy, Babbitt, and Lowes helped to bring American Studies into being. Long-range trends, such as the shifting emphasis from linguistic and belletristic analysis to cultural and intellectual history, helped. Insurgency and dissent, evident in American scholarship during and ever since the Progressive Era, have provided a climate of opinion in which new studies could prosper. The energy of many original minds have powered the American Studies circuits.

So far as formal organization and programing is concerned, the watershed was World War II. "Discrepancy between the position of the United States in the world and its place in syllabuses and curricula had long been growing," Sigmund Skard notes; "after 1945 it proved intolerable. . . . The radical change was brought on by the need for reorientation."[1]

Looking back on the Truman Era, when only the United States had the Bomb, and Pax Americana—like Hoover's desperately sought prosperity—was "just around the corner," one detects a strong self-congratulatory note in postwar writing and planning. The case for America's phenomenal success was sometimes forged into a doctrine of Americanism. If only we could explain this to the old world—especially an exhausted Europe—perhaps others would become partners with the free (and brave) new world. Alarmed by the narrow nationalism of the time, Arthur Bestor raised a tart question in 1952: "The Study of American Civilization: Jingoism or Scholarship?"[2]

Meanwhile the overseas response to American scholarship and materials was dramatic. Of course, the United States paid the bills for our Fulbright scholars, who turned up all over the world; for the U.S. Information Service (USIS) and the Voice of America, which deluged the world's libraries and air waves; for the Marshall Plan as well as tanks and planes to add punch to our argument. Still the world *did* listen, Europe *did* recover, we *did* champion the new nationalism in Asia and Africa.[3]

No one will ever be sure whether American Studies abroad would have taken root without such massive support. Everyone knows that the support was provided and the results—in quantitative terms at least—were impressive.

CREST AT MIDCENTURY

A sort of crest for the movement came at midcentury when the American Studies Association (with its official journal, *American Quarterly*) was founded and the multivolume *Literary History of the United States* (edited by Spiller, Thorp, Canby, and Johnson—Founding Fathers all) appeared. National and international surveys recorded steady growth in the 1950's.[4] Has the situation improved or worsened since then? To what seems a simple question there is conflicting evidence and violent disagreement.

Impressive regional programs and individual achievements are not hard to find, but growth continues to be sporadic and opposition perennial. Like the English sparrow, the American Studies devotees find that the winter can be long and essential support short. The English sparrow analogy is apt, since much pioneering has been done in and through English departments, turning their attention to long neglected American writers like Melville, Twain, and Faulkner. Professor Robert Spiller, a key figure in keeping the national association at Pennsylvania, is a literary scholar; so were a succession of association executive secretaries (Louis Rubin, Charles Boewe, Robert Lucid) and the current *American Quarterly* editor (Hennig Cohen). Under their leadership the association has enjoyed a modest expansion, currently about 200 members a year, according to Mr. Lucid.[5]

The first independent national American Studies Association meeting was held in Kansas during October 1967. The delegates were haunted by the question Henry Nash Smith had raised a decade earlier: "Can 'American Studies' develop a method?" His answer—and he earned the first Ph.D. given in the field—was discouraging. "We shall have to develop one for ourselves, and I am afraid that at present we shall have to be content with a very modest program. The best thing we can do is to conceive of American Studies as a collaboration among men working within existing academic disciplines but attempting to widen the boundaries imposed by conventional methods of inquiry."[6]

CONSENSUS, NOT CONFLICT

By the time Smith's essay appeared, vast changes had occurred throughout the world—political, ideological, intellectual. A tiny object called sputnik had sent its "beep beep beep" around the world, driving American complacency out of the skies. A new group of historians, including Daniel Boorstin, David Potter, Louis Hartz, and Richard Hofstadter, had argued that consensus, not conflict, characterized American history. Still a younger school, labeled the "New Left," had reacted strongly against the consensus.[7] But there never had been a consensus on what American Studies was and how it should meet the challenges of the 1960's.

Most of the men who in the 1940's had declared holy

war against "established" departments had quietly slipped into departmental niches themselves and advised their younger colleagues to do the same. It is one thing to observe, with Howard Mumford Jones, that the departmental system—which, as Laurence R. Veysey notes in *The Emergence of the American University*, is less than a century old—splits us into little groups conducting internecine wars; and quite another thing to restore the peace.[8] David Riesman has summarized the cyclical process which goes on inside the halls of academe:

> . . . in order to find a place in a vested departmental structure, the proponents of a new melange are forced by resistance to claim too much; what they plan is, however, tentative and nearly intractable intellectually even if not faced by external resistance; the traditional going concerns have an easier time and the floor of their work is higher even if the ceiling is lower so that interdisciplinary misfits are conspicuous and easily made targets; then the bloom is off or the boom is over and the vested academic interests easily re-establish themselves.[9]

Sparrow-lovers, alarmed but not dismayed by methodology and departmentalism, argue that what they have is a single *subject matter*—the totality of American experience. Many other disciplines have no single monolithic method. The "Aims and Methods" pamphlet of the Modern Language Association, for example, lists four methods; historians can't agree on four times that number. Adapting to rapidly changing environments, they argue American Studies may never develop a method—thank goodness. "Method" implies rigidity and restriction. "Methods are quite sound when a master uses them," Charles Williams writes in *Descent of the Dove;* "cheapened when they become popular; and unendurable when merely fashionable. Thus, predestination was safe with Augustine, comprehensible in Calvin; tiresome in the English Puritans, and horrible in the New England meeting houses." Can the same be said of New England (or New Mexico) colleges? Might we not, like the durable sparrow, merely peck around, here and there, as circumstances dictate? That way lies survival.

VOICES OF PROTEST

Such survival, insists Alfred Kazin, outspoken critic (once advocate) of the movement, portends an academic disaster. American Studies has gotten out of hand and—like the passenger pigeon—flies toward extinction. There are no intellectual checks on the production of "American Studies," for there can be no genuine demonstrations of causation, Kazin argues.[10] The "field" is never social, economic, literary, or intellectual history but the number of relationships made between facts that we have not discovered for ourselves and which therefore are used as symbols. Who is to deny us Custer's Last Stand, the Greek Revival, slavery in the cities, WPA art, pro-Franco sentiment in New England, and the agrarian radicalism of Mary Ellen Lease? Anything goes in this collective auto-analysis —the sooner the whole business goes, the better. Nor is Kazin's an isolated voice protesting the whole movement. Passenger-pigeon fanciers argue that not only is no "synthesis" of American civilization apparent—none is possible. Ours is a civilization of information, not synthesis. To quote Jean Améry:

> The "configuration" of our industrial and consumer society is a comprehensive but heterogeneous structure of facts, or rather knowledge of facts, that can be coordinated but not fused into a synthesis.[11]

At least this puts the problem on epistemological grounds and takes it out of the faculty cloakroom. "To be sure," writes Norman Charles, dean of humanities at Millersville State College, "campus politics and jockeying for position within a department often have little to do with epistemology or the pursuit of truth. But I am hopeful that sooner or later a superior wisdom must prevail within the intellectual community and that the weight of informed opinion will demand a reversal of the trend toward more and more narrow specialization within the academic departments. The fact that the movement has never quite crystalized or gained a distinctive identity doesn't necessarily mean that it has failed or is failing."[12]

On the other hand, Francis A. Young, executive secretary of the Committee on International Exchange of Persons, observes that American Studies as an organized discipline or union of disciplines has failed to take root in foreign soil and even seems to be losing ground in the U.S. "But," he writes, "I think it will probably continue to exist indefinitely in this country as a loose federation of disciplines concerned with various aspects of the American experience, since the disciplines concerned are all related to the same basic reality and can stimulate and cross-fertilize each other." Concerned, like Dr. Young, with international dimensions of American Studies, Richard W. Downar, director of the American Studies program of the American Council of Learned Societies, questions both the feasibility and utility of comparing or even speaking in similar terms of American Studies in the United States and in foreign countries:

> The U.S. has certainly been a pioneer in the field of area studies, and in part because of our experience there, I continue to feel that a foreign educator wishing to establish an American Studies Department abroad might be well advised to take his guidelines from one of the well-established centers in the U.S. *other than American Studies*. For the same reason, I do not believe that the validity or the future of American Studies Departments abroad should be measured or influenced by the fate of American Studies Departments in the U.S.—but rather by the fate of Russian, or Chinese, or South-East Asian Centers in this country.[13]

Another scholar vitally interested in foreign approaches to American Studies is Professor Walter Johnson, author of the 1963 report for the U.S. Advisory Commission on International Educational and Cultural Affairs.[14] In it Dr. Johnson argued for sending abroad scholars "well trained and established in the individual academic disciplines," rather than men with interdisciplinary training. In effect, he was arguing against the tenets of American Studies and for a return to the confining disciplinary boxes which the movement's Founding Fathers struggled to destroy. He all but implies that the day of the passenger pigeon has already come, at least beyond our shores. There is, however, no rancor in Dr. Johnson's diagnosis; instead he reflects the tranquillity and departmental conservatism which Robert Knapp found to be a possible trademark of the historical profession.[15]

NEW AGE OF CIRCUITRY

Whatever the fate of American Studies programs abroad, those at home must take into account the new cultural patterns of the 1960's which, as Susan Sontag points out in *Against Interpretation,* are built on nonliterary foundations. The basic texts for this new Age of Circuitry are found in the writing of Wittgenstein, Marshall McLuhan, John Cage, Claude Levi-Strauss, Siegfried Gideon, Norman O. Brown, and Gyorgy Kepes. They stress new dimensions, a more open way of looking at the world. Do their ideas find a place in most English or American Studies courses? If not, why not?

Of course academic enterprises, old or new, cannot follow every fad; but it is important to know how young people are viewing the world, what material they place a high premium on, how the gap between the past which scholars study and the present in which they function can be bridged. "Woe to the teacher who isn't competent and relevant!" warns John M. Culkin, interdisciplinary director of the Center for Communications at Fordham University in New York. "The students want the big thing, the real, the now. The generation gap may be the gap between intellectual and emotional development. What gets starved in the traditional culture comes out in the popular culture."[16]

Such statements seem pivotal for scholars seriously concerned with American culture; but where are the programs in the United States, or abroad, which explore Culkin's "generation gap" in more than a cursory fashion?

One formidable problem lies not inside the academy but in the culture itself. As Gertrude Stein reminded us, America is the oldest nation, being the first to enter the 20th century. That meant it was the first to confront the new technology, alienation, and automation; the first to explore the terra nulla of the Circuitry. This gives American area studies a different dimension from others and makes the old 19th century thought patterns—still used extensively in graduate research and dissertations—hopelessly inadequate. The difference is the environment. It took man centuries to move from the natural to the mechanical; then, almost instantly, to electrical. Paradoxically, with change too fast to be discernible, everything is suddenly visible: segregation, poverty, Senators' expense accounts, the wart on Nasser's nose. In an important recent collection of student essays (edited by Otto Butz) called *To Make a Difference*, Janet S. Schaefer entitles her essay "Beyond Categories." She argues that we must be willing quickly to relinquish categories and stereotypes if we are to understand America. Passenger pigeons, take note.

CHANGING GENERATIONS

The job of every new generation is to seek new modes of expression. When you cut the timespan of "generation" from 25 years to 10—which the 20th century has done—it is hard to tell a mode from a fad; and impossible to age grace-fully. So great is the acceleration that one is "out" before he fully realizes that he is "in."

Modes may be verbal, aural, visual, physical—an expres-sion, a sound, a look, a gesture. It is the never-ending battle of Ancients vs. Moderns. Changing generations never has been, never can be, easy.

Phoenix-lovers remind us that we confront not only such "ultimate" problems as nuclear bombs, rocketry, and anni-hilation, but staggering daily realities such as increasing population, uncheckable hunger, rural and urban deterio-ration, accelerated disease, resources-depletion, traffic trauma, energy overload, racial warfare, air-water pollution: staggering, poorly analyzed problems which bear on our individual well-being. "Show us a group of scholars who will tackle *these* problems in a fresh, interdisciplinary way," they say, "and we'll show you the new philosopher-kings!"

When the new royalty appears, it will introduce compar-ative cultural research that shifts the emphasis of American Studies from chauvinism to comparison, and develops a whole new set of landmarks by which the territorial impera-tive of a truly relevant field could be determined.[17]

Darwin speaks to the whole academic community, not merely the biologists. To survive, a movement must be able to adapt to new environments, to struggle with new prob-lems. Many courses being taught, and these being written, under the rubric of American Studies, are attempting to answer questions no one is asking in 1967. Too often they are demonstrating the same kind of routine, pedestrian coverage which made the Founding Fathers take action in the 1940's. In Darwinian terms, such courses invite com-parison to the sad fate of the passenger pigeon.

FAST-CHANGING WORLD

Today's world is changing at a rate which defies description, let alone comprehension. The world alters as we walk on it. Recently I returned from a lecture tour in Eastern Europe—the fourth in 4 years. The young people there are talking, reading, dressing, dancing differently. Not only memories, but photographs, texts, discussions prove it. We *do* live in a global village, wired for sound. Neither bamboo nor iron curtains avail in the Age of Circuitry. All men, to some degree, are bombarded by the new media. The school, church, and universities are no longer inside buildings, but wherever sound and sight penetrates. Recitations and resurrections have different dimensions. Phoenix-watchers, take note.

WE BEGIN with a single question, and end up with several new ones:

What are the conditions for the survival and growth of American Studies, here and abroad?

Why are our offerings well received in some foreign countries (Japan, Italy, Norway) and less so in others (India, France, Denmark)?

If the movement does survive—as probably it will—can it also prevail?

If the medium is the message, what does that message say to interdepartmental scholars?

How much cohesion is necessary in academe?

How do we instigate and then perpetuate the skeptical, relentless, furious search for truth, whatever labels we carry?

TO ASK SUCH QUESTIONS is to doubt and to wonder. The sense of wonder, like doubt, is an angel which echoes what Isaac Newton said of his own achievements: The great ocean of truth still lies all undiscovered before us.

[1] Sigmund Skard, *American Studies in Europe* (Philadelphia: University of Pennsylvania, 1958), II, p. 641.

[2] Dr. Bestor's article appeared in the *William and Mary Quarterly*, 3d Series, IX, No. 1 (January 1952). See also Marvin Wachman's "Chauvinism and American Studies: Colgate's Approach to the Problem," *American Studies*, IV, No. 2 (November 1958).

[3] See *International Educational Exchange: The Opening Decades, 1946–1966* (Washington: Government Printing Office, 1966).

[4] See especially Robert Walker, *American Studies in the United States* (Baton Rouge: Louisiana State University, 1958) and Sigmund Skard, *op. cit.* The annual summary in the *American Quarterly* is also helpful.

[5] Letter to the author dated Sept. 27, 1967. On the question of the adaptation of English departments to the ends of American Studies, one might do well to ponder David J. Palmer, *The Rise of English Studies* (London: Oxford, 1965).

[6] The essay is reprinted in Joseph J. Kwiat and Mary C. Turpie, eds., *Studies in American Culture* (Minneapolis: University of Minnesota, 1960).

[7] See John Higham, "The Cult of the American Consensus," *Commentary*, XXVII (February 1959), 99–100; William A. Williams, *The Contours of American History* (New York: World, 1961); and the journal *Studies on the Left*.

[8] Howard Mumford Jones, *Education and World Tragedy* (Cambridge: Harvard University, 1947).

[9] Letter to the author dated Sept. 13, 1967.

[10] See Kazin's review of Alan Trachtenberg's *Brooklyn Bridge: Fact and Symbol*, in *New York Review*, July 15, 1965.

[11] *Preface to the Future* (New York: Ungar, 1964) p. 211.

[12] Letter to the author dated Sept. 22, 1967.

[13] Letter to the author dated Sept. 15, 1967.

[14] The Commission published the report under the title *American Studies Abroad*.

[15] To quote Knapp in *The Origins of American Humanistic Scholars* (Englewood Cliffs: Prentice-Hall, 1964): "No professional schism, few rigid methodologies or ideologies, and indeed little bitterness are found among American historians." See also Donald R. McCoy, "Underdeveloped Sources of Understanding American History," in *Journal of American History*, LIV, No. 2 (September 1967).

[16] Interview with John M. Culkin in *Pace*, September 1967, pp. 12–13.

[17] For an example of such a plea, see Lawrence W. Chisolm's essay on "Cosmotopian Possibilities," which begins on page 298.